Churchill's Mum

The Story of Jennie Jerome, an American Heiress

By

Sandi Jerome and David R. Stokes

Churchill's Mum

Published by Smiling Eagle Press

2nd Edition

Printed in the United States of America

ISBN: 978-1-969767-06-7

Cover by: Nilesh Prabhu doggiesouz@gmail.com

Contents

Introduction 5
Prologue 8
I Want to Matter 14
Beginnings 38
War in Paris 60
London and Married Life 84
Blenheim 109
USA and Ireland 125
London House of Politicians 142
Snow and Russia 157
Randolph in India 176
Resignation 184
Sandringham 196
Russia, France and Berlin 214
Lord Randolph and Birmingham 236
Jennie's World Tour 255

Jennie – The Writer.. 284

The South African War 296

Famous Letters Received..312

Final Years..318

Comments and References 328

About the Authors...332

Introduction

This book is a hybrid; part biography, part historical fiction, part recovered memoir.

We used source material that came directly from Jennie Jerome's own words, published in 1908 as ***The Reminiscences of Lady Randolph Churchill.*** Her memoir, written when she was in her early fifties, reads like a journal of the era: a record of travels, social events, and name-dropping that was fashionable for women of her station. She wrote in the restrained style of her time, rarely revealing her inner thoughts or private struggles. The prose can feel formal to modern ears because it *is* formal; these are the words of a Victorian lady writing for public consumption, not posterity's psychological analysis.

We have preserved much of this material, converting it from first to third person and adding historical context about the places and people she mentioned. When you encounter passages dense with names, dates, and social minutiae, you are reading Jennie's world as she recorded it. We translated many French words and correspondence to English.

But Jennie's memoir left gaps. She tells us what happened; she rarely tells us what it *felt* like. To honor the full woman, not just the society hostess but the fierce mother who shaped one of history's greatest leaders, we have woven her documented experiences into dramatized scenes. These narrative sections, which you will recognize by their dialogue and interior moments, imagine the emotional reality behind the facts.

We have also created a fictional frame: Sophia Carter, an American journalist interviewing the elderly Winston Churchill at Chartwell in 1964. These conversations never happened. But they allow us to see Jennie through her son's eyes and to understand why her story matters beyond the footnotes of history.

Think of this book as a restored painting. The original canvas, Jennie's actual life and documented experiences... remains intact. We have filled in colors that time had faded, added details that modesty had obscured, and highlighted connections that hindsight makes clear.

When the prose grows formal and the names multiply, that is Jennie speaking across the centuries. When the scenes breathe and the dialogue sparks, that is our storytelling craft, bringing her fully to life. Both are necessary to tell her story. This was personal to Sandi Jerome; her husband is the 4th cousin of Jennie Jerome.

Prologue

Sunlight, almost American in its intensity, poured over the rolling Kentish hills and pooled in golden puddles along the flagstone walkways of Chartwell. Sophia Carter had traveled three thousand miles from New York to the English countryside. Each step brought her closer to the man who had, in her childhood, been little more than a silhouette behind the microphone, all gravel and defiance and resolve.

She rehearsed her opening line as she walked through the anteroom. Chartwell, every corridor a memory, every room a campaign. As she walked, she listened for the sound of the old man's breath, or perhaps the hush of brush against canvas, but heard only the slight ticking of clocks. The studio door stood open.

Churchill was at his easel. His hair, once a battlefield of cowlicks and stubborn tufts, now lay thin against his skull. The hand that held the brush trembled slightly. He did not turn when she entered. Instead, he gestured with the brush toward the window, where the gardens sloped down to the lake.

"You see, Miss Carter, the willows are at their loveliest in late July. But they will not stay lovely. Nothing does, in the end." He gestured to a chair and she took a seat.

The cracked leather chair gave a small sigh beneath her. On the table beside her, a silver tray held a solitary cup and saucer, the tea cooling in the draft from the garden doors. Across from her, a faded portrait of Randolph Churchill, Winston's father, peered out from the frame with the same relentless blue stare she had seen in the newsreels.

Sophia introduced herself, and he gave a small nod before returning his focus to the canvas. She wondered how much of Churchill's public self was still a performance. She wondered if he, like so many of her subjects, would be more forthcoming with a woman than with his old fourth estate adversaries.

She began with the familiar litany of questions. Did he foresee the outcome of the war? What sustained him through the Blitz? How had he managed, in the darkest hours, to rally not only a country but a continent? Churchill answered with stories she already knew from the half-dozen books on her hotel nightstand. But then, as if tiring of the choreography, he set down his brush and fixed her with that legendary gaze, now watery but undimmed.

"You want to know what kept me from despair." His voice was a rasp, but the syllables still bore the shrapnel of old battles. "It was not the Empire, nor even the people. It was my mother."

Sophia, who had spent her career extracting secrets from men who believed themselves inscrutable, blinked in surprise. "Your mother?"

He nodded, once. "American. Brooklyn-born, as you may have read. Fierce in her affections, ruthless in her ambition. It was her blood, not my father's, that gave me the courage to be hated, and the stubbornness to be right."

It was not what she had expected. She had come to Chartwell to record the valedictory wisdom of a world leader, and here was an old man speaking about his mother, as if she were in the next room, ready to defend him against the laughter of the boys at Harrow or the sneers of back benchers in Parliament.

"She was beautiful," Churchill went on, his eyes refocusing on the far end of the garden. "Not in the English way, you understand. Hers was an American beauty. She could have been a queen, had this been a different country. Instead, she was a general in disguise."

Sophia found her carefully prepared notes suddenly irrelevant. She set them aside and leaned in, coaxing the old man to continue. "Tell me about her," she said.

Churchill smiled, the edges of his mouth creasing into the familiar parenthesis. "I will. But you must promise to listen as a daughter would, not as a reporter."

Sophia nodded, feeling for the first time in years the childlike awe that had driven her to journalism in the first place.

He began to conjure Jennie Jerome, not as a figure of historical footnote, but as a force of nature. The daughter of a Wall Street tycoon, who crossed the ocean and scandalized London with her wit, her laughter, indifferent to the boundaries of class or custom. She ruled her son's childhood with an iron whim, teaching him French, fencing, and above all, the art of never admitting defeat.

"She lived for pleasure," Churchill said, "but never at the expense of pride. She was the reason I survived my father's neglect, and she was the reason I never truly feared the Germans, or the bombs, or the howling of the mob on Downing Street."

Sophia listened, her pen forgotten. She realized, with a kind of ache, that this was the real interview, not the recitation of battles and parliaments, but the confession of the last private loyalty in a life conducted almost entirely in public. She wondered if, in the brief time they had together, she might convince him to share one memory, one secret, that had never made it into the history books.

As Churchill paused to collect his thoughts, Sophia noticed how the light had shifted. The sun now angled directly through the studio window as he reached for the brush once more. “You see,” he said, gesturing again to the unfinished landscape, “the willows bend, but they do not break. That is the lesson of both America and England, and perhaps, of mothers and sons, as well."

"You know, Miss Carter," he continued, "her American odyssey began not in ballroom or drawing room, but as a little girl chasing her father’s fortunes across the shifting chessboard of two continents." He placed his hands, knotted by time and memory, flat upon the table, and closed his eyes briefly as if summoning the spectral Jennie Jerome from the hazy past. "She told me, in a rare moment of candor, that she had no true childhood home, not in the manner the English like to imagine, with ancestral keys and nursery firesides. The Jeromes, you see, were ruled by restless enterprise. One season in Manhattan, the next in a villa at San Remo, then Paris for the polish of proper education, and so the pattern went."

Sophia, leaning in, could not help but be drawn to the way his voice grew steadier, almost younger, whenever he spoke of his mother. There was a tenderness, unexpected in a man so renowned for his granite resolve. "Was it difficult for her, all the moving about? Never quite belonging anywhere?" she ventured softly.

Churchill’s eyelids fluttered open. "On the contrary, my dear, it made her formidable. Adversity, as I have long said, is the grindstone of character. Jennie took every new environment as a stage to be mastered. She understood, instinctively, that adaptability is the only true security for one’s soul. She could become Parisian or London grande dame at will, and at her best, she made the transformation seem innate rather than imposed."

He shifted in his chair and gestured toward the half-finished canvas on his easel. The landscape, a study in turbulent skies over tranquil waters, was an apt rendering of his mother's nature. "It was this lesson, the art of survival by reinvention, that she imparted to me. A lesson I clung to in my own wanderings, from Sandhurst to the cavalry in India, from the battlefields of South Africa to the corridors of Whitehall, Parliament, and Number Ten. You see, for all the pageantry, politics is merely the art of improvisation in the face of the unforeseen."

Sophia's pencil was moving furiously against the paper, making a tapping sound from her notebook.

"I remember a particular episode, when Mama was still just a girl, no more than nine or ten, her father was suddenly summoned to Europe on urgent business. The family uprooted overnight, their belongings packed in crates, every cherished memento left behind in New York. Young Jennie, bracing herself against the Atlantic crossing, made a private vow to make the world her playground, not her prison. By the time they settled in the Via di Porta Pinciana, she had already mastered enough Italian to charm the Roman grocers as if she were some miniature empress."

He chuckled, the sound half fondness, half fatigue. "That sense of command, of bending the situation to her own advantage, never left her. It was her greatest gift and perhaps her greatest curse. For when she entered English society, with all its rigid codes and unsmiling dowagers, she simply did not recognize defeat. She saw the world as a banquet and expected a place at the head table, no matter what the host or hostess might have in mind."

Sophia scribbled furiously. "Do you think she ever regretted the instability of her upbringing?" she asked.

"Regret?" Churchill rolled the word on his tongue as though tasting it for the first time. "I rather doubt it. In fact, I suspect she found conventionality insufferable. The routine of an unchanging household would have suffocated her. No, if my mother mourned anything, it was the world's chronic lack of imagination. Adaptability and audacity, a rare combination, and one that served her prodigiously when she crossed the Atlantic to marry Lord Randolph. She was expected to be merely ornamental, a decorative adjunct to the Churchill lineage. Instead, she became its engine, its diplomat, its secret weapon."

Churchill's gaze drifted toward the window, where the black swans, his pride and joy, glided across the lake, their passage creating only the softest of ripples. "You will find, Miss Carter, that the greatest strength a person can possess is not brute force or even intellect, but the ability to shape oneself to the demands of fate. The most American of virtues is the capacity for endless self-invention."

I Want to Matter

"She had the gift of making everyone she met feel important: the rare accomplishment of inspiring others to give of their best."

— Winston Churchill on his mother, Jennie Jerome Churchill

Chartwell, 1964

Churchill reached for his tea, the cup trembling slightly in his grip. "You ask about the sources of my strength during the war..." Sophia Carter adjusted her notepad as Sir Winston Churchill set down his paintbrush with trembling hands. The afternoon light filtering through the studio windows caught the still-wet oils on his canvas, a serene view of the lake he'd personally designed and built in the grounds below.

"Everyone expects me to speak of parliamentary debates or military strategy." He paused, gazing out at his beloved gardens. "But the truth is, Miss Carter, it began with an American girl who refused to be ordinary."

Sophia leaned forward, intrigued. She had come to interview the great wartime leader, but something in his tone suggested a more personal revelation was coming.

"She was my mother, you see. Jennie Jerome from Brooklyn." Churchill's eyes brightened with memory. "People always said she was just another dollar princess who married into the British aristocracy. They were quite wrong about that." He turned from his easel to face her directly. "She didn't just marry into our world; she transformed it. And in doing so, she created the man who would one day stand against Hitler."

The old statesman's gaze grew distant. "To understand how an American heiress shaped the destiny of an empire, Miss Carter, you must first understand what it meant to be a young woman who dared to want more than society offered. She once told me that she didn't want merely to shine, she wanted to matter."

COWES, ISLE OF WIGHT, 1873

The summer breeze carried the salt of the Solent across Cowes harbor, ruffling the Union Jack that flew from the stern of their chartered yacht. Jennie stood at the bow, her dark hair whipping across her face as she studied the Isle of Wight sprawled before her, another temporary home in a life full of temporary homes for the Jerome family.

Jennie's appearance that afternoon would have raised eyebrows among the more conservative English ladies present. Having spent recent months in Paris, she wore a walking dress of emerald silk taffeta with a daringly fitted bodice, a stark contrast to the loose styles favored by proper English misses. Her bustle was smaller and more artfully arranged than the enormous crinolines still popular in England, and her hat, a confection of peacock feathers and silk roses, was distinctly Parisian in its bold sophistication. Everything about her costume whispered of Continental elegance and marked her as deliciously different from the other young ladies at Cowes. Behind her, the British Royal Navy vessels bobbed in perfect formation, their polished brass catching the July sunlight. It was 1873, and Cowes Week was in full spectacle.

The regatta had been drawing aristocracy to these waters since 1826—nearly fifty years of racing cutters and schooners around the Isle of Wight, with courses marked by vessels stationed off Yarmouth and buoys near Southsea Castle. Queen Victoria herself often watched from the royal balcony. For one week each summer, the small town of Cowes became the center of the British social universe, and Jennie found herself unexpectedly at its heart.

"Rather magnificent vessels, aren't they? Though I must say, American racing yachts have a certain boldness of design the British still resist."

Jennie turned, startled by the masculine voice. A young man in naval whites stood nearby, studying her with frank interest. He wasn't particularly tall or handsome, but there was an intensity to his blue eyes that made her breath catch. "You must be Miss Jerome," he said with a slight bow. "The American beauty everyone's talking about."

"And you are?" Jennie asked, raising an eyebrow.

"Lord Randolph Churchill." He smiled, revealing a flash of unexpected charm. "Second son of the Duke of Marlborough, reluctant naval enthusiast, and chief disappointment to my illustrious family."

"Impressive credentials," Jennie replied, fighting a smile. No proper Englishman introduced himself with his failings.

"Not nearly as impressive as yours, I hear," he countered. "Fluent in three languages, educated in Paris, and already scandalizing London society with your forthright opinions."

Before she could respond, the steward approached with a bow. "Miss Jerome, your mother requests your presence below deck."

Jennie sighed. "Tell her I'll be down shortly." The words came out sharper than intended. At nineteen, she tired of her mother's constant arrangements and social maneuverings.

"Family obligations?" Lord Randolph asked as the steward retreated. "I know them well. Perhaps we'll continue this conversation at the Duchess's garden party tomorrow?"

"Perhaps," Jennie replied noncommittally, though something about his irreverent manner intrigued her.

She lingered a moment longer after he departed, watching a sleek, racing yacht cut through the water. The vessel belonged to the Prince of Wales, the future King Edward VII, whose scandalous affairs were whispered about even in New York drawing rooms. How strange to find herself in his orbit now, part of this ancient, rigid society that simultaneously fascinated and frustrated her.

Below deck, the yacht's salon had been transformed into an extension of any London parlor. Mrs. Clara Jerome sat surrounded by calling cards and invitations, her steel-gray dress a testament to her unshakable propriety. The Jerome women had been in England less than a season, but Clara had navigated their entry into society with military precision.

"The Duchess of Marlborough is hosting a garden party tomorrow at her summer residence," Mrs. Jerome announced without preamble. "The whole family will attend."

"Another party." Jennie sank into a velvet chair, her sapphire silk dress rustling. "Another parade of eligible British nobility."

"You could show more enthusiasm." Mrs. Jerome shuffled the cards with practiced hands that bore the finest diamond rings Leonard Jerome's Wall Street fortune could buy. "We didn't cross an ocean and leave New York to hide away on boats."

"We left because of the war in France." Jennie touched the pendant at her throat, a gift from the Empress Eugénie before everything fell apart at Sedan. The Jerome family had been in Paris during those glittering Second Empire days, when Jennie had been educated among European royalty. "Not to hunt for titled husbands."

"The Franco-Prussian War is over. And you could do worse than a British title." Mrs. Jerome's voice softened as she studied her daughter. Jennie was not conventionally beautiful by Victorian standards. Her olive complexion, raven hair, and voluptuous figure were a stark contrast to the pale, willowy English roses. But there was something about her, a vibrant intelligence, a barely restrained passion, that drew every eye in a room. "You shine here, Jennie. Even the Queen notices American girls now."

"I don't want to shine. I want to matter." The words hung between them, heavier than the humid summer air.

Mrs. Jerome looked up sharply, recognizing the dangerous ambition in her daughter's voice. "Then make yourself matter."

The next afternoon, Jennie stood in the Duchess's garden, her yellow dress a spot of sunlight among the muted English pastels. The Marlborough estate was a modest summer residence by ducal standards, merely twenty rooms with a view of the Solent. Lords and ladies moved through the crowd like chess pieces, calculated, predictable, each movement dictated by centuries of protocol.

The band played Strauss while footmen circulated with champagne. Jennie took a glass and moved away from her mother, pretending to admire the roses. Three months in England had taught her that British aristocrats considered enthusiasm vulgar.

Better to display boredom than reveal her fascination with this world of ancient titles and crumbling estates.

"Still finding our English gatherings tedious, Miss Jerome?"

She turned to find Lord Randolph Churchill approaching, looking more comfortable in his formal attire than he had in his naval whites the day before. His blue eyes held the same amused intensity that had caught her attention on the yacht.

"Lord Randolph," she acknowledged with a slight nod. "I was beginning to think our conversation yesterday would go uncontinued."

"I never break a promise, particularly to beautiful American revolutionaries." He smiled, taking up position beside her. "Though I've been detained explaining to my mother why I was conversing with the notorious Miss Jerome on a yacht rather than paying court to Lady Hunston's daughter as instructed."

"Notorious?" Jennie raised an eyebrow. "And here I thought I'd been the model of decorum."

"That's precisely what makes you notorious. Genuine intelligence in a society that prefers its women decorative." He leaned closer. "Your mother has her sights on a duke for you, I hear."

"Your intelligence network is impressive," she said, surprised.

"A necessary tool in politics." He sipped his champagne. "Speaking of which, what do you think of British politics, Miss Jerome?"

The question startled her. Englishmen rarely asked women, especially young, foreign women, for political opinions. "I think it needs new blood." She smiled. "And possibly a revolution. But I prefer to scandalize them." Jennie met his gaze. "It's more entertaining."

"Even better!" Randolph's eyes sparked with interest. His face came alive when he smiled, transforming from ordinary to magnetic. He offered his arm. "Shall we plot the overthrow of Parliament over tea?"

As they walked through the garden, Jennie felt the weight of disapproving stares. A cluster of aristocratic mothers watched with predatory interest as the Duke of Marlborough's second son escorted the American girl past the fountain. On the terrace, the Prince of Wales himself paused mid-conversation to observe their passage.

"You've made quite an entrance into society," Randolph noted, guiding her to a secluded bench beneath an ancient oak. "They say you've refused two offers already."

"Three," Jennie corrected. "All from men who wanted my father's money to repair their estates and never asked a single question about my thoughts."

"And what are your thoughts, Miss Jerome?" Randolph leaned closer. "Beyond the need for revolution."

For the next hour, they talked about everything, Disraeli's reforms, the American Civil War, the future of the British Empire, the poetry of Byron. Randolph spoke rapidly, his mind jumping between subjects with dizzying speed. He quoted Parliament speeches verbatim, analyzed foreign policy with razor precision, and lambasted the "old wooden-heads" who controlled his party.

"You should be running this country!" Jennie exclaimed when he finally paused for breath.

"That's the plan." His eyes gleamed with ambition. "But I need allies. People who aren't afraid to break with tradition."

For the first time since arriving in England, Jennie didn't feel like an exotic specimen on display. In Lord Randolph's irreverent humor and quick mind, she sensed something rare, a chance to matter beyond her dowry and her beauty.

When Mrs. Jerome finally located her daughter, she found Jennie deep in conversation about Irish home rule with the Duke's second son.

"Jennie, dear, we must be going." Clara Jerome's voice was pleasant, but her eyes telegraphed warning.

Randolph stood. "Mrs. Jerome, your daughter is extraordinary. May I call on you both tomorrow?"

Clara hesitated just long enough to establish her authority. "We receive visitors after three o'clock."

The next day, Mrs. Jerome slapped the morning paper onto the breakfast table. "Impossible, absolutely impossible! "

Jennie looked up from her toast. "What's impossible, Mother?"

"Lord Randolph Churchill has formally asked permission to court you." Her mother's voice trembled with a mixture of triumph and anxiety. "From your father, through the proper channels."

"That's good news, isn't it?" Jennie kept her voice steady, though her heart raced.

"A second son, Jennie. A second son with no fortune and a reputation for trouble." Clara paced the rented villa's breakfast room. "The Duke of Marlborough has made it clear that Randolph's allowance is modest. He expects you to live on your settlement."

"Randolph is brilliant." Jennie pushed her plate away. "He understands that England must change or risk revolution like France faced."

"Change?" Mrs. Jerome laughed bitterly. "We came to England for stability. For position. Not for you to throw yourself away on some reformer with radical ideas. Your father worked too hard for his money to see it wasted on political campaigns."

"The world is changing whether England likes it or not." Jennie stood, her chair scraping against the floor. "Perhaps that's what they need, an American girl with radical ideas."

The door chimed. Both women froze.

"He's early." Mrs. Jerome smoothed her skirts. "Completely improper."

"Good." Jennie smiled, feeling a wild recklessness rising within her. "We can be improper together."

Lord Randolph stood in the parlor, examining a Monet painting with critical interest. He turned as Jennie entered, his face lighting up with an intensity that made her flush.

"Miss Jerome. I hoped to catch you before the vultures descended."

"Vultures?"

"The social climbers. The matchmakers. The entire apparatus of London society that will try to turn you into a proper English lady." He stepped closer. "Promise me you won't let them."

"Is that why you came early? To extract promises?"

"I came early because I couldn't wait." His voice dropped. "And because I need your help."

Jennie raised an eyebrow. "With what?"

"I'm giving a speech in Parliament next week. My first real chance to shake things up." He paced the room, nervous energy radiating from him. "But I need someone who sees England with fresh eyes. Someone who isn't bound by tradition."

"And you think an American girl can help you reshape British politics?"

"I think you can help me reshape the world." He stopped in front of her, close enough that she could smell the sandalwood of his shaving soap. "They underestimate you because you're American, young, female. Let them. While they're busy looking down their noses, we'll change everything. Help me tomorrow, in my study."

Jennie's heart raced. This wasn't the careful courtship her mother wanted. This was revolution wrapped in romance, danger disguised as opportunity. This was everything her conventional education had warned against. But working alone with this handsome man, without a chaperone, was dangerous.

"My mother won't approve."

"Of course not." Randolph grinned. "That's half the fun."

The next day, Jennie sat in Randolph's study at Blenheim Palace, surrounded by political treatises and parliamentary records. Maps covered the walls, the British Empire sprawled across continents in imperial red. Outside, peacocks screamed in the ancient gardens where generations of Churchills had plotted wars, marriages, and political alliances.

"The problem," Randolph said, pacing between towering bookshelves, "is that England thinks power comes from tradition. They cling to the old ways while the world speeds past them."

"Like refusing to let women vote?" Jennie looked up from a draft of his speech. "Or treating the colonies like wayward children?"

"Exactly." He leaned over her shoulder, his breath warm against her ear. "What would you change first?"

"Everything." Jennie turned to face him. "But I'd start with this speech. It's too cautious. You're trying to please everyone."

"And what should I do instead?"

"Shock them." Her eyes blazed. "Wake them up. Make them face the future instead of hiding in the past."

Randolph stared at her for a long moment. Then he grabbed a fresh sheet of paper. "Show me."

They worked throughout the day, drinking tea gone cold and arguing about various strategies. When sunset approached and they would be expected for dinner, they had more than a speech. They had a manifesto.

"It's perfect." Randolph read over the final draft. "They'll hate it."

"Good." Jennie stood, stretching. "Hate means they're paying attention."

He caught her hand. "Marry me."

Jennie froze. "What?"

"Marry me. Be my partner in everything, politics, life, revolution." His grip tightened. "Help me build a new England."

"I can't." But her voice wavered. "We've known each other less than a week."

"Three days," he corrected her. "I know you better than people I've known all my life." His blue eyes burned with conviction. "Your mother would never allow it."

"No, she wouldn't."

"Then we'll elope." His eyes sparkled with conspiracy. "Paris. The British Embassy. Quick and quiet before anyone can stop us."

"You're mad." But Jennie smiled. "Completely mad."

"Is that a yes?"

She looked at their joined hands, at the speech that might change history, at the man who saw her as more than just a pretty American heiress.

"Yes." Her heart soared. "Yes to everything."

As the saying goes, "The course of true love never runs smooth," and Jennie's engagement to Lord Randolph Churchill was no exception to the rule. The Duke of Marlborough, her prospective father-in-law, would not consent to their marriage until Randolph had secured a seat in Parliament. Moreover, the Duke likely wished to test the stability of their affections, as they had arrived at their momentous decision rather hastily.

During the year of their engagement, Jennie remained with her family in Paris, contenting herself with flying visits from her fiancé, with whom she maintained an animated correspondence. He tried to initiate her in the mysteries of English politics, of which she was at that time in blissful ignorance. She looked forward greatly to the impending General Election, which, apart from the dignity Randolph was to acquire by becoming a member of Parliament, meant the end of their long probation.

In one of Randolph's letters of 1874, he spoke about Mr. Disraeli, for whom he had a profound admiration:

"I advise you to get a copy of today's 'Times' if you can, and read Disraeli's great speech. He has made a magnificent one to the Conservatives of Glasgow... it is a fine specimen of perfect English oratory."

In 1874, Benjamin Disraeli became the Prime Minister of the United Kingdom for the second time, leading a Conservative government after defeating William Gladstone's Liberal Party in the general election held in January and February of that year Jennie and Randolph were apart.

This was a significant achievement as it marked the first clear Conservative majority in the House of Commons since the 1841 election. Disraeli had previously served as Prime Minister briefly in 1868, but that was a minority government that only lasted for about ten months before being defeated by Gladstone. In 1874, Disraeli was approximately 70 years old and at the height of his political power.

Jennie remembered a great controversy in Randolph's letters over her having used the word "prorogued" in a wrong sense, apropos of Bazaine's trial. After the Franco-Prussian War of 1870-1871, Marshal François Achille Bazaine faced a historic military trial for his surrender of the fortress of Metz and his entire Army of the Rhine (approximately 140,000-180,000 men) to the Prussians on October 27, 1870. The trial took place at the Grand Trianon at Versailles, and Bazaine was tried "for his life on military charges devised by the first Napoleon, enraged by the surrender by General Dupont at Baylen in 1808 during the Peninsular War." Following France's crushing defeat in the war, "national pride demanded a scapegoat, and it was Bazaine who was blamed for just about everything that had gone so very wrong." He became "the victim not only of a wholly unjustified accusation of treason by the Government of National Defense," which had seized power after the fall of the Second Empire.

After the war, "Marshal Bazaine was convicted by a French military court" for his actions. The charges centered not only on military incompetence but also accusations of potential treason. Bazaine's leadership was widely criticized. Prior to the surrender, he had conducted negotiations with the Prussians while holed up in Metz, and many questioned his motivations, especially as he was known to be a Bonapartist loyalist even after Napoleon III's capture and the establishment of the republican government.

The trial represented one of the most significant military tribunals in French history, as France sought to make sense of its devastating defeat by finding someone to blame. Many historians have since debated whether Bazaine received a fair trial or was simply made a convenient scapegoat for France's larger military and political failures during the war. Jennie mentions Bazaine more in the next chapter.

Much to Randolph's indignation, she had quoted in her defense the opinion of the Comte de Fenelon, a young Frenchman of their acquaintance whom she thought, in virtue of his descent, a good authority. From Blenheim, Randolph wrote angrily with maybe a touch of jealously?

"Hang le petit Fenelon... little idiot! What do I care for him? He may be a very good authority about his own beastly language but I cannot for a moment submit to him about English. Whether you use the word prorogation as a French or an English one I don't know. In the former case, as the word is a Latin one and as there can be no doubt as to its meaning, I apprehend you are wrong, but still would not attempt to lay down the law to you on the meaning of any French word. If you use it as an English word you are undoubtedly not only using an inaccurate expression, but a meaningless and unintelligible one. To prorogue, means to suspend something for a definite time to be resumed again in exactly the same state, condition, and circumstances. Therefore to talk about proroguing the Marshal's powers, would mean that they were to be suspended for a certain time and then resumed again exactly as before. Parliament is prorogued, L'Assemblée is prorogued; that does not in the least mean that the powers of either are lengthened or increased in any way but that they are temporarily suspended. Whatever words the French papers may use, I have never seen any English paper use the word in any other sense and in any other sense it cannot possibly be used."

And in a further letter Randolph ended: "I am looking forward particularly to utterly suppressing and crushing le petit Fenelon. We must really though drop this argument when I am with you, as it is likely to become a heated one, I fear. We will therefore 'prorogue' it."

Was this "crushing" threat a sign of jealously? Did Randolph worry that Jennie was being courted by a handsome Frenchman while their engagement and marriage details were being prolonged?

Randolph's family, the aristocratic Marlboroughs were horrified at the prospect of American blood mingling with their ancient lineage. The Duke and Duchess recoiled at what they perceived as a deeply mismatched union, their noble son entangled with a woman whose father, though wealthy, had made his fortune in finance and newspapers rather than inherited estates. Lady Frances Marlborough reportedly exclaimed to confidantes, "An American? He might as well marry a circus performer!" The Jerome family's New York roots, their connection to the loud world of stock speculation, and Jennie's reputation for vivacity and fashion-forward thinking represented everything the conservative

Marlborough disdained about American society. The absence of aristocratic breeding was considered a stain that even Jerome's considerable fortune could not wash away. In drawing rooms across London, whispers circulated about "dollar princesses" buying their way into British society, with many regarding these transatlantic marriages as little more than crass transactions, American money exchanged for English titles, a perspective that cast a shadow over Randolph and Jennie's genuine affection and "prolonged" engagement.

The engagement announcement triggered immediate tension between the families. Leonard Jerome, Jennie's father and a successful financier, initially offered a generous dowry of £50,000, an enormous sum in those days. However, the Duke of Marlborough demanded more than just money; he insisted on strict controls regarding how the funds would be managed, revealing his distrust of American financial practices. A flurry of tense correspondence crossed the Atlantic as the families negotiated terms.

For eight long months, the young lovers were largely kept apart. Lord Randolph returned to England while Jennie remained with her mother in Paris, their passionate romance sustained through letters exchanged across the Channel.

Meanwhile, Leonard Jerome ultimately compromised by establishing a trust fund of approximately £50,000 that would provide the couple with an annual income of about £1,000, a handsome sum but carefully structured to satisfy the Marlboroughs' concerns about control and respectability.

Finally, on April 15, 1874, after months of family negotiations and financial arrangements, the couple wed at the British Embassy in Paris. Although the Duke and Duchess of Marlborough had reluctantly given their blessing, an undercurrent of aristocratic disapproval persisted.

Nevertheless, the marriage marked one of the early prominent unions between British nobility and American wealth, a pattern that would become increasingly common in the late 19th century as cash-strapped aristocrats sought American fortunes and ambitious American families desired the social elevation that came with noble titles.

This unlikely romance between the impulsive, politically ambitious Lord Randolph and the beautiful, intelligent Jennie Jerome would produce not only a lasting love story but also one of history's most consequential figures, their son, Winston Churchill, born just seven months after their wedding.

But what a wedding it was! Paris sparkled in the January frost of 1874. Jennie stood before the mirror in her hotel room, pinning a small cluster of white roses to her traveling suit. No white gown, no elaborate ceremony, just a quick, quiet wedding at the British Embassy.

A knock startled her. "Come in."

Her mother swept into the room, face tight with anger and exhaustion. She had traveled day and night upon receiving Jennie's letter announcing the engagement. "So, you're determined to go through with this madness."

"Yes." Jennie met her mother's eyes in the mirror. "I am."

"Second son, Jennie. No money, no title, nothing but dreams and radical politics." Mrs. Jerome sank into a chair. "I wanted so much more for you."

"You wanted what you thought would make me happy." Jennie turned. "This is what actually will."

"And when Randolph's dreams fail? When society shuns you? When the money runs out?"

"Then we'll fail together." Jennie knelt beside her mother. "But we'll fail trying to make a difference. Isn't that better than succeeding at being decorative?"

Mrs. Jerome touched her daughter's cheek. "You're so young."

"I'm old enough to know my own mind."

Later, standing in the Embassy's austere chamber, Jennie barely heard the words of the ceremony. She focused instead on Randolph's hand gripping hers, on the future stretching before them like an unwritten page.

"Ready to scandalize England, Lady Churchill?" Randolph whispered as they signed the register.

"I thought we were going to revolutionize it."

"That too."

Three months later, Jennie stood in the Long Gallery of Blenheim Palace, surrounded by centuries of Churchill ancestors. Their painted eyes seemed to judge her, the American interloper who dared to join their ranks. The palace was a monument to ambition, built for the first Duke of Marlborough after his triumph at the Battle of Blenheim. Its massive scale dwarfed most royal residences, a testament to Churchill greatness. Now it was Jennie's home, at least when they weren't in London for Parliamentary sessions.

"They look formidable." The Duchess of Marlborough appeared beside her. "But they were all outsiders once."

Jennie turned in surprise. Her mother-in-law had been cool but correct since the wedding. This was the first hint of warmth. "Even the first Duke?" Jennie gestured to the largest portrait, which showed John Churchill in full battle regalia.

"Especially him." The Duchess smiled slightly. "He changed England through force of will and raw talent. Rather like what you and Randolph plan to do."

"You know about our plans?"

"My dear, everyone knows. The question is whether you have the steel to see them through." The Duchess turned to face her. "Politics is not a game for the faint-hearted. The same society that smiles at you today will savage you tomorrow if they sense weakness."

"I'm not weak."

"No." The Duchess studied her. "You're rather terrifying, actually. An American girl who reads Disraeli for pleasure and discusses reform bills at dinner parties. You make them nervous."

"Good."

"Better than good. Use it." The Duchess touched her arm. "But remember, in politics, timing is everything. Choose your battles carefully."

A few days later, Jennie sat in their London townhouse, reading draft bills while Randolph paced. Already, her presence in the capital was causing ripples. The American beauty with political ambitions had become a fixture in parliamentary gossip.

"The old guard won't support it." Randolph ran a hand through his hair. "We need new allies."

"Then we'll find them." Jennie set down the papers. "The working men's associations, the reform clubs, the, "

A knock interrupted them. A footman entered with a silver tray. "An invitation, my lady. From Windsor Castle."

Jennie's hands shook as she opened the envelope, then she dropped the letter. "The Queen requests our presence next week," Jennie said, her voice shaking as she picked up the invitation.

Randolph stopped pacing. "The Queen never receives Americans." This energized Jennie. She loved a challenge.

"She does now." Jennie stood, mind racing. "This is our chance. If we can convince her that change can strengthen the monarchy rather than threaten it..."

"You're thinking too small." Randolph pulled her close. "This isn't just about one bill or one reform. We're going to build a new kind of power, one that doesn't depend on birth or tradition."

"And how do we do that?"

"By being smarter, working harder, and wanting it more than anyone else." His eyes blazed. "Ready to make history, my love?"

Jennie kissed him. "Always."

Windsor Castle loomed against the twilight sky, its ancient stones washed purple in the fading light. Jennie sat straight-backed in the carriage, every detail of her appearance perfect. One did not meet the Queen of England looking less than immaculate.

"Remember," Randolph squeezed her hand, "she respects honesty above flattery."

"I remember everything." Jennie touched the notes hidden in her reticule, intelligence about the royal household's views on reform, carefully gathered over weeks. Already she had developed a network of informants, servants and ladies-in-waiting who passed her gossip in exchange for American fashions or small favors.

The castle corridors stretched endlessly, lined with armor and tapestries chronicling England's bloody history. Footmen in royal livery led them deeper into the labyrinth until they reached the Queen's private audience chamber. Victoria proved smaller than expected but her presence filled the room. Black-clad and severe as she had been since Prince Albert's death more than a decade ago, her sharp eyes missed nothing as Jennie curtsied deeply.

"So." The Queen's voice carried unexpected warmth. "You're the American girl who's turning London upside down."

"Your Majesty is too kind." Jennie met her gaze steadily. "I merely support my husband's efforts to strengthen the empire."

"By challenging every tradition we hold dear?"

"By helping traditions evolve, Ma'am. A tree that cannot bend in the wind will break in the storm."

Victoria's eyes narrowed. "You speak boldly for a newcomer to our shores."

"I speak as one who loves what England could become."

A long silence followed. Then the Queen smiled. "Well said, Lady Churchill. Perhaps we need fresh eyes to see old problems clearly."

That audience changed everything. Doors that had been closed opened wide. The American beauty and her ambitious husband became the most sought-after guests in London. But with opportunity came danger.

As Jennie and Randolph left Windsor that evening, neither realized they had just set in motion forces that would reshape an empire, and their lives. As their carriage moved through the streets into the gathering darkness, two brilliant conspirators playing a game whose rules they had yet to fully understand.

How had she come to this moment? Jennie wondered as their carriage rolled through the night. From Brooklyn to Blenheim Palace, from a New York brownstone to the corridors of power. Perhaps to understand where she was going, she needed to remember where she had begun.

As she starred into the night, her mind drifted back, past the whirlwind romance, past the European finishing schools, to a little girl watching her father build a fortune from nothing in the chaotic energy of post-Civil War America. Leonard Jerome, speculator and

risk-taker, who had taught his favorite daughter that convention was for those who lacked the courage to defy it...

Beginnings

Chartwell, 1964

Churchill reached for his tea with unsteady hands, the delicate China cup rattling slightly against the saucer. "You know, Miss Carter, people often ask about my early memories of America. They expect tales of my mother's grand New York society." He paused, a wry smile crossing his weathered features. "But the truth is, my mother's American story began long before the glittering ballrooms, it started with a little girl who learned that home was wherever her father's ambitions took the family."

Sophia noticed how his voice grew stronger when speaking of his mother. "She told me once that she never really had a childhood home in the traditional sense. The Jerome family was always moving, New York to Italy, Italy back to America, then off to Paris for her education. Most children would have found such upheaval unsettling."

"But not your mother?"

Churchill shook his head slowly. "Quite the opposite. She learned early that adaptability was strength, that one could make oneself at home anywhere if one had enough spirit. That lesson would serve her well when she crossed the Atlantic to marry my father." He gazed toward the window where his famous black swans glided across the lake. "It would serve me well too, in rooms from the Colonial Office to the White House."

BROOKLYN, NEW YORK, 1854

Jennie (Jeanette) Jerome was born in Brooklyn, New York in 1854, however, some biographers and historical records have listed alternative dates, including, January 9, 1850. This earlier date appears in some older biographies and would have made Jennie four years older than commonly believed. Wikipedia notes that "A plaque at 426 Henry St. gives her year of birth as 1850, not 1854." It also mentions location discrepancies, stating that "on 9 January 1854, the Jeromes lived nearby at number 8 Amity Street.

The confusion stems from several factors. First, during the Victorian era, it wasn't uncommon for women in high society to shave a few years off their age. Second, some of the inconsistency may have originated with Jennie herself, who was known to be somewhat flexible about her birth year in different documents. Adding to the confusion, birth records in Brooklyn from that period are incomplete, and the Jerome family's frequent travels between America and Europe further complicated the documentation of precise dates. Some biographers have suggested that Jennie's mother may have deliberately obscured her daughter's true age to make her appear younger when she entered the marriage market at an age that in British society would have seemed old.

In Jennie's memoir, she claims that Italy gave her that first taste of the good life. She explains that her father,, Leonard Jerome, was working as the American Consul in Trieste for three years, so Italy basically set the tone for her whole childhood vibe. Again, her claim of being born in 1854 is up for debate. In 1852, Leonard Jerome "accepted President Millard Fillmore's nomination as American consul to Trieste, a popular summer destination for nobility. He served for only eighteen months, long enough for his wife Clara to be mesmerized by European society." More confusion because Clara is also the name of Jennie's older sister, Clarita.

Churchill's Mum

According to Encyclopedia.com, "Following the birth of their first child in 1851, Leonard served as American Consul in Trieste and later lived with his family in Paris before returning to America in 1860. The timeline doesn't work out.

But Jennie mentions in her memoir; "Those Italian skies." They're what gave her that lifelong love of heat and sunshine. And get this; she claims that until she was six, she barely spoke anything but Italian, thanks to her "smiling, dark-eyed peasant nurse" who filled her ears with what she'd later call "the most melodious of all languages." There is a chance that these were stories told by her mother and father about their travels before Jennie was born or she was truly born in 1950 in New York before they left for Italy in 1851.

One thing we do know is that Leonard Jerome wasn't exactly the type to settle down in some quiet Mediterranean town for long. A Princeton grad and the most ambitious of nine brothers, he packed up Jennie, her mom, and her two sisters (one of whom would die shortly after) and headed back to America. On the journey home, crossing the Mont Cenis in a horse-drawn carriage, Jennie says she was totally blown away by the deep snow - though she'd soon see plenty of that back in the States. The Mont Cenis crossing from Italy into France in the 1850s was done by "diligence" - a public stagecoach service that moved along the zigzag path of Napoleon's road. These vehicles were drawn by horses with "perpetually jingling bells" that would ascend and descend the mountain pass.

For the next few years, the Jerome family set up shop in New York, where her father was busy making and losing several fortunes. At one point, he practically owned the whole Pacific Mail Line. The guy was all over the place; he even co-edited the New York Times with Henry Raymond for a while. But his real legacy? He founded Jerome Park and the Coney Island Jockey Club - the first two major American racecourses - earning himself the title "father of the American turf" alongside his buddy August Belmont.

Leonard Jerome played a significant role in the founding and development of the Saratoga Race Course, which stands today as one of America's oldest and most prestigious racetracks.

Jerome was among the prominent financial tycoons who helped John "Old Smoke" Morrissey make the Saratoga Race Course a reality when it officially opened on August 2, 1864. Other notable backers included Commodore Cornelius Vanderbilt, John Hunter, and William Travers, the namesake of the prestigious Travers Stakes and Saratoga's first president.

While Morrissey was the driving force behind the racetrack, he understood that "his project would be more widely accepted if men such as Travers and Jerome were fronting the operation" due to their social standing. This arrangement helped give the new venture legitimacy in upper-class society circles.

The Civil War raged across America during these years, but in Jennie's world, it barely registered. The biggest impact on her young life was calling all the Southern kids at dance class "wicked rebels" and trying to pinch them. Oh, and singing some pretty harsh parodies of "Maryland, My Maryland."

One more sober memory that did stick with Jennie was when their Madison Square house was draped from top to bottom in black and white - the day of President Lincoln's funeral, when "the whole of New York looked like one gigantic mausoleum."

After the war came the usual childhood stuff - boring lessons, trips to the opera "to improve their minds," and the fun of sleighing and skating in winter. The real highlight for young Jennie? Getting to ride on her dad's coach to Jerome Park, where she "always occupied the seat of honor next him." Sometimes she'd even see her father's blue and white racing colors cross the finish line first, which was a major thrill for a little girl. Jerome Park was a famous horse racing track in the Bronx, New York, named after Leonard, and built in 1866 by Leonard Jerome and August Belmont Sr. and was the site of the first Belmont Stakes race in 1867.

However, Jerome Park no longer exists today as a racetrack. The site was acquired by New York City in the 1890s to build the Jerome Park Reservoir, which remains today as part of the city's water supply system. The reservoir was completed in 1906. But there is a still a Jerome Park neighborhood in the Bronx named after the historic racetrack, and there's also a small Jerome Park along the reservoir. Additionally, Jerome Avenue in the Bronx is named after Leonard Jerome as well. But if gambling on Wall Street was his hobby, horse racing was his passion.

He once hoisted Jennie onto his most famous racehorse, Kentucky, whose impressive lineage included "Lexington" and "Magnolia" by "Glencoe" - basically horse royalty. Kentucky never lost a single race but met a tragic end when he burned to death on his way to California after Leonard sold him for the then-ridiculous sum of $40,000.

Unlike most American kids, Jennie and her sisters weren't allowed to go to many children's dances. She did remember one fancy ball at Mr. Belmont's place when she was ten. She went dressed as a vivandière; a fancy French canteen girl. She and was so excited she couldn't sleep for days. But when the big night arrived, she ended up in floods of tears because she didn't look "at all as I thought I was going to" - a feeling she'd experience many times throughout her life.

The Jeromes spent some awesome summers in Newport, where Leonard built a charming villa - not one of those over-the-top white marble palaces that were becoming fashionable. In Newport, the Jerome girls were allowed to "run wild and be as grubby and happy as children ought to be."

Mrs. Ronalds, one of the reigning beauties of the day, gave Jennie a small dog-cart and two donkeys named "Willie" and "Wooshey." Jennie would fill the cart with half a dozen kids and tear up and down Bellevue Avenue, using what they called the "Persuader" - a stick with "the business end of a tin tack" - to get those donkeys moving. The cart and its wild pack of children soon became "a terror to the smart folk in their silks and feathers who drove majestically by." For Jennie, these were the golden days.

When Jennie Jerome was so very young, her world was seen through the eyes of her big sister, Clarita Jerome, who everyone called "Clara," the same as her mother. As so many younger sisters do, Jennie lived vicariously through her big sister during those desperate times when she was so eager to know and experience, to feel the meaning of adult life. As a young American girl living in Paris, she wouldn't venture too far down a path of melodrama and say her life was meaningless, but there was an acute sense of boredom, of waiting for... for what?

When her sister, Clara, would come home from rubbing shoulders with Royals at "small dances," Jennie's greedy ears would devour all that was served, but hearing all these delicious tales was no substitute for being in the room. Her sister's eyes would be twinkling, and plenty of her glitter and glee would gladly rub off. Jennie would hear so much about the elaborate gowns, the food and the music.

Oh, the music they played! Waltzes were at the height of fashion, with Johann Strauss II's compositions being particularly popular. His "Blue Danube" waltz, which premiered in 1867, was the new sensation at Parisian balls during this period. Other Strauss waltzes like "Tales from the Vienna Woods" filled her ears with delight. The three-quarter time signature of these waltzes created the sweeping, elegant movement that defined ballroom dancing of the era. But the best part of Clara's stories was about those larger than life personalities and what they would talk about. All of these stories, though, would only accentuate her painful anticipation, waiting to be old enough to attend these functions herself.

Jennie Jerome lived in Paris during her early adolescence, from approximately 1867 to 1870. Her father, Leonard Jerome, moved the family from New York to Paris during the Second French Empire when Emperor Napoleon III ruled and Paris was experiencing its grand renovation under Baron Haussmann. Their family lived in luxurious accommodations in Paris, where Jennie and her sisters received a cosmopolitan education that included music, languages, and the social graces expected of young ladies in European high society. Their time in Paris helped shape Jennie's sophisticated personality and contributed to her later success in British aristocratic circles - part of the recipe for a perfect statesman, Winston Churchill.

Later, as a sixteen-year-old, when Jennie Jerome was deemed a proper age to enter society, when she was no longer troubled by her governesses, she journeyed into those magnificent halls, and ballrooms, and boudoirs. Jennie realized that she was still not at the end of some fairy tale but the beginning of her life. There was even more anticipation and waiting; waiting for married life, which young women during that era were told is wonderful, then waiting for motherhood, which they were assured is sublime, and still more waiting for their children to reach certain stages, which truly is heavenly, and then their children would have children of their own, at which point much of the waiting is no longer anticipation. At that point, looking toward the past became preferable to Jennie, longing for those cherished days of youth when she was so very bored and eager to hurry up and get to what was next.

When would that day of peace arrive, not looking forward nor back, when she might be truly content and happy with who, where, and when she was?

Her memoirs, "The Reminiscences of Lady Randolph Churchill," might have been for money, but they could also be her gift to so many other little girls seemingly trapped in this beautiful world, desperately guessing and attempting to know the unknowable.

Yes, Jennie was in her mid-fifties and had entered what might be considered the third and final chapter of her life. But there is a good chance that the first few chapters of her memoir and some of the stories were inspired by the widely popular novel, *Little Women*, published a few years before Jennie was presented to society. Jennie might have kept a diary as mentioned in the Churchill Project at Hillsdale College; "A surviving diary entry by Jennie (written in 1882 when Winston was seven) records her reading to him and giving him lessons, unusual for a Victorian mother."

The basis for these early years might have been a diary; girls, especially girls from wealthy families did commonly keep diaries. Diary-keeping was a widespread practice among young women and girls during the Victorian era. Diary keeping in the 19th century was common enough that there were even established "rules" for the practice. One article from the period advised that keeping a diary would be "a wise idea" to record events that played out in one's life, suggesting it was a valued activity.

It was as if Jennie's sister, Clara, was Jo March and Jennie the forlorn Amy. Most likely there was many "Lauries" from "*Little Women.*" Decades later, when Jennie had the privilege to be engaged in the service of other fallen soldiers via the American Hospital Ship "Maine," she might have been reminded of those young boys she met, just before she was permitted to enter society and attend those "small dances."

In 1867, when Jennie's mom got sick, the family sailed to Europe so she could see the famous American doctor Dr. Sims in Paris. Jennie had no idea she wouldn't return to America until 1876, by which time she'd already been married for two years. Finding the educational opportunities better in Paris than New York, they decided to stay. Once her health improved, Jennie's mother became quite the hit in French society, where her beauty attracted tons of attention. Back then, a beautiful American woman was still a novelty.

But, Paris in 1869 was living its final moments of glory, though nobody knew it yet. The Second Empire seemed rock-solid, the court was dazzling, and the parties were out of this world. The light-hearted Parisians were loving the daily sight of royal processions and cavalcades. The Bois de Boulogne and the Champs Élysées, where the Jeromes were living, were packed with fancy carriages.

Jennie often spotted Empress Eugénie, whom she called "the handsomest woman in Europe." Empress Eugénie (full name: Eugénie de Montijo) was the wife of Napoleon III and the last Empress of France, reigning from 1853 to 1871.

Born in Spain in 1826 to a noble family, she was educated in France and became known for her beauty and intelligence. Napoleon III, who was the nephew of Napoleon Bonaparte and had established the Second French Empire after a coup d'état in 1851, married her in 1853, partially because she was not from a reigning royal house, which helped him avoid complicated diplomatic entanglements.

As Empress, Eugénie was a major fashion icon who greatly influenced European style and supported the haute couture industry in France. She was particularly associated with the designer Charles Frederick Worth, helping to establish Paris as the world's fashion capital. She also took an active role in politics, serving as regent during Napoleon III's absences and advocating for conservative Catholic positions.

When the Franco-Prussian War broke out in 1870, leading to the capture of Napoleon III and the fall of the Second Empire, Eugénie fled to England. After her husband's death in 1873, she lived in exile, primarily in England, for the rest of her long life. She died in 1920 at the age of 94, having outlived both her husband and their only son, who was killed in 1879 while serving with the British Army in the Anglo-Zulu War.

But Jennie mentions in her memoirs, Empress Eugénie, in about 1868 driving in her daumont with green and gold liveries that made quite the spectacle.

Four horses and postilions weren't just for royalty either - Princess Metternich, the Austrian Ambassador's wife, also rolled like that. The beautiful Madame de Canisy and the Duchesse de Mouchy (the Empress's BFF) cruised around in similar style, adding to Paris's air of elegance that no other European capital could touch. The Duchesse de Mouchy was Anna Murat (1841-1924), who was actually a relative of the Bonaparte family through her grandfather, Joachim Murat (Napoleon Bonaparte's famous cavalry general who later became King of Naples). Anna married Antoine de Noailles, the Duc de Mouchy, in 1865.

The Duchesse de Mouchy was indeed one of Empress Eugénie's closest confidantes and BFF and companions at the French imperial court. She was part of Eugénie's inner circle of ladies-in-waiting and friends, and remained loyal to the Empress even after the fall of the Second Empire in 1870.

Even among those who sensed trouble brewing, no one had spotted "the black shadow cast on the blue sky by the approaching figure of Bellona" (the Roman goddess of war) with "her fierce eyes fixed on happy, smiling, tranquil France." Although Jennie was still too young for society (and still dealing with governesses), she eagerly soaked up all the gossip about the Tuileries balls and Paris's buzzing social scene.

Emperor Napoleon III reportedly had a thing for Americans, and many were invited to official celebrations. Jennie's oldest sister, Clara, made her debut at one of the Tuileries balls. Despite being intimidated by the palace's grandeur and having to walk up the grand staircase between the Cent-Gardes in her first low-cut dress, she later gave Jennie all the juicy details.

Unlike at the English Court, there was no formal procession. When everyone had gathered, the doors would fly open, and they'd announce "Sa Majestél'Empereur," followed by "Sa Majestél'Impératrice." Empress Eugénie would appear looking incredible - one evening, Jennie mentions that the Empress wore green velvet with a crown of emeralds, diamonds, and pearls on her "small and beautifully shaped head."

Jennie goes on to describe how the Emperor and Empress would walk around the circle of guests (who were all curtseying and bowing), saying a few words here and there, then move on to the ballroom. Besides the grand palace functions, smaller and more casual dances called "petits Lundis" had been going on for about ten years. Even the Prince Imperial, though just a boy, was allowed to attend these, probably to help develop his social skills.

Beautiful women in Paris got invited to these events, where court ceremony was ditched in favor of having a good time. After one particularly lively petit Lundi, which had been extra fun because it was Twelfth Night and featured a magnificent "Gâteau des Rois" with gifts for the ladies, Count Hatzfeldt (later German Ambassador to England) made an ominous prediction: "I never saw their Majesties in better spirits than they were last night, and, God knows where they will be next year at this time." Looking back after everything fell apart, this comment seemed eerily prophetic.

The famous beauties who surrounded the Empress (whose portraits lined her Tuileries boudoir) were regulars at these small dances. The Marquise de Galliffet and her sister Madame Cordier would sometimes dress alike, creating a striking contrast between blonde and brunette. The Marquise de Galliffet was Florence Georgina Laffitte, born around 1843, who married General Gaston de Galliffet on October 26, 1859. She was a lady-in-waiting to Empress Eugénie and was considered one of the great beauties of the Second Empire.

Princess Metternich described Florence in her memoirs as having "auburn hair" and "strange and beautiful eyes - one green and one chestnut brown," adding that she had lovely teeth that "almost... illuminated her whole face." In 1868 specifically, the Marquis de Galliffet was featured in the painting "Le Cercle de la rue Royale" by James Tissot, showing his social standing in Parisian high society during that time.

It's worth noting that the Marquise and her husband eventually separated - according to an announcement of her death in 1901, they had lived apart "for nearly forty years," which would date their separation to around the early 1860s, though they never formally divorced. But in 1868, the Marquise was known to be "an intimate friend of the Empress Eugénie" along with Madame de Pourtalès, making her an important figure in the imperial court's inner circle.

Her husband, the Marquis de Galliffet, would later become infamous for his role in suppressing the Paris Commune in 1871, after the fall of the Second Empire.

The Comtesse de Pourtalès, with her bewitching face and killer charm, also dabbled in politics, serving as the link between the Legitimists and Bonapartists. The Comtesse de Pourtalès was Mélanie de Pourtalès (née Louise Sophie Mélanie Renouard de Bussière), who was born on March 26, 1836, at the Château de Robertsau in Strasbourg and died on May 5, 1914. She was introduced to the French imperial court by the Austrian ambassador, Richard von Metternich, and was also appointed as a lady-in-waiting to Empress Eugénie.

The Comtesse's salon was regarded as one of the most famed during the Second French Empire, where she became one of the leading figures in Parisian high society and imperial court life. She was described as a "familière de la Cour du Second Empire, salonnière" (a familiar figure at the Imperial Court and a renowned salon hostess). She and her husband, Count Edmond de Pourtalès, owned the Château de la Robertsau in Alsace (which is now known as the Château de Pourtalès), where they hosted illustrious guests including Franz Liszt, Napoleon III, Empress Eugénie, various European royalty, and Princess Metternich.

Years later, Jennie would see Comtesse de Pourtalès at the opera, looking like a vision in tulle, with soft brown hair, gorgeous expressive eyes, and a radiant smile. After Jennie married, whenever she visited Paris, she always found a warm welcome at the Comtesse's house on rue Tronchet. Even in her grandmother years, she remained stunning, with Frenchmen still calling her "La belle Mélanie" and saying "Elle estétonnante" (She is amazing).

These beautiful women ruled the social scene for so long that jealous rivals nicknamed them "La vieille Garde" (The Old Guard). Princess Mathilde, who had a swanky house in the rue de Courcelles, threw cotillions that attracted more aristocratic families than the Tuileries events. The noble set, satisfied that her mother was a Princess of Württemberg and her uncle was Czar Nicholas I, didn't see her as a social climber like they did the Empress.

Undoubtedly the smartest and most interesting woman of the Second Empire, Princesse Mathilde had handled the social duties at the Élysée back in 1848 for her cousin Louis Napoleon when he was President of the Republic. Her marriage to Count Anatole Demidoff had been a disaster, and after some seriously violent behavior on his part, they separated. Her uncle Nicholas I forced Demidoff to give her a massive income - reportedly twelve million francs over sixty years.

The Princess surrounded herself with witty, talented people, and her salon was world-famous, easily matching the legendary salons of the eighteenth century, with the added bonus of royalty and major cash. When she opened her doors for something as frivolous as a dance, it was to please the Prince Imperial and the Empress's nieces. That's where some of the pretty young Americans in Paris, including Jennie's sister (later Mrs. Moreton Frewen), got to mingle with major celebs like Dumas, Sardou, Théophile Gautier, and Baudry. At this point in the memoirs that we noticed how women were known by their husband's name. Jennie wrote these memoirs about the life of Lady Randolph Churchill - instead of Jennie Jerome Churchill and her sister, Clara, becomes Mrs. Moreton Frewen.

But, as we continued through her memoirs, we do notice the Jennie spends a lot of her time discussing the wives of famous men. She continues "name dropping" with more of Eugénie's inner circle. To Jennie, none stood out like Princess Pauline Metternich, the Austrian Ambassador's wife. Though only 22 when she hit Paris in 1860, her wit, energy, and extraordinary "chic" (the only word that really fits) immediately put her among the leaders of Europe's most brilliant court. Her clever comebacks were on everyone's lips, every woman tried to copy her outfits, and everyone who was anyone wanted her at their parties.

Metternich's true passion was the theater. Nothing made her happier than organizing amateur dramatics, and she was the driving force behind all the shows at Compiègne, whether dancing as a black devil in a ballet or dressing as a coachman singing saucy verses. It helped that Octave Feuillet wrote the lyrics and Viollet-le-Duc was the stage manager. Despite these silly pastimes, Princess Metternich remained a true aristocrat.

After the Empire fell, she returned to Vienna and quickly gained the same social power she'd enjoyed for ten years in Paris. A genuine art and music patron, she was solely responsible for getting "Tannhäuser" performed in Paris in 1861, though it bombed spectacularly. The French weren't ready for anything as complex as Wagner yet, but credit to her for understanding and appreciating him twenty years before they did.

By 1888, the Viennese had written a poem in her honor that went:

Es giebtnur a Kaiserstadt;
Es giebtnur a Wien;
Es giebtnur a Fürstin:
Es is die Metternich Paulin.

(There's only one Imperial city; There's only one Vienna; There's only one Princess: It's Metternich Pauline.)

Years later, when Jennie wanted to put on a performance of the "Puppenfee" in London, Princess Metternich sent her detailed instructions showing what a born director she was.

But Jennie did notice some of the famous men. Among the social stars of the Second Empire, Boson de Talleyrand Périgord, Prince de Sagan (later Duc de Talleyrand) was the standout. Along with the Duc de Morny and Count Gramont-Caderousse, he kept Paris society in a constant state of amazement with his parties and extravagance. His name was on everyone's lips.

He was part of the distinguished Talleyrand-Périgord family, with important connections to French nobility. Boson de Talleyrand-Périgord was the son of Napoléon Louis, III. duc de Talleyrand-Périgord (1811-1898) and Anne Louise Charlotte Alix de Montmorency (1810-1858). His family had deep aristocratic roots, with his grandfather being Alexandre de Talleyrand-Périgord and his grandmother being Dorothea of Courland, Duchess of Sagan.

As a cavalry officer, Boson de Talleyrand-Périgord became one of the major figures in French high society in the second half of the 19th century. He was known for his elegance and aristocratic bearing, embodying the refined lifestyle associated with the Prince de Sagan title.

When Jennie first met the Prince after the war in 1872, he was about forty-five. He was quite the sight - snow-white curly hair that stood out like a lion's mane (which he had a habit of running his fingers through), a well-built figure, perfect clothes, a white carnation in his buttonhole, and a monocle attached to a black moiré ribbon that instantly became the fashion. He was the ultimate Parisian dandy - "le dernier cri" (the latest fashion). Newspapers and theaters constantly caricatured him.

Though kind-hearted, he deserved better than the mess of his home life, where his problems with the Princess were public knowledge for years. A descendant of the famous diplomat Marquis de Talleyrand, he stood to inherit a dukedom and massive estates in both Germany and France, including the historic Château de Valançay on the Loire. Though he didn'tactually get his inheritance until he was old and sick, he'd already blown through most of it anyway.

He created the Auteuil race-course and the Cercle de la rue Royale, supported the arts, and helped many artists succeed. Whatever his faults, Jennie thought he probably got as good as he gave. When he was hit with paralysis, fate ironically landed him in his wife's house, where he hadn't lived for years and had sworn never to enter again. He was still living there when Jennie wrote her memoir, the Princess having died a few years earlier. He later became the 4th Duke of Talleyrand upon his father's death in 1898, inheriting the title "His Serene Highness, the 4th Duke of Talleyrand and Herzog zu Sagan."

The Prince organized many fun outings for Jennie and her sister. She remembered one picnic to St. Germain when James Gordon Bennett was driving them back on his coach and they crashed near the Arc de Triomphe, nearly killing everyone. Sometimes she'd ride with her father and the Prince in the Bois de Boulogne, feeling very grand on a seemingly fiery chestnut horse.

In November 1869, the Empress went to Egypt to open the Suez Canal while the Emperor stayed in France for political reasons. Talk about a royal tour - her progress created massive excitement. She left Port Said for Ismailia on the Aigle, which had been tricked out to the max for her, with sixty vessels following behind. Cleopatra sailing up the Cydnus to meet Mark Antony had nothing on this spectacle, and like the Egyptian queen, Eugénie "beggared all description." Every stop featured ridiculous expenditure and display as everyone competed to honor the gorgeous Empress who, "imposing and serene," was then balanced - for one final moment, though she didn't know it - at the peak of her power and glory.

The Duc d'Albe, her favorite nephew who was in her entourage, told Jennie years later about this incredible journey. When the Empress stepped off the boat at Ismailia, she found all the carriages waiting for her painted in the imperial colors, with green and gold liveries and gold bees. Even her villa was furnished exactly like her rooms at the Tuileries so she'd feel at home. Apparently, they did the same thing for Queen Victoria when she and Prince Albert visited the French court in 1855 for the Exhibition.

Verdi composed "Aida" for the Canal opening and in honor of the Empress, who attended the premiere in Cairo.

While Eugénie was in Egypt, the Emperor threw what would turn out to be his last famous party at Compiègne, with Princesse Mathilde helping host.

The Château de Compiègne was a former royal residence built for Louis XV and later restored by Napoleon I. From 1856 onward, Napoleon III and Empress Eugénie made it their autumn residence and redecorated some rooms in the Second Empire style. This magnificent palace became one of the three most important imperial residences in France, alongside Versailles and Fontainebleau.

Compiègne was one of the Emperor's preferred residences because it offered a freer lifestyle, with less emphasis on rigid etiquette compared to other imperial palaces. The palace also played a key role in the imperial couple's personal history, it was here that the relationship between Eugénie de Montijo and Napoleon III blossomed into romance, leading to their marriage just one month later.

During their stay at Compiègne, guests enjoyed various forms of entertainment. Hunts, excursions, games, concerts, and theatrical performances filled their days, allowing them to temporarily forget the constraints of etiquette that normally governed court life. For entertainment, the palace hosted many different activities. Amateur theater was particularly appreciated, with guests participating in charades, pantomimes, tableaux vivants, and other theatrical games. Napoleon According to anecdotes, Empress Eugénie had theater troupes arrive from Paris by train on the day of performances and depart immediately afterward, supposedly because she knew her husband's tendencies and didn't want to risk him becoming infatuated with a young and pretty actress. To further enhance entertainment options, Napoleon III decided in 1866 to build a larger, more modern theater. The Imperial Theatre of Compiègne was designed by the official government architect, Auguste-Gabriel Ancelet, and was connected to the château by a covered gallery that formed a bridge over the road. The Forest of Compiègne was a major attraction and hunting ground. It is a vast wooded area roughly circular in shape with a diameter of about 14 kilometers (9 miles), covering approximately 14,414 hectares (35,620 acres). Stretching forward from the château, the Avenue de Beaux Monts scales the heights of the same name, providing a scenic promenade into the woods.

The forest was lushly irrigated, being adjacent to the rivers Oise and Aisne, as well as many smaller tributaries and streams. It featured picturesque natural attractions with arrays of oak and beech trees projecting what was described as a "noble and ordered beauty." The most prominent tree species were oak, beech, and hornbeam. For centuries, the Compiègne forest had been a prized hunting ground for virtually all the kings of France. Some 350 roads and pathways cross it, adding up to over six hundred miles of trail with stately vintage signposts marking most of the intersections. Interestingly, the oldest signposts include a small red mark showing the direction to the château, these were added by imperial order during the Second Empire after Empress Eugénie once found herself lost in the thick woods.

This party at Compiègne that Jennie discusses in her memoirs was smaller than usual because the Emperor's health was bad and he was worried about politics. Jennie's mother and sister were among the invited guests. The entertainment included hunting, shooting, and dancing. On the first day, there was a grande chasse (stag hunt) that all guests attended, riding or driving. The hunters wore royal colors - men in green coats with gold buttons, ladies in flowing green habits and three-cornered hats. The stag was eventually cornered in a lake, with the Prince Imperial delivering the coup de grâce (mercy killing).

That night came the curée aux flambeaux (torchlit presentation of the kill) in the château courtyard. Everyone gathered on the balconies in the torchlight. The deer's carcass lay in the center, covered with its skin. The hallali (hunting horn) sounded; at a signal the hounds were released, and within seconds the stag had completely disappeared.

The next day, they organized a trip to see Château Pierrefonds, about ten miles away. The party traveled in chars-à-bancs (open carriages) guided by M. Viollet-le-Duc, the famous architect who had just restored the place. Compiègne, where Joan of Arc was captured and which Louis XV rebuilt and Napoleon I decorated, seemed modern compared to this massive castle with its battlements and medieval features.

After touring the castle with Viollet-le-Duc as their guide, they had tea in the beautiful armory, where the Emperor gave each lady a souvenir - a small weapon.

One day there was a Cabinet Council, and guests were told to be quiet and not disturb His Majesty. Who knows what critical issues they discussed? Times were tense, and talks with Prussia weren't going well. The government was fighting with the opposition.

Marshal Bazaine, who had come from Paris for this Council, had recently made major military preparations to stop Opposition members from meeting to change the date set by the Government for the Chambers to convene. The Emperor himself, expecting trouble, had gone to Paris. Thankfully, everything stayed peaceful, and the troops weren't needed. But it shows how precarious things were for the Empire and the new Ollivier Ministry.

At this Compiègne visit, Bazaine brought his Mexican wife, who caused a sensation by wearing a vivid scarlet dress with matching gloves. This was considered très Anglais (very English), as French women avoided such bright colors.

Every night, sixty to a hundred guests had dinner, with the Emperor never letting it last more than 45 minutes. Sometimes they used magnificent gold plates, sometimes precious Sèvres porcelain. Before dinner, people lined up in two rows. The Emperor escorted Princesse Mathilde, sitting across from her at the table's center, with a few honor seats reserved on each side. Everyone else sat where they wanted, with ladies choosing which gentlemen would escort them, as was the custom at Compiègne. After dinner came dancing, which the Prince Imperial, then only thirteen, could join until ten o'clock, when his tutor would approach saying, "Monseigneur, votre chapeau" (Your Highness, your hat) - code for bedtime.

At the end of the visit came a grand lottery where all tickets won prizes. The Emperor stood near two large urns from which numbers were drawn, wishing each guest "Bonne chance" (Good luck) as they received their number. There must have been some behind-the-scenes manipulation, because

Jennie's mother and the American minister, Mr. Washburne, won valuable pieces of Sèvres china, while younger people got less expensive gifts. Jennie's sister received an inkstand shaped like a knotted handkerchief filled with napoleons (gold coins), which prompted the Emperor to joke, "Mademoiselle, n'oubliez pas les Napoléons!" (Miss, don't forget the Napoleons!) - a clever play on words.

War in Paris

Chartwell, 1964

"The Franco-Prussian War," Churchill mused, setting down his teacup with care. He looked past Sophia to the window, where a thin autumn mist had begun to soften the outlines of the rose gardens. "Most people forget that my mother was just a girl when it all began. Seventeen, barely that. And living in the very heart of it all, amidst boulevards that would soon run with the fever of siege and revolution." The timbre of his voice changed, the words carrying an undertone that suggested both pride and mourning.

Sophia watched the transformation, saw how the memory of Jennie Jerome animated the old man. Her notebook rested untouched in her lap. She sensed that she was in the presence of a story that would be told in the pauses and digressions, in the faint glimmer that appeared, unexpected, in the eye of a legend.

"She watched an empire fall, Miss Carter," Churchill continued. "Saw Napoleon III's Second Empire crumble in a matter of months. You must picture it, a city famous for its parties, its salons, every evening a waltz of uniforms and whispered intrigues, suddenly seized by the iron logic of war. Food rationed, streets barricaded, the elegant promenades turned into firing lines and trenches." He chuckled, the sound like gravel tumbling in a tin. "And yet, Paris kept on living. The gaslights burned, the theatre boxes were filled, even under bombardment, because the Parisians, like my mother, knew that panic is the least practical of virtues."

"That must have been terrifying for a young American girl," Sophia said, her voice nearly a whisper.

"Terrifying?" Churchill's laugh was softer now, almost fond. "She found it exhilarating. The Jeromes, her family, were meant to depart for London, like every other respectable American expatriate. But my mother, even then, disdained respectability. She persuaded her father to stay, to see the drama to its end. She argued, with a logic I would later recognize in myself, that true history is not witnessed from a safe distance. It must be inhaled, lived, even if it chokes you." He paused, a distant look settling over his features. "She attended salons where bullets whistled past the shutters. She wrote letters by candlelight as shells shattered the rooftops. When the city starved, she dined on stewed rat in the company of poets and generals, as if Paris would never permit her to be merely ordinary."

Sophia resisted the urge to scribble in her notebook, unwilling to break the spell. "It sounds almost romantic," she remarked.

Churchill's lips tightened. "War is never romantic, not in the sense young men, or magazine writers, forgive me, often hope. But for her, those months in Paris were the crucible. They set her nature. She was a creature of style, yes, but also of resilience. To the end of her days, Miss Carter, my mother preferred danger to dullness. When other women trembled, she laughed."

He rocked back in his chair. "Years later, during the Blitz, when London was burning and Downing Street shook with each new detonation, my staff urged me to evacuate

to the country. Take the government underground, they said. Preserve the chain of command. They had charts and protocols and all the persuasive instruments of bureaucracy. But I thought of her then, seventeen, besieged, and utterly unafraid, and I asked myself how I could possibly run when she had refused to. How could I bear to look in the mirror if I abandoned the city she would have protected at any cost?"

Sophia found herself leaning forward, the question out before she could moderate it. "She shaped your courage." Churchill nodded, not as a gesture of pride, but of acknowledgment. "She shaped my understanding that crisis reveals character, not creates it. The girl who refused to flee Prussian guns became the woman who taught her son never to yield to tyranny. She never said as much. She didn't need to. Hers was an education by example."

He fell silent, the only sound the gentle ticking of the clock. For a moment, Sophia saw not the statesman of history, but an old man adrift in the memory of a mother he had never ceased yearning for.

When Churchill finally spoke again, his voice was quieter, as if addressing his words to the past. "They accuse me of sentimentality, Miss Carter. Of romanticizing adversity. But I assure you, the agony of those years in Paris marked my mother forever. She saw suffering, yes, but she saw too how ordinary people, servants, shopkeepers, even the street sweepers, found dignity in defiance. That was the lesson she passed to me, never underestimate the ordinary man, or woman, in their hour of crisis."

Sophia sensed the interview was shifting, that the old man's defenses had been lowered by the force of nostalgia. She considered her next question carefully, wishing for the subtlety of a Parisian salon rather than the blunt tools of modern journalism. "Do you ever feel," she asked, "that your mother's legend is larger than her life? That perhaps you've made her into a myth?"

Churchill's good eye twinkled, catching the low light like a gem. "All mothers are myths, Miss Carter. It is their privilege. But the myth, as you say, has its uses." The smile returned, sadder and wiser. "Without legends, what are we left with? Lists of dates, tables of casualties, the dull arithmetic of the graveyard. My mother had no patience for such things. She lived her own legend, and forced the world to accommodate it."

Sophia closed her notebook, understanding that the best part of the story would not be found on the printed page, but perhaps, if she was cunning enough, she could capture the essence of it between the lines. "How much," Sophia ventured, "do you think your mother's Americanness made a difference, in the end? Did it set her apart, or simply give her license to defy the rules?"

Churchill considered this. He rose, not without effort, and limped to the window, gazing out at the swans and the relentless drizzle beyond. "It made all the difference," he repeated. "Americans believe that reality itself can be remade by willpower. The English prefer to endure it. My mother believed in both. She taught me to respect tradition, and at the same time, to break it whenever necessary."

He turned, the silhouette of the garden, a landscape of survival, framed behind him. "That is what saved us in 1940. The stubbornness of the English, galvanized by the reckless optimism of the American. A rather potent mixture, don't you agree?"

Sophia smiled. "Unbeatable, I would say."

PARIS, 1870

By spring 1870, Paris was buzzing with unrest and war rumors. Prussia had repeatedly acted aggressively and insulted France. Prévost Paradol, a brilliant journalist whose daughter played with Jennie, described the two countries as "running on the same lines, collision being inevitable." People said the Emperor was too trusting and Bismarck was sneaky; Bismarck wanted war, and he usually got what he wanted. In Prussia too, disturbing rumors had been circulating for a while.

In 1862, King Wilhelm I appointed Bismarck as Minister President of Prussia, a position he held until 1890 (with a brief break in 1873). He was a practitioner of realpolitik - politics based primarily on practical considerations rather than ideological notions.

By 1870, Prussia under King Wilhelm I was emerging as a hegemonic power in Europe. After victories in the Second Schleswig War in 1864 and against Austria at Sadowa in 1866, Prussia had dissolved the German Confederation in favor of the North German Confederation. Wilhelm I became president of this new confederation and Bismarck its chancellor. Napoleon

Bismarck believed that a war against France was necessary to create German nationalism and allow for the unification of the German states. He famously stated: "I knew that a Franco-Prussian War must take place before a united Germany was formed." Some historians argue that Bismarck deliberately provoked France into declaring war to draw the southern German states, Baden, Württemberg, Bavaria, and Hesse-Darmstadt, into an alliance with the North German Confederation dominated by Prussia.

When General Blumenthal was shooting in Norfolk in 1869 with Lord Albemarle, who mentioned wanting to see Prussian military exercises, the General replied ominously: "It is not necessary to come to Prussia; we will have a review for you in the Champ-de-Mars."

The Hohenzollern incident was the last straw, pushing France beyond endurance. When Prince Leopold of Hohenzollern (Bismarck's puppet) became a candidate for the Spanish throne, the French saw it as "unesanglante injure pour l'Empereur Napoléon" (a bloody insult to Emperor Napoleon). Fired up by the press, the whole country demanded war. According to history, peace might have survived if not for the rashness of the Duc de

Gramont (then Foreign Minister) and the bungling of M. Émile Ollivier, who famously said he and his colleagues took responsibility for the war "d'un cœurléger" (with a light heart).

With peace negotiations now impossible, on July 19, 1870, war was declared, much to the Emperor's sorrow. Napoleon was very sick at the time, about to have a serious operation, and had tried everything to prevent war.

Jennie never forgot the excitement. Crowds filled the streets shouting "À Berlin!" (To Berlin!). The war was the only topic anyone talked about. Complete strangers would stop each other to discuss what was happening. Everyone had total confidence in the generals and army. They all believed it would be one straight march to Berlin; nobody doubted it for a second. The Jeromes' sympathies were naturally with the French, and Jennie felt she hated "Ces sales Prussiens" (those dirty Prussians) as much as any Parisian.

Wild incidents kept happening. One day Jennie saw Capoul, the famous tenor, and Marie Sass from the Opera being recognized in an omnibus, then made to stand on top and sing the "Marseillaise" while a growing crowd joined in the chorus. The omnibus was a popular form of public transportation, particularly in cities like Paris and London. It was a horse-drawn, enclosed carriage designed to carry multiple passengers.

One night the Jeromes went to the opera in walking clothes, carrying their hats in case trouble broke out and they had to walk home - which they did. The performance was bizarre, with singers constantly interrupted and forced to perform patriotic songs.

Getting home for the Jeromes proved extremely difficult because the streets were packed with huge crowds chanting "des chassepots, des chassepots" (demanding rifles). "Poor guys," Jennie thought, they soon got all the rifles and fighting they could handle.

July and August were anxious months. The Jeromes followed war news obsessively, tracking events with maps and flags. One day the Emperor was leaving Paris for Metz to join his army of 380,000 men, which to his horror turned out to be only 220,000 poorly equipped troops. Another day brought details of Saarbruck and the Prince Imperial's baptême de feu (baptism of fire). Or they'd hear about Marshal Lebœuf resigning and Marshal Bazaine becoming Commander-in-Chief, which according to M. Barthélemy Saint-Hilaire would "give confidence to the country."

But the terrible news kept coming; the speed of the French army's collapse seemed unbelievable. Soon their maps of France were bristling with the hated Prussian flag, and people were shouting "Nous sommestrahis!" (We've been betrayed!).

Once or twice, rumors of great victories spread. Within minutes, the whole city would be decorated with flags flying from every window and celebrations everywhere, only for the jubilation to end hours later as the truth emerged and the "glorious victory" turned out to be a crushing defeat like Weissemburg, Worth, or Gravelotte, followed by more cries of betrayal from the bewildered Parisians.

As the war advanced, foreigners who could leave Paris did so. The Jeromes were advised to go, but Jennie's mother had a bad sprain and couldn't walk, so they stayed put. Besides, they couldn't believe the Prussians would actually reach Paris, so they kept delaying their departure. Their house became a meeting place for their few French friends who hadn't gone to fight.

Their main visitor was the Duc de Persigny, who had been close with the Jerome family for years. Persigny, a compact, dapper man with piercing eyes and pleasant manners, had been Louis Napoleon's right-hand man - also known as Victor Fialin. He'd shared Napoleon's adventures and imprisonment, and when Louis Napoleon became Emperor, he reaped the benefits of his loyalty. The Emperor once joked about his government: "How can you expect my government to get on? The Empress is a Legitimist; Morny is an Orleanist; Prince Napoleon is a Republican; I am a Socialist, only Persigny is an Imperialist, and he is mad!"

When Persigny became a duke, he married the daughter of the Prince de la Moskowa, whose grandfather was the famous Marshal Ney. The Duchesse de Persigny was definitely eccentric. Stories about her behavior while her husband was Ambassador to England were legendary. Her lateness was notorious - once at an official Embassy dinner for the Lord Mayor, guests were told "Her Grace was in her bath," and she appeared with her beautiful blonde hair (which she was very proud of) still wet and hanging down her back, saying "Pardonnezmoimesamis, c'estcetimbécile de Persigny qui ne m'a pas fait dire l'heure" (Forgive me, my friends, it's that imbecile Persigny who didn't tell me the time).

The Duchess had a quick temper too. At a children's dance in Paris, Jennie vividly remembered getting her ears boxed because she couldn't do the mazurka. The Duchess was a major Anglophile, and their country estate Chamarande was furnished entirely in English style - which, given the early Victorian taste of the era, wasn't exactly attractive. Several rooms were copies of Balmoral Castle, a private royal residence located in Aberdeenshire, Scotland, that served as a beloved retreat for the British Royal Family.

Chamarande was complete with tartan curtains and carpets that made art-loving Frenchmen raise their eyebrows. On the other hand, the bedrooms with English writing-tables and comfortable armchairs showed the French what such rooms could be.

In August 1870, the Empress - who'd been made regent and was living at St. Cloud - received frequent visits from Persigny, who kept the Jeromes informed. This was her third time serving as regent, as she had previously taken on this role in 1859 and 1865. As regent, she presided over the Ministerial Council, though she was prohibited from promulgating any new laws except for those already under discussion. The Palace of Saint-Cloud, located near Paris, had been a favored residence of Napoleon III and Empress Eugénie. The imperial couple had even spent their honeymoon there, and it was used as a summer residence during their reign.

The news grew increasingly alarming until one day he burst in crying, "Tout est perdu; les Prussienssont à nosportes!" (All is lost; the Prussians are at our gates!) and begging them to flee before it was too late.

With great difficulty and heavy hearts, they prepared to leave for Deauville. As a coastal town in Normandy, Deauville provided access to the English Channel and offered an escape route to England. Trains were running irregularly and infrequently. As it turned out, they caught the very last train to depart. They could only take luggage they could carry themselves, so they tied a few clothes in sheets and tablecloths. Jennie's mother had to be carried since she couldn't walk.

While in Deauville, a friend named M. de Gardonne unexpectedly showed up at their hotel and asked to hide in their rooms for the day. He insisted they not mention his name or tell anyone they'd seen him. Naturally, they found this strange, and Jennie's mother grew suspicious, but he claimed it was for "state reasons" that they'd hear about later. After dinner, when it was completely dark, he left as mysteriously as he'd arrived.

Two days later, they were thrilled to learn about the Empress's escape from Paris with Dr. Crane, Dr. Evans (the

American dentist), and Madame Lebreton, their friend M. de Gardonne having helped arrange it. The Empress arrived in Deauville incognito, boarded Sir John Burgoyne's yacht waiting in the harbor, and after a rough crossing landed at Ryde in the Isle of Wight. The dangers of this escape, while less hazardous and more successful than the Flight of Varennes, had been greatly exaggerated in retellings. The Flight to Varennes was a pivotal moment of the earlier French Revolution (1789-1799), in which King Louis XVI of France, his wife Queen Marie Antoinette, and their children attempted to escape from Paris. They made it to the small town of Varennes-en-Argonne, where they were arrested and returned to Paris.

Meanwhile the Emperor, after Bazaine's defeat at Gravelotte and other disasters, repaired to Sedan, where, after the battle, on his own authority, he raised the flag of truce. According to his posthumous memoirs, Napoleon III "understood the gravity of the responsibility which he was incurring and foresaw the accusations that would be raised against him." As an example of these, the letter on the following page, which Jennie included in her memoirs from General Palikao, his late Minister of War, is of interest.

The Comte de Palikao, formerly General Moutauban, took part in the 1860 expedition to China. He was said to have acquired his title (the name Palikao being derived from a town in China) from the fact that he had presented the Empress Eugenie with some splendid black pearls, looted during the sack of the Summer Palace in Peking.

OSTENDE, October 21, 1870.

MY DEAR DUKE,

I arrived in Ostend four days ago, and I found your address at our mutual friends the Bureaus.

Since our separation on the 7th, I have been in Belgium and I would have asked for your news since this time if I had known where to send you a letter. I therefore eagerly seize the opportunity offered to me by the encounter with this excellent prefect of Orleans, to come and chat with you for a few moments.

Threatened in my freedom on the day of September 4, I left the same evening, and I took refuge first in Namur where I was joined by my wife and daughters 24 hours after my departure.

The main purpose of my trip to Namur was to get closer to Sedan, to find out about my son who was causing me great concern. After several days of searching, I finally learned that my son, after being wounded at Sedan, and having had a horse killed, was a prisoner in Cologne, not having wanted to accept the capitulation for himself.

I left Nemours for Spa; the latter place being no longer habitable during the winter, I came to settle in Ostend to await events whose outcome I cannot foresee.

How I wish, my dear Duke, that I had a pen skilled enough to retrace for you all the impressions I have experienced since that fatal Sedan. I came to ask myself how such a disaster could have occurred, without the principal author of this dismal drama having buried himself under the corpses of his army!

I believed that it was easier to die than to dishonor oneself...

The death of the Emperor at Sedan would have saved both France and his son, the capitulation has lost everything. France has become the prey of foreign and internal Vandals, how can this desolation of our unfortunate country end! , unless a general war, which should bring a diversion in Prussian politics, I do not see in which direction we can turn. England seems to have abandoned us, and yet the circumstances which had cemented our alliance of 1856, may reoccur for Her, but then she will no longer be able to count on our support. We have fallen very low!

I had offered my services to the government of national defense but I withdrew my offers as soon as I saw the government call, to the eternal shame of France, a Garibaldi to defend it.

On the other hand, accusations of treason reach all the generals who served the Empire, I did not want to mix my name with all these ignominies.

Farewell, my dear Duke, if you want to give me your news, my family and I will be very happy...for we all have a grateful heart.

All yours,

General de Palikao.

In view of this somewhat cruel letter, Jennie could not refrain from quoting General Changarnier, who, although at one time hostile to the Emperor, spoke of him thus: "...And he has been called 'Coward'! When I remember that this man, tortured by a horrible disease, remained on horseback at Sedan an entire day, watching disappear the prestige of France, his throne, his dynasty, and all the glory reaped at Sebastopol and in Lombardy, I cannot control myself."

And again, Colonel Fabre said: "The Emperor remained passively for two hours under the fire of shells, seeing many of his officers killed round him, before he reentered Sedan."

It is easy to see in her memoirs that Jennie felt deeply for Napoleon III. After his capture, he was initially imprisoned in

Germany at Wilhelmshöhe Castle in Westphalia until March 1871 before being allowed to go to England In England, Napoleon III settled with his wife Empress Eugénie and their son at a small country house called Camden Place in the village of Chislehurst near London where he would spend his final few years.

In October, not being able to return to Paris, Jennie and her family migrated to England, which she now saw for the first time. A winter spent in the gloom and fogs of London did not tend to dispel the melancholy which they felt. Their friends scattered, fighting, or killed at the front; debarred as they were from their bright little house and their household gods, it was indeed a sad time.

Among the refugees who came to London was the Due de Persigny. Broken-hearted, ill, and penniless, their poor friend was put to many straits to eke out a living selling the little he had been able to bring away with him. His devotion to Napoleon III never altered, although the Emperor was often irritated with him and evidently, from the following letter, thought he interfered indiscreetly:

WILHELMSHOHE, January 7, 1871.

MY DEAR PERSIGNY,

I received your letter of January 1, and I thank you for the wishes you make for a better future. Without wanting to enter into the discussion of the ideas you put forward, I will tell you that nothing good can come out of this confusion that results from individual efforts, made without discretion and without authorization. Indeed, I find it strange that people should concern themselves with the future of my son without worrying about my intentions.

I know that you wrote to Mr. de Bismarck who naturally asked me if this was with my authorization and as being in agreement with me. I had him answer that I had not authorized anyone to take care of my interests and those of my son without my consent.

Believe, my dear Persigny, in my friendship,

Napoleon.

The letter was written from Wilhelmshohe (where the Prussians held Napoleon III, and given to Jennie by M. de Persigny as an autograph of the Emperor, the Duke adding at the same time that it compromised no one but himself.

There is good reason to believe that the letter referred to a scheme for placing the Prince Imperial on the throne during the Emperor's captivity, with the Empress as Regent. Persigny died in 1872, preceding by one year his imperial master in 1873.

That autumn and winter of 1870-1871 London society was much entertained and a little scandalized by the doings and sayings of two pretty and lively refugees from Paris. The Duchesse de Carracciolo and the Comtesse de Bechevet, with their respective husbands and a few Frenchmen who preferred shooting birds in England to being shot at in France, took a place in the country. Many were the stories told of practical jokes and unorthodox sporting incidents, the ladies astonishing the country yokels by shooting in kilts and smoking cigarettes, a thing unheard of in those days. All London laughed at the misfortunes of M. de Bechevet, who, being ill, was persuaded by one of the guests, admirably disguised as a doctor, that he was dying. Another guest, travestied as a priest, received his last confession, which eagerly listened to by the rest of the party, hidden behind curtains, their peals of laughter resuscitating the dying man.

While they were in London, and during the siege, Jennie's father, who had just arrived from America, arranged to go to Paris with General Sheridan. They got permission to see Mr. Washburne, the American Minister, who had been through the whole siege. They were blindfolded and taken through the Prussian lines, and a few days later saw the great columns of the victorious army roll down the Champs-Elysees. Her father on his return gave Jennie a graphic description of the triumphal entry and of the vivid scene impressed on him, how the masses of infantry, most of them wearing spectacles, marched by the Arc de Triomphe, which was barricaded, and through the deserted streets of the once gay city singing "Die Wacht am Rhein." Many were the stories of individual suffering and despair, of hair-breadth escapes and brave deeds, told him by the besieged.

That summer Jennie paid her first visit to Cowes. In those days it was delightfully small and peaceful. No glorified villas, no esplanade or pier, no bands, no motors or crowded tourist steamers, "no nothing," as the children say.

The Royal Yacht Squadron Club lawn did not resemble a garden party, or the roadstead a perpetual regatta. Yachts went in and out without fear of losing their moorings, and most of them belonged to the Royal Yacht Squadron. People all seemed to know one another. The Prince and Princess of Wales and many foreign royalties could walk about and amuse themselves without being photographed or mobbed, and many were the gay little expeditions to Shanklin Bay, Freshwater, or Beaulieu, where they threw off all ceremony and enjoyed themselves like ordinary mortals.

After his release, the Emperor Napoleon III and the Empress Eugenie, who were now living at Camden House, Chiselhurst, came to Cowes on a short visit. One day a gentleman called, but finding Jennie and her family out, left a card saying he would come again. "Le Comte de Pierrefonds", who could it be?

They asked the Empress's private secretary, M. Pietri. M. Pietri replied with "Mais c'estl'Empereur!" (But it's the Emperor!), laughing as he said it.

This revealed that the visitor was actually Emperor Napoleon III, who was using the title "Comte de Pierrefonds" as an alias or incognito title after his exile from France. Shortly afterward they were asked by their Majesties to go for an expedition round the Island. The party consisted of the Emperor and Empress, the Prince Imperial, the Empress's nieces the Mesdemoiselles d'Albe (afterwards Duchesse de Medina Coeli and Marquise de Tamamis), and Prince Joachim Murat, the Due d'Albe (Carlos), a few Spaniards, and the suite, which was composed of one or two faithful followers. The expedition was rather a failure, owing to the roughness of the sea, most of the party seeking "the seclusion that the cabin grants." The Mesdemoiselles d'Albe were desperately ill, and lay on the deck in a state of coma. But the Empress enjoyed the breeze. The young Prince Imperial, full of life and spirits, chaffed everyone, some of his jokes falling rather flat on the Spaniards, who were feeling anything but bright, and evidently thought it no laughing matter.

Jennie could see the Emperor leaning against the mast, looking old, ill, and sad. His thoughts could not have been other than sorrowful, and even in her young eyes he seemed to have nothing to live for. She was right, he died a few years later.

After two years' absence (having left for two weeks, as they thought at the time), Jennie and her family returned to Paris, to find their house, goods, and chattels intact, with the exception of the cellar, which had been visited by a shell from Mont Valerien.

But what changes in Paris itself! Ruins everywhere: the sight of the Tuileries and the Hotel de Ville made her cry. St.-Cloud, the scene of many pleasant expeditions, was a thing of the past, the lovely chateau razed to the ground. And if material Paris was damaged, the social fabric was even more so. In vain they tried to pick up the threads. Some of their friends were killed, others ruined or in mourning, and all broken-hearted and miserable, hiding in their houses and refusing to be comforted.

The statues at the Place de la Concorde representing the most important towns of France,, Strasburg, Lille, Nancy, Orleans,, swathed in crape, in which some are still draped on the anniversary of Sedan, reminded one daily, if one had needed it, of the trials and tribulations France had just gone through. Only the embassies and a few foreigners, principally Americans, received or entertained. The Misses King (one of them became Madame Waddington, wife of the Ambassador to England) gave small parties. Mrs. John Munroe, the wife of the American banker, also gave dances for her daughters, who eventually married, one Mr. Ridgeway, well known in Paris and the hero of Bourget's "M. Cazal," the other Baron Hottingue. A few opened their houses, but the French on the whole were shy of going out at all, and if Paris had any gaiety left in those days, it was owing to her cosmopolitan character. As time has gone on, with the fall of the Empire and the advent of the Republic, society in Paris has become a thing of the past. Broken up into small coteries and cliques, each, a law unto itself, thinks the others beneath contempt. The old nobility, which was beginning to get accustomed to the Empire, and was peeping shyly out of its faubourg, has retired into it more pertinaciously than ever. Where there is no recognized head or "fount of honor," so to speak, there can be no recognized grades, and with the exception of a small group, Paris society in the present day, as compared with the past, is like a ship without a rudder.

Among their compatriots who were more or less settled in Paris, their greatest friends were perhaps the Forbeses of New York. Two of the daughters eventually married Frenchmen, one the

Due de Praslin, head of the house of Choiseul, and the other M. Odilon Barrot, son of Louis Philippe's Minister.

Jennie, her sister, Clara, and Countess Hatzfeldt were once invited by the Due de Praslin to visit his beautiful Chateau of Vaux-Praslin. Their host took them all over the huge building, pointing out everything of historical interest, until they came to an ornamented door, before which he paused, but did not enter. "La chambre du feu Due de Praslin" he said in a grim voice, and then passed on. This was the room of the late Duke his father, who had murdered his wife, a deed which filled the civilized world with horror, and which undoubtedly precipitated the revolution of 1848.

The Duchess's unfounded jealousy of their French governess drove the Duke to this terrible act. On their way home they discussed the details with bated breath, how the Duchess had first been stabbed, then smothered under the canopy of the bed, which the Duke pulled down on her; how the Duke was tried by his peers and sentenced to death, but the night before the execution was found dead in his cell, friends having smuggled in poison to him. It was averred, later, that the story of his death was not true, and that in reality he had escaped and lived in exile for many years.

At the trial the French governess pleaded her own cause so eloquently, that she left the court without the slightest aspersion on her character. She went to America and married the Rev. Henry M. Field, brother of Cyrus W. Field of Atlantic Cable fame. By the way, the first time the cable was laid by the Great Eastern it broke in mid-ocean, and Jennie's father, who was much interested in the scheme, lent his steam-yacht the *Clara Clarita* which went out and recovered it. The yacht was afterward sold to the government. Jennie remembered well being taken, as a great treat, on the yacht on its trial trip, and her poor mother's face of dismay at the fittings of pale blue velvet and silver! Her father, in his extravagant manner, had left it all to the upholsterer.

In the autumn of 1873, Jennie recollected going to Bazaine's trial at Versailles. France needed a scapegoat for its humiliating defeat in the Franco-Prussian War, and Bazaine, who had surrendered the fortress of Metz and his army of approximately 150,000 men to the Prussians in October 1870, became the primary target of accusations not just of breaching military discipline but also of treason.

A long, low room filled to suffocation with a curious crowd, many of whom were women, a raised platform, a table covered with green baize and holding a bottle of water, a few chairs arranged in semicircles, completed the mise-en-scene, which seemed rather a poor one for the trial for life or death of a Marshal of France.

The Due d'Aumale, who was president, having seated himself at the table, Bazaine was brought in. All eyes turned on him, and some of the women jumped on their chairs, leveling their opera-glasses at the unfortunate man. This was promptly put a stop to by the gendarmes present, who pulled the offenders down unceremoniously by their skirts. "Fi donc!" Jennie heard a gendarme say, "c'est pas gentil"; nor was it. "Fi donc!" is a French exclamation expressing disapproval or disgust - similar to saying "For shame!" or "How disgraceful!" in English.

"C'est pas gentil" translates to "It's not nice" or "That's not kind."

Bazaine sat unpassive even while MaitreLachaud, his advocate, making a curious defense at one moment pointed with a dramatic gesture to the accused, exclaiming "Mais, regardez-le donc! Ce n'est pas un traitre, c'est un imbecile!" (English

Translation: "But, just look at him! He is not a traitor, he is an imbecile!")

How the mighty had fallen! Jennie thought of him and his wife in the glittering throng of Compiegne only three years before, and of him again as commander-in-chief of a huge army, which now he was supposed to have betrayed and sold. She said supposed, for although he was found guilty and condemned to death (which was commuted to twenty years' imprisonment) there were many who believed in him and thought him a hero. His permitted escape on the 9th of August, 1874, from the Ile Ste. Marguerite had the elements of the grotesque about it, and if he was a martyr, Jennie doubted if posterity would place a halo round his head.

Ever since, those early days Cowes has always had so great an attraction for Jennie that, notwithstanding its gradual deterioration, she rarely missed a yearly visit. To travel from Paris to Cowes in the 1870s, travelers would first take a train from Paris to a French port city like Calais or Dieppe. From there, they would cross the English Channel by steamship to an English port such as Dover, Southampton, or Portsmouth. The Channel crossing typically took several hours and could be quite rough depending on weather conditions.

Her first ball in was at the Royal Yacht Squadron Castle, an entertainment long since abandoned, but then an annual event during the Cowes regatta week. It was there that she had the honor of being presented to the present King and Queen, and made the acquaintance of Lord Randolph Churchill.

In Jennie's memoirs, she mentions the roughness of the sea during an expedition around the Isle of Wight with Emperor Napoleon III and Empress Eugénie, which suggests that sea travel in that era could be quite uncomfortable, with seasickness being a common issue even on relatively short voyages.

Jennie was seventeen years old when the Franco-Prussian War broke out in July 1870. These formative years of her late adolescence were dramatically transformed by the conflict.

What began as a two-week departure from Paris turned into a two-year exile in England, introducing her to British society where she would eventually meet Randolph. When she finally returned to Paris, she was almost twenty and had matured considerably, having witnessed the fall of an empire, the refugees of war, and the transformation of European politics. Her experiences during this period shaped her remarkable social adaptability and cosmopolitan outlook that would later make her one of the most influential women of her era.

Similar to how there was a perfect storm for World War 2, Jennie falling in love with Randolph was the sunshine that chased away the storm clouds. Instead of being a spoiled heiress thrown into British Society, Jennie had already rubbed elbows with royalty. She was not intimidated by her new inlaws. Duke and Duchess? Jennie had danced with a prince and laughed with the Empress. In the first three chapters of her memoirs, she doesn't go deeply into her childhood; Jennie had lost a sister when she was eight and was constantly being moved from her home.

But we know Jennie was a talented pianist who received training from Stephen Heller, a friend of Chopin. Her piano teacher believed she had the potential to reach "concert standard" with sufficient dedication and practice. Her musical ability was considered quite impressive, with some sources describing her as having professional-level piano skills.

Jennie was also linguistically accomplished. She spent significant time in Paris during her formative years, which contributed to her fluency in French. This cosmopolitan upbringing gave her what contemporaries described as "French élan" alongside her "American effervescence", making her stand out in British high society.

One of the most famous descriptions of Jennie's appearance came from Lord d'Abernon, who said there was "more of the panther than of the woman in her look", capturing her exotic and magnetic beauty. Jennie possessed striking physical features including "thick, black, wavy hair, a peaches and cream complexion, and large, magnetic, royal blue eyes that were grey at the centre", making her one of the most captivating women of her era.

Her beauty was so renowned that photos of her appeared frequently in papers, and postcards with her image were sold, similar to how celebrity photographs are marketed today.

She "moved on effortlessly" and "mixed in the highest London society circles" where she continued to attract numerous admirers. Among her reported romantic partners was King Edward VII of England. It was said that "Queen Alexandra especially enjoyed her company, although Lady Randolph had been involved in an affair with her husband the king", suggesting an unusual tolerance of the relationship.

These relationships demonstrate her remarkable ability to maintain her allure and vivacity well into her later years, defying the conventions of her time regarding age and female beauty. But her real power wasn't her beauty; Jennie has been described as "a dynamic behind-the-scenes political force" who helped advance both her husband's and son's political careers.

These diverse talents - musical, linguistic, literary, political, and social - made Jennie Churchill a remarkably accomplished woman for her era, going well beyond the traditional expectations for women of her time.

Our first two chapter highlights her meeting and marriage of Randolph which was rather brief in memoirs. The next chapter in this book picks up her memoirs after this marriage and leads into the birth of Winston, seven months later. Yes, there has been speculation about Winston's conception - was it before or after that wedding? Did Jennie play her hand to move the wedding along?

According to Lord Randolph Churchill's own letter to Jennie's mother, Churchill was born prematurely after his mother had a fall. In this letter, he described his newborn son as "very healthy considering its prematureness," suggesting that the family at least claimed the birth was early.

As Wikipedia notes, "Churchill was reportedly born two months premature. He was supposedly due in January 1875 and it had been intended that he would be born at his parents' house in Charles Street, Mayfair." In another account, Churchill's father wrote that "[Lady Randolph] had a fall on Tuesday walking with the shooters, and a rather imprudent and rough drive in a pony carriage brought on the pains on Saturday night." This explanation about the circumstances leading to his early birth appears in several sources.

According to the National Churchill Museum, "Winston Leonard Spencer Churchill was born 30 November 1874 at Blenheim Palace, the ancestral home of the Dukes of Marlborough." They don't specifically mention premature birth in their brief biography.

However, some historians have questioned whether Churchill was truly premature. William Manchester, in his biography "The Last Lion," suggested that "Premature? The Times bought it. At the head of its birth notices it reported: 'On the 30th Nov., at Blenheim Palace, the Lady Randolph Churchill, prematurely, of a son.' But no one believed it..."

The skepticism arises because Jennie and Randolph had married only seven and a half months before Winston's birth. Some historians have suggested that the claim of prematurity was a way to avoid scandal over a pre-wedding pregnancy, which was not uncommon in Victorian high society.

Our bet is on Jennie doing what it took to get what she wanted and that was Randolph. Next, she had make sure that marrying the second son of a duke was not a mistake and to carve out an amazing future for Randolph and her first born child. Whether Churchill was truly born prematurely or Jennie strategically claimed an early birth to maintain social propriety remains a subject of historical debate. In the next chapter based on her memoirs; you decide.

Churchill's Mum

London and Married Life

Chartwell, 1964

"She was nineteen when she married my father, you know. Nineteen, and convinced that she could fashion an empire from the brittle air of London drawing rooms," Churchill said. The paintbrush quivered slightly between his thumb and forefinger, the blue oil on its tip trembling in anticipation of the canvas. "The English aristocracy didn't quite know what to make of her." He paused.

Sophia, sensing that something lived in the silence, waited. "How so?" she finally prompted.

"Well, for starters, she had opinions," Churchill said. "English ladies of 1874 were expected to be, if not strictly ornamental, then at least decorative. Accomplished in piano, perhaps, or embroidery, but never in the art of argument." He set the brush down with deliberate care. "My mother arrived with ideas about politics, society, even fashion that rattled the establishment."

Sophia leaned forward. "She refused to be invisible."

"It was more than that," Churchill replied. "She was incandescent. She could light an entire ballroom with her laughter." His gaze drifted from the window to the painting, then back again. "She wore colors, scarlets, emeralds, even American blue, that made other women look as if they were in mourning. She spoke to men as equals, not as superiors to be placated. There were times, I am sure, when the Dowager Duchesses and Lord Chamberlains of London society believed she was some manner of foreign sorceress, sent to bewitch their sons and sow chaos among the pedigreed ranks."

Sophia smiled at the image. "She sounds ahead of her time."

"Indeed," Churchill said, with a tone of pride. "But more than that, she had the intelligence to know precisely how far she could push, the restraint to cause just enough scandal to be interesting, not enough to be banished. There is a delicate dance, Miss Carter, in the halls of power and influence. My mother was a masterful choreographer."

He tapped the brush on the edge of the water glass. "If I inherited any measure of cunning, or resilience, or even taste for the theatrical, it was from her. Though I suspect I was rather less subtle in my methods." He laughed softly, the sound dry as autumn leaves.

Sophia considered this for a moment, then asked, "Did she want you to make your own mark on the world?"

"Oh, she wanted nothing less," Churchill replied. His voice took on a reflective cadence. "She knew, even when I was a child at Harrow, that the world would be unkind to anyone who failed to announce themselves with sufficient bravado. She wrote letters, hundreds of them, always instructive, sometimes scolding, never dull. She believed that I was destined for greatness, and when I failed, she believed more fiercely still."

He reached for his glass of whiskey and found it empty. Sophia, ever the reporter, made a note but did not offer to refill it. Churchill's hand lingered on the glass all the same. "There are those who say the sons of great men are either smothered by expectation or crushed by neglect. I suppose I was lucky to have a mother who preferred to goad rather than shelter."

He looked up at Sophia, his eyes fierce and suddenly lucid. "Americans love the idea of a self-made man, Miss Carter. There is no such thing. Every man is stitched together from the ambitions and follies of his parents."

Sophia shifted, feeling the weight of Churchill's attention settle on her. "Did she ever regret leaving America?"

"Never," he said, the answer immediate. "She felt that destiny lay eastward across the Atlantic, not in Gilded Fifth Avenue mansions. She carried America with her wherever she went, but it was always in service of some larger purpose. When she met my father, she saw not a man, but a culmination of opportunity and challenge. She believed that together they could shape history, and for a time, they did."

He closed his eyes, as if reciting from memory rather than invention. "My father was brilliant, and brittle. My mother was vivid, and indomitable. Their marriage was a battlefield, but it was also a forge." Churchill opened his eyes and fixed Sophia with a look that was half plea, half warning. "If you wish to understand the mind of a politician, look first to the heart of his mother."

Churchill seemed content to let the conversation settle. After a moment, Sophia said, "I would like to hear more about her. About how she, and you, survived in a world that would rather have seen you fail."

LONDON, 1874

Immediately after her marriage in April 1874, Jennie settled in London, to enjoy her first season with all the vigor and unaided appetite of youth. After the comparatively quiet life of Paris, she seemed to live in a whirl of gaieties and excitement. Many were the delightful balls she went to, which, unlike those of the present day, invariably lasted till five o'clock in the morning. Masked balls were much in vogue. Holland House, with its wonderful historical associations and beautiful gardens, was a fitting frame for such entertainments, and she remembered enjoying herself immensely at one given there.

Disguised in a painted mask and a yellow wig, she mystified everyone. Her sister who was staying with them, had been walking in the garden with young lord, who was a parti and much pursued by designing mothers with marriageable daughters.

"Parti" is a French term that was commonly used in Victorian and Edwardian high society to refer to an eligible bachelor who was considered a good marriage prospect, particularly one with wealth, status, or title. It appears that Jennie wanted to protect his real identity in her memoirs.

The term derives from the French "bon parti" meaning "good match" or "good catch." When Jennie referred to this young lord as "a parti," in her memoirs, she means he was a highly desirable potential husband, someone with the right social standing, wealth, and connections that would make him an attractive marriage candidate for young women of society.

Introducing him to Jennie, her sister pretended Jennie was her mother. Later in the evening Jennie attacked him, saying that her daughter had just confided to her that he had proposed to her, and that she had accepted him. To this day she could still see his face of horror and bewilderment. Vehemently he assured her that it was not so. But she kept up the farce, declaring that her husband would call on him next day and reveal their identity, and that meanwhile she would consider him engaged to her charming daughter. Deficient in humor and not overburdened with brains, he could not take the joke, and left the house a miserable man.

Generally speaking, there was no doubt that English people were dull-witted at a masked ball, and did not understand or enter into the spirit of intrigue which was all-important on such occasions. One reason may have been that both sexes were masked in England, whereas abroad this was not the practice, nor would it have been understood. The license a man might take if his identity were to remain unknown would never be tolerated. Besides, it stood to reason that unless one of the two remained unmasked there could not be much mystifying. Some women refused to say anything but "Yes" and "No" in a falsetto voice, and thought they had had a glorious time as long as their identity was not discovered. "You don't know me. You don't know me," was the parrot cry of one lady. "And I don't want to," said Lord Charles Beresford, fleeing from her, "if you've nothing else to say."

Another masked ball was given by M. and Mme. de Santurce, the head of the Murietta family. They had a charming house in Kensington, like many others long since closed. Madame de Santurce, a beautiful woman of the Spanish type, was very popular, and entertained lavishly at Wadhurst, their country place in Sussex.

Some years later, Jennie was there with Randolph when an amusing incident occurred at which they all laughed heartily. Thought-reading was the fashionable amusement of the moment, and one evening Lady de Clifford, a very pretty and attractive woman, insisted on making Randolph, who was reading peacefully in a corner, join in the game. Having duly blindfolded him, she led him into the middle of the room and made various passes with her hands, saying, "Don't resist any thought which comes into your head; do exactly what you feel like doing. I am willing you." Without a moment's hesitation Randolph threw his arms round the lady, and embraced her before the whole company. To her cries and indignant remonstrances he merely replied, "You told me to do what I felt like doing, so I did."

The London season of the 19th century was far more prolonged and its glories more apparent than the early years of the 20th century when Jennie wrote her memoirs. It was looked upon as a very serious matter which no self-respecting persons who considered themselves "in society" would forego, nor of which a votary of fashion would willingly miss a week or a day. The winter session which usually assembled in February, as it does now, and sat for six weeks, brought to London the legislators and their families; but from October to February the town was a desert. Religiously, however, on the first of May, Belgravia, the Belgravia described by Lord Beaconsfield, would open the doors of its freshly painted and flower-bedecked mansions.

Belgravia was one of London's most fashionable and exclusive residential districts in the late 1800s. It ranked among other prestigious London neighborhoods such as Tyburnia and Mayfair during this period and maintained its reputation as one of London's most fashionable residential areas since its

The transformation of Belgravia began in the 1820s and 1830s on land owned by the Marquess of Westminster. This massive development project was led by master builders Thomas and William Cubitt, who were celebrated figures in London society by the early 1840s. The name "Belgravia" was originally a nickname applied to Belgrave and Eaton Squares and their immediate surroundings, but eventually became the popular collective name for the entire "City of Palaces" that stretched southwest from Hyde Park Corner toward Pimlico and Chelsea. The grand terraces of white stucco houses that characterize Belgravia were constructed between 1830 and 1847. The area's focus was on the elegant Belgrave Square and Eaton Square.

Belgravia's architecture is remarkable for its grandeur and sense of unity, with much of it surviving intact to this day. The district features luxurious Victorian mansions in the late Georgian style, with meticulously planned pedestrian zones and well-groomed gardens and parks.

In the late 1800s, there were heated discussions about which of London's fashionable districts was superior. According to Charles Dickens Jr.'s 1879 Dictionary of London, the rivalry between Tyburnia and Belgravia was so intense that it was suggested they should "settle the vexed question of superiority by an appeal to arms" or "Meet and have it out in Hyde Park."

In Victorian England, Belgravia was extremely popular with members of aristocratic families as well as wealthy manufacturers and bank owners. The truly wealthy maintained townhouses in Belgravia in addition to their country estates.

Some notable residents of Belgravia in the late Victorian era included: The poet Matthew Arnold (1822-1888) lived at No. 2 Chester Square, while Mary Shelley (1797-1851), author of Frankenstein, resided at No. 24 of the same square. Admiral John Liddell (1794-1868) lived at No. 72 Chester Square. Eaton Square in Belgravia was home to several British Prime Ministers during various periods, including Lord John Russell, Stanley Baldwin, and Neville Chamberlain.

Lowndes Square, which dates from about 1838, was built on land owned by the Lowndes family, descendants of William Lowndes who had been Secretary to the Treasury during Queen Anne's reign. The square was home to many distinguished residents throughout the Victorian era.

The late Victorian period saw a high level of formality in upper-class households. Servants in Belgravia were paid higher wages than in other parts of London, which was meant to place them "above considerations" of the perquisites or "rights" that household staff previously expected. The Austrian Embassy, the oldest embassy in the area, opened in Belgravia during the 19th century, beginning the district's long association with diplomatic residences.

In Jennie's memoirs, she talks about the dinners, balls, and parties succeeding one another without intermission till the end of July, the only respite being at the Whitsuntide recess. A few of the racing people might go to Newmarket for a week, but the fashionable world flocked only to the classic races, the Derby, Ascot, and Goodwood.

Parties were arranged for Hurlingham to see the pigeon-shooting, or for the fashionable flower-shows then held at the Botanical Gardens, or again to Wimbledon to see the shooting for the Elcho Shield, which in those days was a feature of the London season. To be Commandant of the Camp was a coveted post, and Jennie remembered Lord and Lady Wharncliife living in large tents and entertaining for a whole fortnight in the most sumptuous manner. They would drive down on coaches in Ascot frocks and feathered hats, and stay to dinner, driving back by moonlight.

Chiswick House, which was let at that time by the late Duke of Devonshire to the Prince and Princess of Wales, was the scene of many garden-parties and dinners. One night Jennie and Randolph dined there to meet two Russian Grand Dukes. Her elder sister, Clara, who had arrived from Paris and was staying with them, was also invited. They were pressed to play the waltzes of Waldteufel, whose lovely music was only just beginning to be known in England, although he had for years been band-master at the Tuileries. When the royalties were departing the company stood on both sides of the hall, the Prince and Princess of Wales gracefully bowing and saying a few words to each guest as was their way. The Russian Grand Dukes, on the other hand, marched out without so much as a look or a bow to the courtesying ladies. This was very much commented on and murmurs of "Cossacks!" and "Grattez le

Russe" [English Translation: "Scratch a Russian"] were heard on all sides.

The French Embassy was a great feature of that season. Sosthenes de La Rochefoucauld, Duc de Bisaccia, had been appointed Ambassador to London, and he and his wife (Princesse Marie de Ligne) were immensely liked, the prestige of his great name adding luster to the importance of his post. Their dinners and balls were most sumptuous, everything being done on a princely scale. On state occasions their gala coach vied in splendor with the finest English equipages, the purple and red liveries of the La Rochefoucauld family having rarely seen the light of day since the reign of Louis XVIII.

Much to everyone's regret the Duke was recalled after a few months. Appointed by Marshal MacMahon, he so far forgot that he was Ambassador of the Republic as to make a speech in the Chamber during a week's leave in Paris, in which he warmly advocated the reestablishment of the Monarchy!

The sight which impressed Jennie the most was Rotten Row, the wonder and admiration of foreigners, whose Prater, Pincio, Unter den Linden, or Allee des Acacias, were but a faint copy. Its glories are, alas! a thing of the past. In 1874, between the hours of twelve and two, the Park was still the most frequented place in London, the fashionable world congregating there to ride, drive, or walk. It was a brilliant and animated scene which filled the foreigner with admiration and envy, no capital in Europe being able to compete with it.

Rotten Row is a famous bridle path located in London's Hyde Park that has a rich historical significance dating back to the late 17th century. Rotten Row was established around 1690 as an avenue for King William III to safely travel between Kensington Palace and St. James's Palace. It was lined with 300 oil lamps, making it celebrated as the first artificially lit highway in Britain. The unusual name "Rotten Row" is widely believed to be a corruption of "La Route du Roi," French for "King's Road," which was its original designation. However, some suggest the name might actually come from the materials used for the road surface - a mix of gravel and crushed tree bark that created a firm yet pliable surface for horses.By the 18th century, Rotten Row had become a popular meeting place for upper-class Londoners. Particularly on weekend evenings and at midday, people dressed in their finest clothes would ride along the row to see and be seen. The adjacent South Carriage Drive was used by society people in carriages for the same social purpose.

During the Regency Era, Rotten Row was the ultimate place for people-watching. The fashionable hour began around 5:00 in the afternoon when members of the ton (high society) would descend on Hyde Park. Well-dressed men and women on horseback shared the bridle path with peers riding in expensive carriages.

In Victorian London, Rotten Row continued to be a fashionable ride and promenade. According to The Queen's London from 1896, Hyde Park featured "unbroken lines of sumptuous equipages drawn by the finest coach-horses money can purchase, and occupied by some of the best dressed and most beautiful women in the world."

The claim to the finest horsemanship in the world had with justice been awarded to English men and women. Mounted on thoroughbred hacks, the ladies wore close-fitting braided habits, which showed off their slim figures to advantage. The men, irreproachably attired in frock-coats, pearl-gray trousers, and varnished boots, wore the inevitable tall hat, a great contrast to the neglige "Rough Rider" appearance of the present day, when all elegance is proscribed in favor of comfort. For two hours a smartly dressed crowd jostled one another, walking slowly up and down on each side of the Row. Well-appointed vehicles of all kinds made the Park look gay, from the four-in-hand coach and pony-carriage to the now obsolete tilbury, with its tiny groom clinging like a limpet behind. In the afternoon the stately barouche made its appearance, with high-stepping horses, bewigged coachmen, and powdered footmen in gorgeous livery. A few of these still survive, but formerly they were the rule rather than the exception.

One day much excitement was caused by the sight of a man galloping furiously up and down in pursuit, so it seemed, of the Heir Apparent. It was found out afterward that he had no nefarious intentions, but unfortunately he went a little too close, and cannoning against the royal personage, knocked him over. This incident gave rise to an amusing popular song called "The Galloping Snob of Rotten Row."

Up to 1834 carriages were allowed in the Row, but in Jennie's 1880s, its tanned roadway is kept entirely for riders. The Duke of St. Albans, Hereditary Grand Falconer, however, has the privilege of driving through the Row if he chooses.

This reminded Jennie of a story told of Lord Charles Beresford, who accepted the wagers of some friends that he would drive up the Row without being molested by the police. But on the day fixed for the experiment, the friends, who had repaired thither en masse, looked in vain for him until in the much-abused driver of a water-cart, which was careering up and down splashing everyone, they spied the laughing countenance of the triumphant Lord Charles.

Pepys says in his gossipy diary: "April 30th, 1661. I am sorry that I am not at London, to be at Hide-Parke to-morrow, among the great gallants and ladies, which will be fine." And again: "April 16th, 1664. To Hide-Parke, where I had not been since last year;

where I saw the King with his periwigs, but not altered at all; my Lady Castlemaine in a coach by herself, in yellow satin and a pinner on; and many brave persons. And myself being in a hackney and full of people, was ashamed to be seen by the world, many of them knowing me." And again: "March 19th, 1665. Mr. Povy and I in his coach to Hide-Parke, being the first day of the tour there. Where many brave ladies, among others, Castlemaine, lay impudently upon her back, in her coach, asleep, with her mouth open."

The Pepys that Jennie refers to was Samuel Pepys - a rising civil servant in England during the early Restoration period. At this time, he was serving as Clerk of the Acts to the Navy Board, a position he had obtained in 1660 shortly after Charles II was restored to the throne.

Having been brought up in France, Jennie was accustomed to the restrictions and chaperonage to which young girls had to submit, but she confessed to thinking that as a married woman she would be able to emancipate herself entirely. In matters of propriety, however, London was much more strict and conventional than it is now. A lady never traveled alone without taking her maid with her in the railway carriage. To go by oneself in a hansom was thought very "fast", not to speak of walking, which could be permitted only in quiet squares or streets. As for young girls driving anywhere by themselves, such a thing was unheard of.

Etiquette and the amenities of social life were thought much more of than they are now. The writing of ceremonious notes, the leaving of cards, not to speak of "visites de digestion," [English Translation: "after-dinner visits"], which even young men were supposed to pay, took up most afternoons.

Jennie complained in her memoirs of the early 1900s that extraordinary restlessness and craving for something new had caused manners to deteriorate from those days of the 1880s, curtailing the amenities of social life on which past generations set such store. A nod replaced the ceremonious bow, a familiar hand-shake the elaborate courtesy. The carefully-worded beautifully-written invitation of thirty years ago is dropped in favor of a garbled telephone message, such as "Will Mrs. S. dine with Lady T. and bring a man, and if she can't find one she mustn't come, as it would make them thirteen"; or a message to a club, "Will Mr. G. dine with Lady T. tonight? If no, will he look in the card-room and see if any of her lot are there, and suggest somebody."

The motor and the telephone were unknown in the 1880s, and the receipt of the shilling telegram was still unusual enough to cause feelings of apprehension. There was none of that easy tolerance and familiarity which is undoubtedly fostered by the daily, not to say hourly, touch and communication of modern society in the 1900s when Jennie wrote her memoirs.

The strict observance of Sunday filled Jennie with awe and amazement. She had lived most of her life in Paris, where everything gay and bright was reserved for that day, and could not understand the voluntary, nay, deliberate gloom and depression in which everyone indulged. There was then no Queen's Hall to while away a wet afternoon and improve one's knowledge of good music. The fashion of going to the country for the week-end was not known, whereas in the 1900s, motors have made the country so accessible that the eyes of all sensible people are open to the folly of wasting days when not obliged in a hot, evil-smelling and noisy metropolis.

Innumerable were the country-house parties with golf, lawn-tennis and the river to amuse and keep one out of doors. Mothers with broods of marriageable daughters find this kind of entertainment a better market to take them to than the heated atmosphere of the ballroom, which the desirable partis shun for the greater attraction of air and exercise.

Gardening, too, had become a craze. The lovely gardens which formerly were left by their owners to bloom unseen are now sought after, and reveled in. Everyone aspires to be a Miss Jekyll or a Mrs. Boyd, and the rival merits of Japanese, Friendship or Rock Gardens form a favorite subject of discussion.

It was not until well on in the eighties that people began to give dinner parties on Sundays. Very few had out their carriages, and as Randolph objected to the practice, their modest brougham was replaced by the common cab.

On one occasion Jennie and Randolph dined at Marlborough House. In the 1880s, Marlborough House served as the London residence of Edward, Prince of Wales (later King Edward VII) and his wife Princess Alexandra of Denmark. During this period, it functioned as the social center of London high society.

As it was a very hot night in July, and the party a small one, the Prince of Wales accompanied his departing guests to the door. At that moment a footman in stentorian tones announced, "Lady Randolph Churchill's carriage stops the way," whereupon a decrepit carriage, dragging the most dilapidated of four-wheelers, well filled with straw, crawled up to the door. As she prepared to get in, their royal host chaffingly remarked that her conscience was better than her carriage. Not to be outdone, Jennie retorted: "Is it not, Sir, the Queen's carriage? How can I have a better?"

Speaking of cabs reminds Jennie that it was always said that the late Lord and Lady Salisbury, who were not given an adequate allowance in the early years of their marriage, and who, as everyone knows, increased their income by the work of their pens, went about habitually in four-wheelers. Lady Salisbury, it is added, used to stick straws in her ball dress to draw attention to the parsimony with which they were treated.

Thirty years ago there were very few Americans in London: Miss Consuelo Ysnaga, afterwards Duchess of Manchester; Miss Stevens, now Lady Paget; and Mrs. William Carrington, were among those Jennie knew.

In England, as on the Continent, the American woman was looked upon as a strange and abnormal creature, with habits and manners something between a Red Indian and a Gaiety Girl. Anything of an outlandish nature might be expected of her. If she talked, dressed and conducted herself as any well-bred woman would, much astonishment was invariably evinced, and she was usually saluted with the tactful remark, "I should never have thought you were an American," which was intended as a compliment.

As a rule, people looked upon an American young woman as a disagreeable and even dangerous person, to be viewed with suspicion, if not avoided altogether. Her dollars were her only recommendation, and each was credited with the possession of them, otherwise what was her raison d'être? [English Translation: "reason for being"] No distinction was ever made among Americans; they were all supposed to be of one uniform type. The wife and daughters of the newly-enriched Californian miner, swathed in silks and satins, and blazing with diamonds on the smallest provocation; the cultured, refined and retiring Bostonian; the aristocratic Virginian, as full of tradition and family pride as a Percy of Northumberland, or a La Rochefoucauld; the cosmopolitan and up-to-date New Yorker: all were grouped in the same category, all were considered tarred with the same brush.

The innumerable caricatures supposed to represent the typical American girl depicted her always of one type: beautiful and refined in appearance, but dressed in exaggerated style, and speaking, with a nasal twang, the most impossible language. The young lady who, in refusing anything to eat, says, "I'm pretty crowded just now," or in explaining why she is traveling alone remarks that "Poppa don't voyage, he's too fleshy," was thought to be representative of the national type and manners.

So great in society was the ignorance even of the country that it was thought astonishing if an American from New York knew nothing of one from San Francisco, as though they came from neighboring counties. On the Continent the ignorance was still greater, many went so far as to include South America. Jennie remembered once a Frenchman asking if she knew a certain Chilian lady, and when she replied in the negative, he exclaimed, "Mais n'êtesvous pas toutes les deux Américaines?" [English Translation: "But aren't you both Americans?"]

American men were myths, few being idle enough to have leisure to travel. But they were all supposed to be as loud and vulgar as the mothers were unpresentable, and the daughters undesirable, unless worth their weight in gold.

A great deal of water has flowed under the bridge since those early days, Jennie thought. Instead, she remarked that the steady progress of American women in Europe can be gauged by studying their present position. It is not to be denied that they are sharing many of the "seats of the mighty," and the most jealous and carping critic cannot find fault with the way they fill them. In the political, literary, and diplomatic world they hold their own. The old prejudices against them, which arose mostly out of ignorance, have been removed, and the American woman is now generally approved of.

In those days Parisian fashions made their appearance in London about two years after they were the mode in Paris. In the matter of dress the Englishwomen have so improved of late years that it is difficult to realize how badly and inappropriately they used to attire themselves. Having formed her opinion by what she had heard abroad, Jennie fancied that they generally wore a muslin and a sealskin, and perhaps she was not far wrong; but the genial climate of England, with its variation of from fifteen to twenty degrees in a day, might be offered as an excuse.

What would now be thought proper only for a dinner could then be worn at Ascot. Jennie remembered appearing on the Cup Day in her wedding-dress of white satin and point lace, with roses in her bonnet. On the other hand, black was alone thought possible for a lady to wear at the play, and once when she appeared in pale blue, Randolph implored her before starting to change it, as it was "so conspicuous."

The late Lord Dudley, like Napoleon I, disliked black and dark colors, and never allowed any member of his family to wear them. Not knowing this, Jennie went to a ball at Dudley House in what she thought a particularly attractive costume, dark blue and crimson roses. To her discomfiture her host came up to her and nearly reduced her to tears by asking why she came to his ball in such a "monstrous dress." An otherwise most kind and attentive host, he certainly was an autocrat in his own house respecting dress. At Witley Court, his famous place in Worcestershire, when there was a shooting party he would come to breakfast in a velvet coat, and insisted on his guests wearing shoes and morning coats instead of the hobnailed boots and rough and often weather-beaten tweeds donned by the sportsmen.

There is no doubt that even in sporting pursuits elegance in dress was thought more of than comfort. In looking at the old pictures of the Prince Consort, it seemed strange that he could stalk in the costume he is invariably represented as wearing, tight-fitting trousers and a long cutaway coat, not to mention a flyaway felt hat, and a plaid on his shoulders by way of cape.

Before leaving the subject of dress, Jennie remarked that it was only fair to recognize that Englishwomen have set the fashion to all the world in country clothes. There they are at their best, and their practical and sensible garments, now so widely adopted by all, were a revelation to Jennie, with her Louis XV heels and plumed hats. When she first came to England and was taken for walks in the country, she had many bitter experiences with long gowns and thin paper-like shoes, before realizing the advantage of short skirts and "beetle-crushers."

The term "beetle-crusher" originated in the mid-19th century as "a vulgar and disgusting expression, implying that a foot is big enough, and flat enough, to kill Black-beetles," according to a caption from an 1856 Punch magazine cartoon.

Even Englishwomen, however, have had to wait for the evolution of fashion in that respect. A granddaughter of Sir Hugh Hume Campbell, a Scotchman of the old regime, told Jennie once how shocked and horrified he was the first time he saw her in an Ulster. An Ulster was a specific type of overcoat that became popular in the Victorian era.

He dubbed it "fast and mannish," only one removed from bloomers, and declared that no grandchild of his, or even any lady, who wore one should be allowed to enter his house. "Mr. Punch," who at that time caricatured women smoking cigarettes in short tailor-made dresses and hard pot hats as something improbable, nay, impossible, little knew what a prophet he was. It is not to be denied that smoking is much on the increase among women in England, and it is now more or less an accepted fact, and is tolerated even in the most old-fashioned houses. This has its advantages, making life more sociable, as men seek their own dens less, knowing that they can have their cigarettes in the company of the ladies.

In the early fifties it was supposed to be the height of ill-breeding and vulgarity for a man to be seen smoking a cigar in the street, and the smoking-room in a country-house was generally some miserable room considered too unattractive for anything else, and as far removed from the living rooms as possible.

Jennie told an old story is told of a lord who was an inveterate smoker. While staying at Windsor in the lifetime of the Prince Consort, he was one day discovered in his bedroom, lying on his back, smoking up the chimney. This was repeated to Queen Victoria, and thenceforward, it is said, a smoking-room was provided.

Although women smoke in restaurants it is unlikely that the practice will spread farther, for in Russia where they smoke more than in any other country with the exception of Austria, a lady who would indulge in thirty or forty cigarettes a day will not smoke in a public place, such as a street or railway-station. In the most aristocratic Austrian circles, on the other hand, ladies are frequently seen smoking cigars at balls and receptions.

Jennie commented that when one sees the number of restaurants there are at the present day, crowded with well-dressed and often well-known people, it seems incredible that thirty years ago none existed. Sometimes Randolph and Jennie would be passing through London in August, and their house being closed they were sorely put to it to know where to dine. The only possible place was the St. James's Hotel, which later became the Berkeley. There, if necessity took you, you could get, in a small, dingy dining-room lighted with gas, an apology for a dinner. Smoking was never allowed, and two people of opposite sex seen together were looked at very much askance. Later, in the early 1900s, the Bachelors' Club and the New Club at Covent Garden became the fashionable resorts at which to dine, although to do so anywhere but in a private house was thought quite "emancipated."

Small dances were given at the New Club, at one of which, Count Kinsky being the host, the Prince of Wales, the ill-fated King of Portugal then Duke of Braganza, the King of Greece, and the unfortunate Archduke Rudolph of Austria were present. It was most animated, and they danced till the early hours of the morning to the music of the Tziganes, then a new importation. An American young lady was so carried away with the excitement of the moment that she was heard calling the King of Greece, with whom she had been dancing, a "bully King", much to his amusement. Jennie often met the King in later years at Aix-les-Bains. He was then extraordinarily like his sister Queen Alexandra, and had the same voice. At one time he was much interested in a playhouse which was being built at Athens, to be called the National Theater, and discussed the project at length with Jennie.

Madame Duse, happening to be at Aix at the time, was very anxious to inaugurate it. Jennie spoke to the King on her behalf, and was instrumental in bringing about the interview between them. Unfortunately nothing eventually came of it, as Madame Duse fell ill. It was a great pity that the finest actress alive should have missed this opportunity of opening the finest theater in the most classic of all cities. Although very attractive, she was a woman of moods, and a difficult person to cultivate. But genius excuses everything.

In those days it would have been absolutely impossible for ladies to appear in public places in full dress. Now people dine at restaurants attired as for a ball, with jewels and tiaras. Once at the Carlton Hotel Jennie saw a large party of well-known people having supper in the public room, who, from their costumes, had evidently been performing in tableaux vivants (table pictures). It was a comical, if not very edifying, sight to see Boadicea, with her shield and spear, her hair hanging to the ground, sitting beside a youth travestied as a cherub, with a wreath of roses on his foolish head, while Madame de Pompadour in powder and patches faced them with Julius Caesar!

Another night it was a wedding party which held high revels in the same place. The young, well-born, and handsome couple were to be married the next day, and had chosen this form of public amusement to celebrate their last hours of "single blessedness." Each sat at a long table decorated with white flowers, the prospective bride with her girl friends, the bridegroom with his boon companions. As the dinner progressed and the fun increased, the throwing of notes and flowers to one another occasioned shrieks of laughter, which startled and amused the general company, not to speak of the waiters, who were having provided for them a show for which they were not asked to pay.

One custom which had changed very much is the short interval necessary before a married couple can appear after their "honeymoon." Two or three days is all that was required after the wedding in the early 1900s; whereas formerly it was supposed to be quite extraordinary, if not actually improper and embarrassing, to mix with your fellow-creatures for at least a month.

Shortly after her marriage, Jennie was presented to the Czar, Alexander II, at a ball given in his honor at Stafford House. On being told that she had been married only a few weeks, he exclaimed, fixing his cold gray eyes on her with a look of censure, "Et ici déjà!" [English Translation: "And here already!"]

Jennie had many new experiences in those early years, not the least trying being her attempt at housekeeping, which was very erratic, owing to the ignorance she often had cause to bemoan. At the first dinner party they ever gave the chef they had brought from Paris became "excited," and, to her consternation, she saw the entree, in the shape of patties, floating in the soup, whereas the poached eggs intended for it appeared in solitary grandeur. These are things never to be forgotten by a young housewife.

Although Randolph did not trouble the House of Commons very much at that time, being satisfied with a perfunctory attendance, he delighted in the society of politicians and men older than himself. Lord Beaconsfield, then Mr. Disraeli, sometimes dined with them. On one occasion Randolph and Jennie were discussing the evening, after their guests had departed, and he commented on Mr. Disraeli's flowery and exaggerated language saying, "When I offered him more wine, he replied, 'My dear Randolph, I have sipped your excellent champagne, I have drunk your good claret, I have tasted your delicious port, I will have no more.'" This Jennie found amusing, as having sat next to him at dinner she had particularly noticed that he drank nothing but a little weak brandy and water.

Mr. Disraeli was always kind and talked to Jennie at length, which occasioned much chaff among her friends, who invariably asked her what office she had got for Randolph. He was very fond of dragging in French words, a language he spoke with a weird accent. Jennie remembered once his saying to her, speaking of a prominent politician of the day and a great friend of theirs: "I think him very gross, like an episeer" (epicier) [English Translation: "grocer"], at which pronunciation Jennie could hardly keep from laughing. Sometimes he was rather cross, and if bored or vexed, did not hesitate to let people know it. On one occasion when Lady Lonsdale (Lady de Grey) gave an evening party at Carlton House Terrace, a lady whose antics were generally a source of amusement ambled up to Lord Beaconsfield, and tapping him archly with her fan, made some foolish remark. Turning a stony stare on her, he said in an audible voice to his neighbor, "Who is that little ape?"

In the late 1880s, Lady de Grey was a prominent member of the Marlborough House set, the risqué social circle that surrounded the Prince of Wales (later King Edward VII). She was described as "six-foot tall and a great beauty" with a "quality that can only be described as dazzling."

During this period, she was so closely associated with the Royal Italian Opera House (Covent Garden) that one publication noted: "Lady de Grey, who is so closely associated with the opera nowadays that on entering the house one instinctively turns towards the left-hand stage box to look for her stately presence." Rather than accepting the conventional roles typically available to women of her background, Lady de Grey was "at heart Bohemian" with "an indefatigable entrepreneurial spirit" that she channeled into rejuvenating London's opera scene through the Royal Opera House in Covent Garden, of which she was patron from the 1880s until World War I. By the 1880s, opera in England had become lackluster and was in steep decline. In 1888, Lady de Grey and Lady Charles Beresford took impresario Augustus Harris under their wing to secure the lease of Covent Garden, establishing a subscription system for opera boxes that made them exclusive to high society.

Throughout her lifetime, Lady de Grey was "an important patron of the arts in Britain and a supporter of talented individuals, particularly Nellie Melba, the Australian opera singer." Her patronage helped establish Melba's success in London. Lady de Grey was a close friend of Oscar Wilde, who dedicated his play "A Woman of No Importance" to her. She also had celebrated friendships with opera singer Nellie Melba, dancer Vaslav Nijinsky, and ballet impresario Sergei Diaghilev. Her presence in the public dining rooms at The Savoy, at the invitation of César Ritz, helped establish the fashion for aristocratic women dining out in public.

BLENHEIM HOUSE.

Blenheim

Chartwell, 1964

"Blenheim Palace," Churchill said, "Do you know it, Miss Carter?" He peered at her expectantly, eyes glittering beneath famously hooded lids.

Sophia shook her head, pen hovering above her shorthand pad.

"Magnificent," Churchill intoned, each syllable ringing with the resonance of a bell. "Overwhelming. The largest private residence in all of England, an edifice meant to remind every visitor, friend or foe, of the victory at Blenheim and the absolute preeminence of its family." He traced the outline of the palace in the photograph, then turned his attention back to Sophia. "They built it as a monument to the first Duke, my ancestor. But also as a fortress, a symbol. Every arch and column is calculated to overawe and humble any who might enter. Even, especially, an American girl of seventeen."

He sipped his tea with measured delicacy. "When my mother first saw it, she was not invited as a guest. She was presented, paraded before the family and their assorted hangers-on as the object of my father's affection. The reluctant future Duchess, the American interloper. The family expected her to be struck dumb by the grandeur." A crooked smile crept onto his lips. "But she was not easily cowed, my mother."

"She wasn't intimidated?"

"Not in the slightest. The way she later told the story, she took one look at those endless galleries, the acres of ornate ceilings and marble, and thought, 'What a wonderful stage for entertaining.' Can you imagine it? A girl from Brooklyn, walking into the Grand Saloon with its walls covered in Rubens, sizing it up as if it were a theatre and she the impresario." He chuckled. "Within months, she had turned the place on its head. Where others saw a mausoleum, she saw a canvas. She orchestrated balls, concerts, even amateur theatricals, some scandalous for the era, all memorable. She had a gift for making people forget themselves and remember only the moment."

Sophia scribbled furiously.

Churchill leaned forward, elbows on knees. "Understand, Miss Carter, that when my mother arrived, Blenheim might as well have been a sarcophagus. My grandmother, the dowager, ruled it like a garrison. There were rooms that hadn't been opened since the Crimean War, staff who had never learned her name. The place was beautiful, but it was dead." He reached for his cigar, then seemed to think better of it, settling for the gentle tap of his fingers on the armrest. "My mother brought the whole enterprise roaring back to life. She opened the doors, sometimes literally, to anyone with wit or talent or even the suggestion of good gossip. Suddenly there were Americans, Russians, French, scientists, painters, writers, mingling with the powdered relics of English high society. It was like oxygen, after a drought of centuries."

He allowed himself a moment to recollect, eyes drifting again to the Blenheim landscape. "I was born in that palace, you know. Born into a world my mother had already begun to reshape. Some said she was frivolous, that she cared only for parties and fashion. They never understood. Her world was a kind of theatre, and she was determined to play the lead, on her own terms. She understood something the Marlboroughs had forgotten, perhaps never learned, great houses are not meant to entomb their inhabitants, but to be lived in, to reflect the spirit of their age. She made Blenheim reflect her."

Sophia paused, her pencil stilled. "Did you love it there? Growing up in such a place?"

Churchill's eyes narrowed, the smile fading into introspection. "It was a splendid prison, Miss Carter. As a boy, I knew every secret passage, every hidden stair, every echoing corridor. I loved the gardens best. The staff were my true family, for my father was distant and my mother, though luminous, was always in motion. But Blenheim gave me perspective. One cannot live among such ruins and remain ignorant of either one's insignificance or one's duty."

He shifted in his seat. "She taught me a certain kind of resilience, not the English kind, which is all stiff upper lips, but the American kind, which is all improvisation and audacity. She taught me that appearances could be manipulated, that reputation was a currency, and that one should never apologize for being larger than life. All of which, I imagine, made me a rather difficult child." The twinkle returned to his eye. "And a nearly impossible Prime Minister."

"Do you think that's what England needed? Someone impossible?"

"Not needed, perhaps," Churchill admitted, "but deserved. After all, we are a nation of contradictions. We worship tradition and despise mediocrity. We revere ancestors and then promptly sell their furniture. My mother understood this perfectly, long before I did. She played the role expected of her, but always with a wink to the audience. In the end, I suppose that is what I inherited from her: the sense that history is not merely endured, but performed. And that the trick is not to be cowed by the size of the stage."

He looked at Sophia, measuring her reaction. "You see, Miss Carter, I am not an original. I am the sum of all her fearless reinventions. If I have ever shown courage, it is because she taught me that the only alternative is cowardice. And that, above all, is unforgivable."

The room was silent except for the faint ticking of the mantel clock. Sophia reviewed her notes, but the story had outpaced her shorthand.

Churchill picked up his brush again. "My mother's death nearly unraveled me. I was already a young officer, armored by the rituals of Harrow and Sandhurst, but nothing prepared me for her absence." He set the tip of the brush to the canvas, painting a ripple on the surface of the lake. "The world seemed suddenly smaller, as if the oxygen had gone out of the room. But," he said, turning to Sophia with a flash of the old defiance, "it was also then I realized that one does not so much inherit a legacy as become possessed by it. To fail is to betray not only the memory, but also the possibility."

He was quiet for a long moment, the scrape of the brush punctuating the stillness.

Sophia finally broke the silence. "Do you ever miss it? The performance?"

He looked at her, the question settling over him like a familiar cloak. "Every day, Miss Carter. And not only the applause. The sense, however fleeting, that one is shaping events rather than merely enduring them. That is the true addiction, not power, but possibility." He set down the brush. "But even the greatest performances must end. And it falls to the next generation to decide whether to preserve the memory, or to make something new upon its ashes."

Sophia closed her notebook, realizing she had filled every page. She looked at the old man, surrounded by his paintings and trophies and ghosts, and saw not the weight of history, but the relentless, undying urge to outwit it.

Churchill cleared his throat, voice suddenly brisk. "Now, Miss Carter, shall we have a look at the garden? There is an azalea I am particularly proud of, and it doesn't like to be kept waiting."

BLENHEIM PALACE, 1874

Jennie's first visit to Blenheim was on a beautiful spring day in May, 1874. Some of the Duke's tenants and Randolph's constituents met them at the station to give them a welcome, and insisted on dragging them through the town to the house.

The place could not have looked more glorious, and as they passed through the entrance archway, and the lovely scenery burst upon her, Randolph said with pardonable pride, "This is the finest view in England."

Looking at the lake, the bridge, the miles of magnificent park studded with old oaks, Jennie found no adequate words to express her admiration, and when they reached the huge and stately palace, where she was to find hospitality for so many years, she confessed that she felt awed. But her American pride forbade the admission, and she tried to conceal her feelings, asking Randolph if Pope's lines were a true description of the inside:

"See, sir, here's the grand approach; This way is for his grace's coach: There lies the bridge, and here's the clock; Observe the lion and the cock. The spacious court, the colonnade, And mark how wide the hall is made! The chimneys are so well design'd They never smoke in any wind. This gallery's contrived for walking, The windows to retire and talk in; The council chamber for debate, And all the rest are rooms of state." "Thanks, sir," cried I, "'t is very fine. But where d'ye sleep, or where d'ye dine? I find by all you have been telling, That 't is a house, but not a dwelling."

The imperious Sarah, known to her contemporaries as "Great Atossa," who with herself, or others, from her birth, finds all her life one warfare upon earth, demolished the older and probably more comfortable hunting lodge which stood in the forest. Tradition asserts that it occupied the site of the "Bower" in which "Fair Rosamond" hid her royal amours.

To this day "Rosamond's Well," concealed among the trees, is the object of a favorite walk. Pope also took exception to the noble bridge which in his day spanned the narrow river only, the large lake through which it now runs having been made later.

That poem Jennie mentioned is from Alexander Pope's "Moral Essays, Epistle IV: To Richard Boyle, Earl of Burlington" (published in 1731). In that section, Pope satirizes the pretentious architecture of grand houses that prioritize appearance over functionality.

As for "Sarah," who Jennie mentioned is referred to as "Great Atossa," this is Sarah Churchill, Duchess of Marlborough (1660-1744). She was an influential figure in the English court during the reigns of Queen Anne and the early Hanoverian monarchs.

How strange life in a big country-house seemed to Jennie, who until then had been accustomed only to towns. The Duke and Duchess of Marlborough lived in a most dignified, and, indeed, somewhat formal style. Everything was conducted in what would now be considered a very old-fashioned manner. At luncheon, rows of entrée dishes adorned the table with massive silver covers being placed before the Duke and Duchess, who each carved for the whole company, and as this included governesses, tutors, and children, it was no small deal.

Before leaving the dining-room, the children filled with food small baskets kept for the purpose for poor cottagers or any who might be sick or sorry in Woodstock. These they distributed in the course of their afternoon walks.

When the house was full for a shooting-party, even breakfast was made a ceremonious meal, and no one dreamed of beginning until all had assembled. The ladies would be dressed in long velvet or silk trains, and Jennie remembered one morning laughing immoderately when Lady Wilton (the second wife of the "wicked" Earl, as he was called), on appearing in an electric blue velvet and being asked who made it, she said with conscious pride, "It's a Stratton," as who would say, "It's a Vandyke." On the other hand, luncheon for the shooters was not in those days the glorified affair it is at time of her memoirs.. People were quite content with something cold, eaten in haste, often not under cover, instead of the carpeted tent and elaborate feast provided in the early 1900s; hot, from the soup to the coffee. There is no doubt the generation at the time of her memoirs treated a country-house more or less like a hotel, coming and going as they like, to suit their own convenience, and seldom consulting that of their hosts.

But in the 1870s, the guests having been duly told by which train to come, were expected to arrive by it, unless a very good excuse was forthcoming. They used to sit solemnly through an elaborate tea, exchanging empty civilities for an hour or more, until the hostess (who wore a lace cap if middle-aged, then about forty) gave the signal to rise, uttering the invariable formula, "I am sure you must need a little rest." The guests, once immured within their rooms, were not to reappear until the dining-hour. However, if bored by their own society, or disturbed by the unpacking maid, there they were supposed to remain. Sometimes it was the hostess who suffered. A friend of Jennie's, a rather shy lady, who was entertaining a prim princess, timidly proposed after half an hour of uphill small talk, to take her to her rooms. "Thank you," said the princess in icy tones, looking at her watch, "it is now half-past five. I will go to my room at seven."

Nous avonschangé tout cela. *English Translation: We have changed all that.* Jennie compared to the 1900s when some of the modern hostesses did not take the trouble to communicate at all in respect of trains and such details. The guests then would find their own way, and choose their own time, at their own sweet will and proper responsibility. Perchance the host and hostess are not even at home to welcome their guests. They may be hunting, golfing or motoring, and excuses when they do appear are thought hardly necessary by them or by their guests.

When the Churchill family were alone at Blenheim, everything went on with the regularity of clockwork. So assiduously did Jennie practice her piano, read, or paint, that she began to imagine herself back in the school-room. In the morning an hour or more was devoted to the reading of newspapers, which was a necessity, if one wanted to show an intelligent interest in the questions of the day, for at dinner conversation invariably turned on politics. In the afternoon a drive to pay a visit to some neighbor, or a walk in the gardens, would help to while away some part of the day. After dinner, which was a rather solemn full-dress affair, they all repaired to what was called the Vandyke room. There one might read one's book, or play for love a mild game of whist. Many a glance would be cast at the clock, which sometimes would be surreptitiously advanced a quarter of an hour by some sleepy member of the family. No one dared suggest bed until the sacred hour of eleven had struck. Then they would all troop out into a small anteroom, and lighting their candles, each in turn would kiss the Duke and Duchess and depart to their own rooms.

The Duke was extremely kind, and had the most courteous and grand seigneur appearance and manner; his wife, Frances Anne, Duchess of Marlborough, Jennie's mother-in-law, was a very remarkable and intelligent woman, with a warm heart, particularly for members of her family, which made up for any overmasterfulness of which she might have been accused.

She ruled Blenheim and nearly all those in it with a firm hand. At the rustle of her silk dress the household trembled. An amusing instance occurred to Jennie of the way in which her opinion was consulted even by distant members of the family. Jane, Duchess of Marlborough, who was the third wife of the sixth Duke, a simple and amiable woman, asked the Duchess what redress she could get for not being invited to Court balls, although she attended the Drawing Rooms. The Duchess advised her to write to the Lord Chamberlain on the subject. A few days later she received a gushing letter from Jane, Duchess, thanking her for her advice, which had been most efficacious. "I am told it was a clerical error," she added, "although I cannot see what the clergy have to do with it."

Owing to the admirable taste and knowledge of the present Duke, people who visit Blenheim in the 1870s would see its pictures, tapestries, and art treasures, can scarcely believe that it has been shorn of many of its glories.

When Jennie first went there the far-famed Sunderland Library was still in existence. The beautiful old leather bindings decorated as nothing else can the immense long gallery with its white, carved book-cases and vaulted ceiling. Cabinets of Limoges enamels gave the old-world look and Renaissance coloring to the Duchess's sitting-room. There, too, were the "Marlborough gems," besides rooms full of priceless Oriental, Sèvres, and Saxe china. And what of the four hundred and fifty pictures all recklessly sold regardless of the remonstrances and prayers of the family and without a thought of future generations! Little did Lord Cairns think when he made his Act affecting the sale of heirlooms that it could be stretched to such a point.

Lord Cairns (Hugh McCalmont Cairns, 1st Earl Cairns) was a prominent British statesman and lawyer who served as Lord Chancellor of Great Britain. In 1882, he was responsible for enacting the Settled Land Act, which made significant changes to English property law, particularly concerning settled estates and the handling of heirlooms.

The Settled Land Act of 1882 was considered "one of the most important Acts for the simplification of land transfer" since earlier reforms regarding entails. The primary purpose of the legislation was to "release the land from the fetters of the settlement – to render it a marketable article notwithstanding the settlement," as Lord Halsbury later explained in the case of Bruce v. Ailesbury [1892].

A key provision regarding heirlooms was contained in Section 37 of the 1882 Act. This section specifically addressed how heirlooms connected to settled estates could be sold:

Under Section 37 of the 1882 Act, the tenant for life gained the power to sell heirlooms, but only if they obtained a court order first. This was demonstrated in the case of Re Earl of Radnor's Will Trusts (1890).

An heirloom in English law was traditionally a chattel (personal property) that "by immemorial usage is regarded as annexed by inheritance to a family estate." The word "loom" originally meant a tool.

Genuine heirlooms were considered to be made by family custom, not by settlement. These could include items such as family bibles, antiques, weapons, or jewelry that had been passed down through generations.

The judicial oversight required by Section 37 was not merely procedural. The courts took their role seriously in determining whether heirloom sales should proceed:

The court would only sanction a sale of settled chattels if "it could be shown that it was to the benefit of all parties concerned." Additionally, if the article proposed to be sold was of unique or historical character, the court would consider both the intention of the settlor and the wishes of the remainder men.

When land was involved, the court would only intervene if the exercise of the power would financially affect the beneficiaries, as seen in Re Earl Somers (1895). However, where the financial loss was only speculative, the court would not intervene, as established in Thomas v. Williams (1883).

The court would also intervene if the transaction was not bona fide or appeared to involve fraud, as seen in the case of Middlemas v. Stevens (1901).

Lord Cairns' Act represented a careful balance between modernizing land law and respecting traditional property rights. The Act gave tenants for life much greater powers to deal with settled land than they had previously under common law, while still protecting the interests of subsequent beneficiaries.

The Settled Land Act of 1882 was part of a series of acts known collectively as the Settled Land Acts 1882 to 1890, which gradually reformed English property law. The provisions regarding heirlooms were eventually updated by the Settled Land Act 1925, which consolidated earlier legislation but maintained the principle that the tenant for life could sell heirlooms only with proper oversight, with proceeds being treated as capital money under the settlement.

Through these reforms, Lord Cairns sought to modernize property law while respecting traditional rights and the intentions of settlors when creating family settlements.

But as Jennie complained, no doubt a certain number could have been spared, such as Rubens's "Progress of Silenus," "Lot and his Daughters," and a few others which, though works of art, were startling, to say the least, and, oddly enough, hung in the dining-room. If familiarity breeds contempt, it also engenders indifference, and the most prudish of governesses, sitting primly between her charges, never seemed to notice these pictures, nor did any members of the family.

The best twenty-five pictures of the collection alone were valued at £400,000 [$2,000,000]. Of these the "Madonna Ansidei," by Raphael, which had been given by the King of Prussia to John, Duke of Marlborough, was purchased for a sum of £70,000 [$350,000] by the National Gallery; also a portrait of Charles I by Vandyke for £50,000 [$250,000]. Rubens's portrait of himself with his wife Helen Forment and infant, and another, of his wife and son, were sold for £50,000 [$250,000] to the late Baron Alphonse de Rothschild. Several family portraits, notably "The Fortune-Teller" (Lord Henry and Lady Charlotte Spencer) by Sir Joshua Reynolds, were sold. Luckily the famous Marlborough Family, also by Sir Joshua, was not allowed to go.

Many interesting stories were told about this picture. When Sir Joshua went down to Blenheim to paint in the younger members of the group, little Lady Anne Churchill, a child of four, on being brought into the room, drew back, caught hold of the dress of her nurse, and cried, 'I won't be painted!' The watchful painter immediately transferred a note of the natural attitude of the child to the canvas, where we see her clutching the dress of her eldest sister, just as he had done with the obstreperous young Russell in the Bedford group. To account for this attitude, he placed her next eldest sister with a mask before her face, as if frightening the younger child. This incident is borrowed from an antique gem, but it is as good an illustration as another of Reynolds's facility and resource.

It is said, too, that while he was painting the picture at Blenheim he dropped his snuff about, and the Duchess, anxious for her carpet, sent a footman to sweep it up. 'Go away,' said the painter, with a proper sense of his dignity, 'the dust you make will do more harm to my picture than my snuff to the carpet.'

It surprised Jennie that in Mr. Boulton's book upon Sir Joshua Reynolds, from which the above is quoted, he should have overlooked the interesting point that the young Marquess of Blandford standing near his father is holding in his arms one of the ten red jewel cases which contained the celebrated Marlborough gems. The Duke himself, who during the latter part of the eighteenth century formed one of the finest collections of gems, intaglios and cameos ever made in England, has in his hand his favorite sardonyx with a cameo head of Augustus. This gem was sold later on for £2,350 [$11,750].

Note: in the 1870s a pound was worth about $5 dollars compared today when a pound only fetches about $1.30 dollars. It appears that in her memoirs, Jennie always noted the value in brackets and US dollars.

Tourists, with whom most show-places in England are infested, abounded at Blenheim, and at certain times of the year and for several days in each week one had, for a little privacy, to take refuge in one's own rooms. Occasionally, for fun, some of them would put on old cloaks and hats, and, armed with reticules and

Baedekers, walk round with the tourists to hear their remarks, which were not always flattering to the family. Baedeker's (often referred to as "a Baedeker") is a series of travel guidebooks that were first published in the 19th century by Karl Baedeker, a German publisher. These guidebooks became famous for their detailed information, maps, and practical advice for travelers.

One day they nearly betrayed themselves with laughter at one of Jennie's compatriots exclaiming before a family picture: "My, what poppy eyes these Churchills have got!"

Foreigners visiting Oxford would often come over to see Blenheim. The famous tapestries, representing the victorious battles of the first Duke, and given to him by various towns, were always an object of great interest. On one occasion a Frenchman, who had been listening in sullen silence to a glowing account of the French defeats, could stand it no longer. Thrusting his stick through a bit of the tapestry representing a fleur de lis flag and trophies in the possession of the British, he tried to tear it up, shouting with rage, "Ce n'est pas vrai! cen'est pas vrai!" *English Translation: "It's not true! It's not true!"* To this day the long rent can be seen.

This reminded Jennie of her father-in-law's favorite anecdote in respect to Blenheim. She thought it was his grandfather who had as his guest the French Ambassador of the day, evidently a man who was somewhat cynical, not to say disagreeable, for he kept asking the Duke most unnecessary questions as to who had given this and who had given that. "The house, the tapestries, the pictures, were they all given? And the Raphael, Was that the gift of the King of Prussia? Was there anything that had not been given?" The Duke, slightly annoyed, said at last: "If your Excellency will come with me, I will show you one of the glories of Blenheim which has not been given." Taking his visitor outside, he pointed to the stone trophies and the effigy of Louis XIV which adorn the south front of the house, "These," he said, "were taken, not given, by John, Duke of Marlborough, from the gates of Tournaic." When the Emperor Frederick, while Crown Prince, once came to stay at Blenheim, he was delighted with this story. He was a very charming man and during the few days he was there made himself most agreeable. Absolutely simple in his manners and tastes, English life seemed rather luxurious to him. Jennie remembered his face of astonishment when he saw at breakfast a gold tea-service which was produced in his honor. "Ach! much too good, much too good," he kept saying, and every morning he spoke of its magnificence.

Among the many new acquaintances Jennie made was that of the Duchess of Cleveland, widow of the third Duke, one of the grandes dames of a former generation. She had a liking for Randolph, and asked him to bring Jennie to see her. She was very kind although she received Jennie in a ceremonious manner, not shaking hands but courtesying. A woman of caustic wit, many stories are told of her and her imperious ways. The family doctor having written to her "My dear Duchess," she wrote back, "Sir, I am not your dear Duchess." Her successor, the late Duchess of Cleveland (Lord Rosebery's mother), was an equally interesting character whose energy was remarkable. When long past seventy, she was still an habitué of the Row, never missing her morning gallop. Not long before her death she went to India accompanied only by her servants.

A delightful man who came to stay at Blenheim, was Sir Alexander Cockburn, Lord Chief Justice of England. But he was dangerous! One day out shooting, while Jennie was walking with him from one covert to another, he let his gun off by accident. Luckily the shot went over her head. "I must be careful," he said placidly. Jennie fled. She remembered asking him what had been the most amusing experience of his legal career. In reply he told her the story of a young barrister who came into court late, having evidently, from his appearance, dined well but not wisely, the night before. Sir Alexander reprimanded him, asking what excuse he could offer. "None," retorted the culprit, "unless it is that I had the honor of dining with your lordship last night, and bad wine tells on an empty stomach." This anecdote may not be original, but Sir Alexander Cockburn told it to Jennie as such.

When one night the snipe, which abound at Blenheim, ran short, the Lord Chief Justice, to his annoyance, was given only half of one. On leaving, he wrote in the Visitors' Book some lines to the effect that he would share almost everything in life, even his wife (he not having one), but not a snipe!

A Visitors' Book (also called a guest book or guest register) was an important social record kept in Victorian country houses and estates, particularly among the aristocracy and wealthy landowners of the 1870s. These books served multiple purposes that went beyond simply recording guests.

The Visitors' Book was a formal record where guests would sign their names upon arrival at a country estate. This practice was part of the elaborate social rituals that characterized Victorian high society. The book typically resided in the entrance hall or drawing room of the estate, where guests would be invited to sign shortly after their arrival.

The physical Visitors' Book was often an elegant, leather-bound volume with high-quality paper pages. Some were quite ornate, featuring decorative bindings, gilt-edged pages, and sometimes personalized with the family crest or estate name embossed on the cover. The interior pages typically had designated spaces for guests to sign their names, indicate their arrival and departure dates, and sometimes add comments or small sketches.

USA and Ireland

Chartwell, 1964

Churchill slowly pushed himself up from his chair, moving to the window that overlooked his beloved gardens. "American and Ireland," he said simply. "Three years that changed everything for our family." Sophia joined him at the window, noting how his reflection in the glass seemed to overlap with the landscape beyond. "My father was made Lord Lieutenant, and we all decamped to Dublin Castle. I was just a small boy, but I remember the change in my mother."

"What kind of change?"

"Purpose," Churchill replied without hesitation. "In London, she had been the brilliant American wife of a rising politician. In Ireland, she became something more, a force for change in her own right." He pointed toward his garden, where peacocks strutted across the lawn. "She learned to hunt, which scandalized the ladies. She learned politics, which worried the men. Most importantly, she learned that she could make a real difference in people's lives."

Sophia watched his profile as he spoke. "The Duchess of Marlborough's relief fund?"

"Among other things, yes. But it was more than charity work. She discovered that she had gifts, for organization, for persuasion, for turning her social connections into genuine political influence." Churchill turned to face her. "When we returned to London years later, she wasn't just Lady Randolph Churchill anymore. She was a power in her own right."

AMERICA, 1876

In 1876, Jennie and Randolph Churchill decided to go to America. Randolph had championed his brother Lord Blandford in an unfortunate affair, resulting in serious differences of opinion with various influential people. Feeling in need of solace and distraction, they made a trip in company with Mr. Trafford and the late Lord Ilchester.

They went first to Canada, where they seemed to spend most of their time eating melons and having cold baths due to the overpowering heat. The travelers saw Niagara Falls, of course, and made a visit to Newport. Though the life there was a great contrast to that of Cowes, savoring more of town than country, they found it one of the most fascinating seaside places. The hospitality and kindness shown to them by friends of Jennie's family were most gratifying.

They also visited Saratoga, where the beauty of the ladies and the gorgeousness of the dresses astonished the men of their party. Having found the hotel at that place absurdly expensive, Jennie asked her father to remonstrate with the proprietor, who replied: "The lord and his wife would have two rooms, hence the expense."

From there they went to the Philadelphia Exhibition, which occupied them for several days and was a source of great interest and amusement. They were accompanied by Jennie's uncle, the late Mr. Lawrence Jerome, father of the then District Attorney of New York, William Travers Jerome. While there, her uncle, remembered as one of the wittiest men of his day, kept them in transports of laughter. When they stopped at different stalls, he would come up to them as though they were strangers, and taking up some article or new invention, would extol its merits in such an inexpressibly funny manner and language that a crowd soon collected, many ending by buying the article. Mr. Jerome would then receive with pride a commission from the delighted shopman.

During their stay they had occasion to meet several prominent Philadelphians. Jennie remembered one in particular who entertained them vastly by remarking to Mr. Trafford that Randolph was a "bright fellow," but it was a pity he had such an "English accent." The same man asked her if she knew Cyrus B. Choate, and when she answered in the negative, exclaimed, "Not know Cyrus B. Choate! Why, he is one of our most magnificent humans!"

One notable Cyrus B. Choate was involved in the high-profile corruption trial of William M. Tweed of Tammany Hall. He also worked pro bono to overturn the court-martial of General Fitz-John Porter.

They left Philadelphia with regret, and staying only a few days in New York, returned to England, feeling invigorated and refreshed by contact with the alert intellects of Jennie's compatriots despite their short stay.

On their arrival in London, they found that the Duke of Marlborough had been appointed Viceroy of Ireland. Lord Beaconsfield had pressed him to accept this post, thinking that it might distract his thoughts from certain family worries which at that time were weighing rather heavily upon him. Hating to be parted from Randolph, his father and mother persuaded him to go with them to Ireland. Not being in favor with the Court, from which London society took its lead, they were loathing to go. Randolph was to act as unpaid private secretary to the Duke, an unofficial post that proved to be of the greatest interest and value to him, diverting his mind from the frivolous society to which he had till then been rather addicted and which now had ceased to smile upon him.

Accompanying the new Lord Lieutenant, they took part in the State Entry into Dublin, which was conducted with the usual military display and viceregal etiquette. The Duke in uniform rode with a glittering staff around him. The rest of the family, in carriages with postilions and outriders, drove through the crowded streets to the black and grimy old Castle, which for centuries had witnessed these processions come and go.

Jennie reflected on the strange persistence of the Irish Viceroyalty despite repeated attacks throughout the previous century. In the old days of slow travel and no telegraph, when it took a week to get to Dublin, she could understand the pomp and circumstance with which the representative of the Sovereign necessarily surrounded himself. In India, the Eastern mind had to be impressed with the glamour of royalty. In distant colonies like Canada, Australia, and New Zealand, Government House was a great feature, and the governors were men of responsibility. But what was the raison d'être (English Translation: reason for existence) of the Dublin Court, which was within a few hours of London and in direct communication by telegraph and telephone with Downing Street?

The Lord Lieutenant, however intelligent and ambitious he might be, if not in the Cabinet was but a figurehead, a purveyor of amusements for the Irish officials and the Dublin tradespeople, on whom he was obliged to lavish his hospitality and his money, with no return and no thanks. The wives of the Viceroys labored in good works, each in turn vying with the other in charitable ardor. But these philanthropic works could be carried on just as well if they did not emanate from the Castle. The ingratitude of the people must be very disheartening to each successive Viceroy. However popular the Lord Lieutenant and his wife might have been, however successful their attempts to cajole, conciliate and entertain, though out of their private means they might have spent money like water, in a week all was forgotten. The new regime became paramount: *Le roiest mort: vive le roi!* (English Translation: The king is dead, long live the king!)

If the Lord Lieutenant carried out with tact and success the policy of the Government, the credit was taken by the Ministry. If, on the other hand, the policy was a failure, he got the blame, or, worse still, was repudiated in the House of Commons and told that the opinion of the Lord Lieutenant was of no account. It was a marvel to Jennie that anyone could be found to accept so ungrateful a post.

The Duke of Marlborough was preceded by the Duke of Abercorn, whose delightful personality and extraordinary good looks were long remembered. "Old Magnificent," as he was called, was very fond of effect, and when making his State Entry into Dublin insisted on the ladies of his family wearing long flowing veils that streamed behind as they drove in the procession through the streets. Stories were told of his having the Drawing Room stopped while he combed and scented his beard, disarranged by the chaste salutes of the debutantes, who, if they were pretty, were made to pass the dais again.

Of late years the Dublin Drawing Rooms had become so conventional that they no longer afforded the amusement they once provided. In old days St. Patrick's Ball, which always took place on the 17th of March and marked the close of the season, was a regular bear garden, at which sentries were needed to prevent the company from appropriating the plate as well as the food. People picnicked sitting on the floor of the supper rooms. As for the clothes, they were fearfully and wonderfully made! Curtains often did duty for trains. Jennie had herself seen a lady in a black dress with a white train, and, in order to carry out the magpie effect, one shoe was white, the other black!

Jennie and Randolph, now with their boy Winston, took up their abode at the Private Secretary's lodge in the Phoenix Park. She found the Irish life very pleasant with its various occupations and amusements, and she delighted in the genial character and ready wit of the people. During the three years they lived there she could not remember meeting one really dull man. From the Lord Chief Justice to the familiar carman, all were entertaining.

Momentous political work was going on. The Government was struggling with the feeling of revolt which at that time was smoldering beneath the surface, besides trying to cope with a famine which was breaking out. The Duchess of Marlborough at this juncture came forward with her usual energy and started an Irish Relief Fund, which ultimately reached the figure of £135,000 ($675,000). This sum was distributed in such a practical and businesslike manner that even the Nationalist Press was obliged to praise these viceregal endeavors. The success of the scheme added greatly to the Duchess's popularity, and to that of the Lord Lieutenant.

Queen Victoria, whose sympathy and appreciation were always very keen in any matters connected with charity, was greatly pleased, and complimented the Duchess in a letter:

Windsor Castle. April 19, 1880.

Dear Duchess,

I, as every one is, am filled with admiration at the indefatigable zeal and devotion with which you have so successfully labored to relieve the distress in Ireland. I am therefore anxious to mark my sense of your services at this moment when alas! they will so soon be lost to Ireland, and wish to confer on you the Third Class of the Victoria and Albert Order.

I will wait till you come over to invest you with it.Believe me always,Yours affectly,Victoria, R. I.

The Duchess was very proud of this letter, and her grandson, the Duke at the time of Jennie's writing, told her a somewhat pathetic incident in connection with it. A little while before her death she sent for him and gave it to him "to be kept in the archives of Blenheim," adding, "I may seem a useless old woman now, but this letter will show you I was once of some importance and did good in my day."

Hunting became Jennie and Randolph's ruling passion. Whenever she could "beg, borrow or steal" a horse she did so. They had a few hunters of their own which they rode indiscriminately, being both light-weights. Some of her best days with the Meath and Kildare hounds she owed to a little brown mare she bought from Simmons at Oxford, who negotiated the "trappy" fences of the Kildare country and the banks and narrow doubles of Meath as though to the manner born. Many were the "tosses" she "took," as the Irish papers used to describe them, but it was glorious sport, and, to her mind, even hunting in Leicestershire later on could not compare with it. With the exception of the Ward Union Stag Hounds and the Galway Blazers, she and Randolph hunted with nearly every pack of hounds in Ireland.

Colonel Forster, who was then Master of the Horse, as he had been to several previous viceroys, was a beautiful rider, and many were the pleasant hunting days they had together. Jennie remembered once when he, Randolph and she sallied forth, each on a gray, hers, which she afterward sold to the King of the Sandwich Islands, had a tail like a shaving-brush, looking for all the world like one of Leech's pictures. The trio fancied themselves, to say the least of it, and vast sums would not have bought them at their own estimation. But alas! in a very short time their pride had a fall in every sense. Colonel Forster's horse lamed itself early in the day; Randolph's animal, after refusing for half an hour to face a yawning chasm, was pushed into it by its irate owner, while Jennie's was caught broadside by a heavy gate she was going through, and horse and rider were upset in the adjoining deep ditch.

Luckily she fell clear, but it looked as if she must be crushed underneath him, and Randolph, coming up at that moment, thought she was killed. A few seconds later, however, seeing her all right, in the excitement of the moment, he seized her flask and emptied it. For many days it was a standing joke against him that she had had the fall, and he the whisky!

The ready wit of the Irish was proverbial and they had many opportunities of judging of it during their stay. One day they met their friend Colonel Forster being driven to a meet in an Irish car. He was laughing heartily and told them that he had just passed a young man riding who evidently fancied himself, from the way he was first gazing at his boots, then smoothing his coat and patting his waistcoat. "Who is it?" inquired Colonel Forster. "Ah, bedad, Colonel, I'm thinking that maybe he is not knowing it rightly himself, by the way he is looking at himself," answered the car driver.

Another witty carman was driving a relation of Jennie's to a meet of the Ward Union Hounds, who, fearing to be late, pressed him to whip up his horse. "D'ye see that?" said the jarvey, pointing to a monument in Glasnevin Cemetery, which they were passing. "That was put up to the gintleman I was driving the last time I sthruckth' auld mare!"

Returning from Punchestown races once, the crowd was so great that the viceregal carriage got blocked, when someone, pointing at the aide-de-camp in full uniform and cocked hat who was sitting opposite the Lord Lieutenant, shouted, much to the poor man's confusion, "Faith, it's the Captain that's doin' the escortin' and chaperonin' to-day!"

Every sportsman knows what it is to ride over a country while looking out of the window on a railway journey. How bold one is! How small the fences seem! and how one wishes with Jorrocks that one could be "an eagle a-soaring o'er the hounds!" Colonel Forster who was traveling was vaguely tapping with his fingers on the arm of his seat, when a stranger, who was at the opposite window suddenly said, "You were wrong, you should have 'trigged' at that fence," meaning that if the Colonel was hunting, which he of course thought he must be, the horse would have kicked back, and this ought to have been illustrated by two taps of his fingers, not one.

At that time the great excitement in the hunting field was the advent of the Empress Elizabeth of Austria, who had taken a place in Meath for a few months. The whole country was agog, and crowds used to flock to the meets to catch a glimpse of her. The Empress, although her reputation for physical endurance and love of riding was great in the sporting world, astonished everyone by the indefatigable life she led. Arriving at Summerhill from Vienna without a break, she donned a habit in the train, got on a horse, and before going into the house went for a school over a small course which had been specially prepared by her orders.

Lord Langford, the owner of Summerhill, had, with much care and at considerable expense, furnished a boudoir for her which was hung in blue damask, and decorated with pictures and china. However, before the Empress had been there twenty-four hours, disdaining such feminine frivolities, she converted it into a gymnasium, in which to exercise daily before going out hunting.

With a wonderful figure and a beautiful seat on a horse, her Majesty made a fine appearance. She rode gallantly and knew no fear, but her riding was of the haute école order, and like most women she could seldom make a horse gallop. This was a source of perpetual worry to her hard-riding pilot, Captain Bay Middleton, whose "Come on, Madam, come on!" was constantly heard in the field.

The Empress wore the tightest of habits buttoned down and strapped in every direction, the safety skirt not having as yet made its appearance. She found herself in many a ditch, and whether she fell clear of her horse or not, it was impossible for her to stand up until the buttons and straps had been unfastened. Under the circumstances it was a marvel that she did not hurt herself. It was her invariable custom to ride with a large fan, which she held opened between her face and the crowd, whether against the rays of the sun or the gaze of the people Jennie never made out. Another curious habit of hers was to use small squares of rice paper in the Japanese fashion instead of pocket-handkerchiefs; by these she could be traced for miles, as in a paper chase.

Much to the chagrin of the Viceregal Court the Empress never came near it, not wishing to lose a single day's sport while in the country. But all those who came in contact with her were fascinated by her graciousness and her imposing beauty. It was sad to think that one who had never harmed anyone, and was beloved by all in her own country, should have met a tragic end at the hands of an obscure miscreant.

The following year the Viceroy had occasion to entertain the Archduke Rudolph, who had come to Ireland on a short visit. At a grand ball given in his honor in St. Patrick's Hall an unfortunate occurrence happened. The Lord Mayor of Dublin being present, and being in his own province, had an arm-chair on the dais next to the Viceroy, but by some oversight none was placed for the Archduke. This gave great offense, and to add to the "tempest in a tea-cup," the Lord Mayor was made to take precedence of the Heir

Apparent of Austria and Hungary, and went in to supper before him. Next day many apologies were offered and the viceregal staff were properly trounced, but the royal visitor, unappeased, departed. Who could have prophesied that he, too, in a few years would come under the ban, and share the evil fate of the House of Hapsburg?

During the three years of the Duke of Marlborough's tenure of office they saw a good deal of Ireland, as he took various places. At Knockdrin Castle, in Westmeath, where they stayed for a few months, they enjoyed the hunting, for the foxes were as wild there as the people were untamed. They thought nothing of going to the meet fifteen or twenty miles on an outside car, and often rode their horses to a standstill in very long runs. After one of these Jennie remembered shocking the Lord Lieutenant's local guests by falling asleep during dinner.

One winter her father-in-law had Lord Sligo's place at Westport, County Mayo, where the snipe-shooting afforded excellent sport. Among the works of art in the house was a celebrated statue of a tinted Venus, whose blue eyes and golden locks were rather too realistic to Jennie's mind for true beauty. In their walks they had many opportunities of seeing the heartrending poverty of the peasantry, who lived in their wretched mud hovels more like animals than human beings. Alas! she feared these deplorable conditions must ever prevail in Ireland, where neglect and misery had rooted the people in their shiftless and improvident habits. No philanthropic scheme seemed really to touch them.

They also visited Galway and Connemara, whose melodious name prepared one for the beauty of its scenery, enhanced as it was by the delights of trout-fishing. Muckross Abbey, on the Lake of Killarney, famed alike for its shooting and its scenery, had been taken by Lord and Lady Wimborne, with whom they often stayed. From there they sometimes went over to Kenmare close by, one of the show-places of Ireland, where the details of the house were carried out in such perfection that even the door-handles were made of old watchcases.

But this magnificence was exceptional and Jennie was often reminded of the descriptions in "Charles O'Malley" of the improvidence and extravagance of the Irish. Sometimes on the roadside one might see a splendid gateway, whose stone pillars and iron-wrought gates stood in solitary grandeur leading to nothing, all the money having been spent on the approach, and none being left for the house.

Among the most delightful personalities Jennie met during those three years was Father Healy, vicar of Bray near Kingstown. He was one of the most celebrated Irish wits of the day, and his genial manner and kind heart made him a most pleasant companion. He and Mr. Isaac Butt often dined with them at their little house in the Phoenix Park.

Mr. Butt was very friendly, not to say homely, but although he could tell a good story in an amusing way, Jennie confessed she thought him rather too serious, constantly dwelling on the miseries and oppression of his countrymen. He would appeal to her as an American to agree with him and when in rash moments she did, would then declare she was a Home Ruler. The words "Home Rule" were the invention of Butt. He thought the old cry of "Repeal" would frighten the English, while the phrase Home Rule would commend itself to everyone as reasonable and innocent. The echoes of their conversations would sometimes reach the ears of the Viceroy, and be thought great heresy.

Of their many habitués, besides Professor Mahaffy of Greek fame, Dr. Nedley another Irish wit, Lord Morris, and Lord Ashbourne (Lord Chancellor of Ireland), Lord Justice FitzGibbon was the most intimate. It was there that the friendship began which lasted to the end of Randolph's life. FitzGibbon had a house at Howth, where every Christmas he assembled a select number of boon companions, Randolph invariably being of the number.

Lord Randolph Churchill was obliged to be in London a good deal during this time to attend to his parliamentary duties. The letters he wrote to Jennie in Ireland were full of politics. One such letter, dated January 28, 1878, from St. James' Club, revealed his conflicted thoughts about a debate in which he could make "a telling speech against the Government" but was cautioned by "old Bentinck." He mentioned that Northcote had made "a very feeble speech" and that Russia's peace terms were "monstrous." He closed by mentioning a pleasant evening at Dilke's with Harcourt, G. Trevelyan, Dicey, and Sir Henry Maine, assuring Jennie she need not "be afraid of these Radicals."

Jennie's visits to London at that time were few and far between, but on one of these, in the summer of 1878, she had the privilege of going with a few other ladies to the "Peace with Honor" banquet which was given in the Wellington Riding School in honor of Lord Beaconsfield and Lord Salisbury on their return from their successful participation in the Berlin Conference. She went with the Duchess of Wellington, arm-chairs being placed in the center of the huge building. It was a wonderful sight, and the enthusiasm was boundless when Lord Beaconsfield, looking like a black sphinx, rose to speak. It was on that occasion that, pointing with a scornful finger at Mr. Gladstone, he declared that he was "inebriated with the exuberance of his own verbosity."

The following year, the Duke of Marlborough having given up the Viceroyalty and left Ireland for good, they also departed, returning to London.

In the summer of 1881 Jennie and Randolph went again to the United States on a short visit. When in New York they heard of the Phoenix Park murders. The Kilmainham Treaty had just been arranged, Parnell having promised to put down outrage. Mr. Forster had resigned, and Lord Frederick Cavendish had been appointed Chief Secretary for Ireland in his place. Jennie remembered a reporter calling at her father's house in Madison Square and telling her the news. They were greatly shocked and could hardly believe it until it was confirmed the next day. She had never met Lord Frederick Cavendish, but Mr. Burke, the other victim, who with his sister lived at the Under Secretary's lodge in the Phoenix Park, they knew quite well. The outcome of this dastardly deed was of course the Prevention of Crimes Act, which was passed at once.

Curiously enough, Jennie had occasion later to see the murderers, just before their condemnation. Although they had left Ireland, she rarely missed paying a visit, either to the Castle during the season, or to the Viceregal Lodge for the Punchestown races. She was staying in Dublin for the Horse Show when she met an official of Kilmainham Gaol, who, owing a debt of gratitude to Randolph, wanted to show her some civility, and therefore thought of nothing better than to invite her to see Kilmainham and the murderers.

She confessed that she did not feel any great desire for this entertainment, but being told that it was nearly impossible to get permission to see them, and that without exception no one was allowed in the prison, she began to feel more interested. Under the seal of the greatest secrecy she found her way to the gaol, where she met Mr. , . He took her into a small room and told her to stand behind his chair while he interviewed the prisoners one by one. They looked apprehensively toward her, but her friend reassured them by saying they need not mind as she was a relation. He only kept them a minute or two putting some trivial questions. The youngest of them, as he was passing out, suddenly turned and asked her to help his wife if he "had to go." This depressed her dreadfully, nor were her spirits raised by being taken round the prison by the Governor, whom Mr. , had somehow "squared."

The tier upon tiers of tiny cells, each containing a miserable-looking man, the food brought in baskets which she saw prodded through and through with swords for fear that something might be smuggled in them, were a more than unpleasant sight. She saw Carey, the informer, who was occupying the same room in which Parnell had been imprisoned. Carey was in his shirt-sleeves and glared at them. Just as she was going to leave and while standing in the middle of the building, talking to the Governor and Mr. , , an electric bell rang and a warder came running up and whispered something to the Governor. He became rather pale and passed his news on to her friend, who seemed equally disturbed.

They both looked at her, and when she asked what had happened, the Governor said the Inspector-General was coming to pay a surprise visit to the prison and was at that moment at the gates, and that if she were found there without a permit signed by the Lord Lieutenant, they would get into great trouble. "Well, let me fly," she exclaimed. "Impossible," they cried; "there is no outlet." "Well, hide me." "You can't hide in a prison!" "One moment," said the Governor hesitatingly, "would you mind a cell?" "Of course not," she replied, and forthwith she was hurried into a cell, a black cell, as being safer from the Inspector's prying eyes.

The door was shut on her, and she felt not "on velvet," but in velvet of the blackest dye. After a time the velvet became thick black wool, and she was certain it was closing round her. Hours seemed to pass and she began to think she was forgotten. Her mind wandered from black wool to rats, and she felt sure she saw little beady eyes looking at her, when the door opened just in time to save her from screaming. She was in that cell twenty minutes at the outside, but it was enough of such an experience. Later she could not help laughing to think of the face of the Inspector, an acquaintance, by the way, had he happened to visit her dungeon. She kept her counsel for more than three years after the execution of those wretched men, and never mentioned her visit to a soul for fear of doing harm.

Under such terrorism did everyone live at that time in Ireland that Lord Spencer, who was then Viceroy, never moved without an escort of Constabulary even when hunting. It was comical to see them in full uniform, their swords bounding in the air as they careered over the fences after the sporting Lord Lieutenant.

During the Jubilee year of Queen Victoria, Jennie revisited the Viceregal Court when Lord Londonderry was Viceroy. Ireland was again suffering under the Crimes Bill, which had been carried by the closure. Mr. Balfour (than whom, with his back to the wall, there was no better fighter) was Chief Secretary, and was beginning that policy of repression which only a strong man could have carried out. There was much unrest in the country and the air was full of disquietude and rumors. The Government no doubt was again going through anxious times, but the visitors at the Castle saw only the sunny side.

The festivities of the Dublin season were taking place with perhaps even more animation than usual, owing to the popularity of the Lord Lieutenant and Lady Londonderry, who was not only a perfect hostess, but the most indefatigable worker in the many charitable schemes she had set on foot. Later, when having left Ireland she returned to London, her salon became and has continued to be a political center, of which she is the presiding genius. An omnivorous reader, blessed with a retentive memory, her conversational powers were great and her influence and interest in the political world have been most valuable to her family and friends. If her receptions were perhaps too crowded, the battalions of a large Conservative Party were to blame.

Everything that year was dubbed "Jubilee," from knights and babies to hats and coats. "God save the Queen" was heard ad nauseam on every conceivable occasion, until the tune became an obsession. This led to a practical joke at the Castle which caused much amusement. One morning, speaking of the Jubilee craze, Jennie pretended that she had received as an advertisement a "Jubilee bustle" which would play "God save the Queen" when the wearer sat down. This, of course, created much curiosity and laughter. Having promised to put it on, she took her hosts into her confidence. An aide-de-camp was pressed into the service, and armed with a small musical box was made to hide under a particular arm-chair. While the company was at luncheon she retired to don the so-called "Jubilee wonder," and when they were all assembled she marched in solemnly and slowly sat down on the arm-chair where the poor aide-de-camp was hiding his cramped limbs. To the delight and astonishment of everyone, the National Anthem was heard gently tinkling forth. Every time she rose it stopped; every time she sat down, it began again. She still laughed when thinking of it and of the astonished faces about her.

London House of Politicians

The new Parliament of 1880 found Jennie and Randolph Churchill established with their household goods in a little house they had taken in London in St. James's Place. It was next door to Sir Stafford Northcote, then leader of the Opposition. Little did the kind old gentleman realize at that time his proximity to the hornets' nest which was being built by the Fourth Party.

Randolph had been reelected for Woodstock, defeating the Liberal candidate, Mr. W. Hall. The contest was not an exciting one, although many of the constituents were dissatisfied and full of grumblings and complaints. They fancied themselves neglected, due to the owners of Blenheim being absent in Ireland for so many years. Nevertheless, Jennie was confident that they would win, having too many good friends in the constituency to fear a rebuff.

Randolph, whose interest in politics had become very keen during his stay in Ireland, now became entirely absorbed by them. During this session the Bradlaugh incident arose in which he took a prominent part. Jennie, too, caught the fever, and went frequently to the House of Commons, listening with growing interest to the debates. The Ladies' Gallery, for which one ballots, and the Speaker's Gallery, to which one is invited by the Speaker's wife, were not in those days the fashionable places of resort they have since become. Only a few ultra-political ladies frequented them.

In the Speaker's Gallery, Mrs. Gladstone, picturesque and dignified, always occupied a reserved seat, from which she was seldom absent. Miss Balfour, too, was generally there. Mrs. Cavendish Bentinck, a tall, handsome woman, whose flashing eyes and raven locks had gained for her among her friends the name of "Britannia," and whose son married Miss Livingston of New York, was also a regular attendee and literally seemed to live there. Later, Mrs. Chamberlain joined the group. But the gay butterflies of society thought it too serious a place for them.

This had quite changed by the time Jennie was writing her memoirs. The generation that followed were full of the desire of being, or appearing to be, serious. To be beautiful and rich was not sufficient; the real social leaders of the day were not content with these accidents of birth and fortune. They aspired to political influence, or to be thought literary and artistic, and society followed the lead. For an interesting debate, or to hear a popular politician, they would make strenuous efforts to get into the Speaker's Gallery. On such an occasion, many of the youngest and prettiest women in London could be found there.

Hidden in Eastern fashion from masculine sight, fifty or more would sometimes crowd into the small, dark cage to which the ungallant British legislators had relegated them. The ladies in the first row, in a cramped attitude, with their knees against the grille, their necks craned forward, and their ears painfully on the alert if they wished to hear anything, were supposed to enjoy a great privilege. Those in the second row, by the courtesy of the first, might get a peep of the politicians below. The rest had to fall back on their imagination or retire to a small room in the rear, where they could whisper and have tea.

Some took the opportunity to polish off their correspondence, hoping, perhaps, that these letters, written on House of Commons paper, might convey a political flavor to the unpolitical recipients. Silence was supposed to be the rule, but the thread of many an interesting speech had been lost in the buzz of stage whispers and the coming and going of restless ones.

"Is that Mr. , ?" a pretty blonde might exclaim to her neighbor. "Do lend me your glasses. Yes, it is he. I wonder if he would dine with me tonight." ("Shhh!" from a relative of the man who was speaking.) "We are thirteen , so tiresome. I think I must send him a note by the usher." ("Shhh!" "Shhh!") "Who is that odious woman hushing me? Darling, keep my chair; I will return in a moment," and amid a jingling of beads and chains and a rustling of silk petticoats, the fair one would fly off to scribble her note.

Meanwhile the front row would settle down once more to the speech to which they were listening. "What an immoral argument! Just like a Radical's impudence to say such things!" might exclaim in no dulcet tones a Conservative peeress, who would be better occupied waking up her lord in the Upper House, than crowding out the wife of some Member of Parliament in the Lower. "Be careful!" her neighbor might warn; "his wife is next to you."

Jennie remembered an enthusiastic wife whose husband was making an important speech, betraying her too intimate knowledge of it by giving her unwilling listener the best points beforehand. Next to speaking in public oneself, there was nothing which produced such feelings of nervousness and apprehension as to hear one's husband or son make a speech. There was no doubt, however, that the frequent recurrence of it minimized the ordeal, particularly if the speakers were sure of themselves. In this respect Jennie could claim to being specially favored, though Randolph, even after years of practice and experience, was always nervous before a speech until he actually stood up.

This subject reminded her of a painful sight she once saw at a big political meeting. A young member of Parliament with more acres than brains, who sat for a family pocket borough, was making his yearly address to his constituents. Shutting his eyes tight and clenching his hands, he began in a high falsetto voice: "Brothers and sisters, Conservatives!" and for thirty minutes he recited, or rather gabbled, the speech he had learned by heart, while his wife, with her eyes riveted on him, and with tears pouring down her cheeks from nervousness, unconsciously, with trembling lips, repeated the words he was uttering.

Those years (1880-84) of political activity when the Fourth Party was at its zenith, were full of excitement and interest for Jennie. Their house became the rendezvous of all shades of politicians. Many were the plots and plans which were hatched in her presence by the Fourth Party, who, notwithstanding the seriousness of their endeavors, found time to laugh heartily and often at their own frustrated machinations. They would often joke about the "goats," as they called the ultra-Tories and followers of Sir Stafford Northcote! Great was to be their fall and destruction.

Sir Henry Drummond Wolff, whom Jennie had met at Cowes before her marriage, was a godsend if anything went wrong, and a joke from him saved many a situation. With a pink-and-white complexion that a girl might have envied, and a merry twinkle in the eyes which hid behind a pair of spectacles, he was the best of company. But she confessed she thought rather dangerous his habit of treating the most serious questions in a flippant manner, and of turning everything into ridicule. Sometimes, to hear him and Randolph discussing the situation, the uninitiated might have thought the subject was a game of chess. It saddened her to think that Fortune had been so little kind to Sir Henry, for, notwithstanding his many services to the State and his private life of unselfishness and abnegation, cares and misfortunes came heavily upon him in his old age.

Sir John Gorst , then Mr. Gorst , was a very different type of man from Sir Henry Wolff. His stern countenance belied him, and he could make himself very pleasant. Jennie remembered his defending her in some trivial case in the County Court, and winning it; the appearance of a Queen's Counsel in silk gown and wig creating a sensation. Randolph accompanied them, and they drove away in a four-wheeler, feeling very triumphant until the wheel came off, and they were ignominiously precipitated into the street.

Sir John had a music-loving soul, and many were the occasions when he and Jennie and Arthur Balfour went off to the "Monday Pops," to listen to the sweet strains of Joachim and Norman Neruda. Her fashionable and frivolous friends, spying the three of them walking together, often teased her about her "weird" companions, one solemn with beard and eye-glass, the other aesthetic with long hair and huge spats. Mr. Balfour's knowledge of music was remarkable, considering the little time he was able to devote to it, and he was no mean performer at the piano, reading and playing classical music. They often played Beethoven or Schumann together. But it was not without difficulty that he could get away from his parliamentary duties, which increased yearly, and often she was disappointed of his company.

Letter from Arthur James Balfour, 1888, House of Commons:
In this letter, Balfour expresses his regret at missing a music concert with Jennie. He writes that he is "groaning and swearing on this beastly bench" listening to Irish grumblings while she is enjoying Wagner. He laments that instead of sitting next to her, he must remain in Parliament as the Irish have "a talent for turning everything into an Irish debate" and when they speak, he must answer.

As regards the Fourth Party, Jennie was full of grievances against Mr. Balfour. He never seemed quite certain whether he belonged to it or not; it depended how Randolph, Wolff, and Gorst were behaving, how much his uncle, Lord Salisbury, remonstrated, or how political events were shaping themselves for the party. If badly, Mr. Balfour would, as she often had reason to tell him, "retirer son épingle du jeu" [English Translation: "withdraw his pin from the game" - meaning to pull out or disengage himself] and repudiate with indignation the idea that he was a member of it. This did not prevent him, however, from secretly hankering after the "wicked" three, whose company had for him all the fascination of forbidden fruit.

Be it as it may, history, that often untruthful jade, would probably write him down as the fourth member of the party, although he may have only coquetted with it. A contemporary said of him, "An apostle of modern intelligence, a depositary of universal knowledge, a standard of mental infallibility, Mr. Balfour would have constituted an important Party in himself if he had not been a chosen vessel designed by nature, by culture, and by the eternal fitness of things to be the Fourth Party's fourth man."

During the time that Randolph and his friends were struggling in Opposition, Sir William Harcourt, Sir Charles Dilke, and Mr. Joseph Chamberlain came frequently to their house. This was looked upon with much disapproval by the "goats," who regarded these politicians as very dangerous company for young people properly imbued with true Conservative principles. The Duke of Marlborough, Jennie's father-in-law, was particularly incensed, and took Randolph seriously to task for having had Mr. Chamberlain to dinner , "a man who was a Socialist, or not far from one; who was reputed to have refused to drink the Queen's health when Mayor of Birmingham," etc. "How could the influence of such a man be anything but pernicious?"

Indeed, London society thought as much, and since they were not in favor at Court at that time, this association with advanced Radicals was made another subject of grievance against them. Randolph, however, pursued the even tenor of his way, and Jennie was glad to think that, notwithstanding their sometimes very acute political differences, he remained to the end of his life an ardent admirer and friend of Mr. Chamberlain.

Sir William and Lady Harcourt used to give the most delightful dinners and parties at their house in Grafton Street, restricted enough in numbers to make conversation possible. Unlike the present day, people were content to remain where they were being entertained, and were not troubled with anxiety to be seen at half a dozen places in the course of one evening. The pleasantest people in London were to be met there, attracted not only by Sir William's wit and conversation, but also by Lady Harcourt's geniality and her art of making everyone feel at home. Jennie was always proud to think that the daughter of that most illustrious historian, Motley, was a compatriot.

She remembered at one of these dinners having an amusing passage-at-arms with her host, Sir Charles Dilke, and Mr. Chamberlain. At that period she had taken up painting very violently, martyrizing many models, paid and unpaid, covering miles of canvas with impossible daubs, and spending a small fortune in paints and pigments. Her first picture, a life-size copy in oils of Sant's "Inexorable" was to her discomfiture mistaken by an admiring friend for a brilliant piece of wool-work! Her three Radical friends having been told of her artistic efforts, chaffingly implored her to hand them down to posterity by painting their portraits. "Why refuse to paint us?" "Where can you find more attractive or noble models!" "Come, here is a chance to immortalize yourself and us."

"Impossible," she cried. "I should fail; I could never paint you black enough."

Jennie used to accompany Randolph to most of his political gatherings in the country. They would stay with some local magnate, who probably would be taking the chair at the meeting. Men on those occasions fared better than their women folk, for, on the plea of having to prepare speeches, they could seek the solitude of their rooms. Not so the wife, who had to sit, perhaps for hours, talking platitudes to the wives and daughters of the political supporters who had been invited to meet her. But their desire to please, and the hospitality they so cordially extended to her, made up for it.

Letter from Lord Goschen, August 17, House of Commons: In this letter, Lord Goschen apologizes for not being able to accept Jennie's invitation as he has friends coming to stay at his country home. He laments being stuck in Parliament without amusements or ladies, describing it as "deplorable." He flatteringly tells Jennie that there is "not a woman in London I like more to take into dinner." He apologizes for what he calls a "Philistine letter" written with a House of Commons inkstand rather than the romantic one she had given him from her first literary earnings.

Of all the statesmen Jennie had met, she thought the late Lord Salisbury and Mr. Gladstone were the pleasantest companions at dinner. Both had the happy knack of seeming vastly interested in one's conversation, whatever the subject, or however frivolous. There was no condescension or "tempering of the wind to the shorn lamb" about it. At the same time, she had to own that any feeling of elation for having had, as one considered, a success was speedily destroyed; for the next woman, whoever she might be, who had the privilege of sitting beside either of these great men, would receive exactly the same courteous attention.

As for Mr. Gladstone, having once started him on his subject, an intelligent "Yes" or "No" was all that was required. But if you ventured a remark (to which he listened in grave silence), he had a disconcerting way of turning sharply round, his piercing eye fixed inquiringly upon you, and his hand to his ear, with the gesture so well known to the House of Commons. His old-world manner was very attractive, and his urbanity outside the House remarkable.

On one occasion Jennie had been at the House hearing Randolph make a fiery attack on Gladstone, which he answered with equal heat and indignation. The hour was late, and Randolph and she had just time to rush home and dress to dine at Spencer House with Lord and Lady Spencer. The first person she met as she went in was Mr. Gladstone, who at once came up and said: "I hope Lord Randolph is not too tired after his magnificent effort." What an object lesson to those foreign politicians who would look upon it as an insult to be asked to meet in the same house!

The autumn of 1883 was marked by the formation of the Primrose League, which subsequently proved to be an event of great political importance, and a tower of strength to the Conservative Party.

The Fourth Party, with the exception of Mr. Balfour, and the addition of Sir Alfred Slade, had drawn up the statutes and ordinances of this new political society, which was to "embrace all classes and all creeds except atheists and enemies of the British Empire." Sir Henry Wolff, who had originated the idea from seeing Conservatives wearing primroses on the anniversary of Lord Beaconsfield's death, came to Blenheim, where Jennie was staying at the time, to initiate them.

All the female members of the family who happened to be there were enrolled as dames, and were given a badge and a numbered diploma. Jennie's was No. 11. The Duchess of Marlborough was made President of the Ladies' Grand Council, which was being formed. They laughed immoderately over the grandiloquent names , the "Knights Harbingers" (or "Night refugees," as they dubbed them), the "Ruling Councillors," the "Chancellor of the League," "Dames," "Dame President," "Habitations," and what not. They criticized freely the gaudy badges and "ye ancient" diplomas printed on vellum. Little did they know the power the League was to become.

As a "dame," Jennie was determined to do all she could to further its aims. The first years of its existence were a struggle. The wearing of the badge exposed one to much chaff, not to say ridicule; but they persisted. Recruits joined steadily if slowly, and by the time of her writing, after twenty-one years of existence, the League could boast of having 1,703,708 knights, dames, and associates upon its rolls, and of having materially helped to keep the Conservative Party in power for twenty years.

For many years Jennie worked strenuously on behalf of the League. She became the "Dame President" of many Habitations, and used to go all over the country inaugurating them. The opening ceremonies were often quaint in their conceptions, a mixture of grave and gay, serious and frivolous , speeches from members of Parliament, interspersed with songs and even recitations, sometimes of a comical nature. The meeting would end with the enrolment of converts.

A strange medley, the laborer and the local magnate, the county lady and the grocer's wife, would troop up and sign the roll. Politics, like charity, were a great leveler. The late Lady Salisbury, when President of the Ladies Executive Council of the Primrose League, once at a committee meeting rebuked a member who thought that a certain form of entertainment to be held at one of the Primrose League Habitations, though attractive to the masses, might be thought slightly vulgar. "Vulgar? Of course it is vulgar," exclaimed the President; "but that is why we have got on so well."

Among the many entertainments of this kind, Jennie particularly remembered going with Mr. Balfour to Manchester just before the general elections of 1886 to open a large Habitation. A few days later, on the seventh of June, Mr. Gladstone was defeated on his Home Rule Bill. In view of this, she permitted herself to recall her remarks on that occasion, as they proved prophetic.

Trembling with excitement, her notes hidden in her fan, she had said: "I am proud to have the privilege of inaugurating this most important Habitation. It is not necessary for me to dilate on the usefulness of the Primrose League. We have had ample proof of the great work it did at the recent General Election (1885), and we shall soon have an opportunity of showing to our opponents that not only is its power undiminished, but that it is increased tenfold. But to make this a certainty, I think that every member of the Primrose League must put his or her shoulder to the wheel. When Mr. Gladstone appears in his new role of undertaker, let us hope that, with the exception of a few hypocritical mourners, he may be left to bury his doomed Bill alone. When that melancholy rite is accomplished, and he appeals to the country, I trust with all my heart that it will answer with one voice in favor of that Party which is pledged to support all that is dear to England , religion, law, order, and the unity of the Empire."

The local press were good enough to add that "Lady Randolph was ably supported by Lord Salisbury's nephew, Mr. Balfour, M.P.!"

The year 1888 saw them in a new house in Connaught Place. "Tyburnia," their friends called it, as on the railings opposite their windows, which faced Hyde Park, there was a small tablet to mark the site of Tyburn Gate. Often Jennie thought of the thousands of poor wretches who had been hanged there, and sometimes wondered if the house would be full of wailing ghosts: but frankly she never saw or heard one.

She was very much occupied that winter furnishing, and disposing in the new house what her brother-in-law Blandford used to call her "stage properties." In a former house which they had bought shortly after their marriage, she had, in her ignorance of the climate, covered the walls with silks and stuffs, and nearly cried with dismay when she saw the havoc wrought upon them by the fogs and smuts of the dirtiest of towns. Her dearly bought experience stood her in good stead when furnishing again. The paneling and clean white paint, which was so popular in later times, formed the principal decoration of their next dwelling, which, by the way, was the first private house in London to have electric lights.

They had a small dynamo placed in a cellar underneath the street, and the noise of it greatly excited all the horses as they approached their door. The light was such an innovation that much curiosity and interest were evinced to see it, and people used to ask for permission to come to the house. Jennie remembered the fiasco of a dinner party they gave to show it off, when the light went out in the middle of the feast, just as they were expatiating on its beauties, their guests having to remain in utter darkness until the lamps and candles, which had been relegated to the lower regions, were unearthed.

The electric light did not prove to them an unmitigated blessing, inasmuch as Randolph, having spoken enthusiastically in the House of Commons in favor of an Electric Lighting Bill, felt he could no longer accept the gift of the installation which, by way of an advertisement, a company had offered to put into their house, free of cost. Unfortunately, there being no contract, they were charged double or treble the real price.

It was curious how fond one could become of inanimate objects apart from their intrinsic value. They had many nice bits of old furniture which they had picked up in Dublin, where they had found their way from the dismantled houses of impecunious Irish landlords. Things could be bought cheaply in those days, the artistic craze being confined to the eclectic few. Now collecting millionaires had bought up nearly everything, and what was left was held at fabulous prices. On the other hand, owing to the taste of the present day, the "House Beautiful" was now within the reach of all. They were far from the heavy and uncomfortable monstrosities of the Early Victorian epoch. Taste and common-sense, with a desire for knowledge, even if allied to a limited purse, would go farther to please the eye of the senses than the riches of a Croesus spent for him by upholsterers. Once the eye was accustomed to the purest styles and perfect models, it unconsciously rejected base imitations and inharmonious lines; just as the man who lives surrounded by fine pictures even if he be not an artist, retains an impression of the warmth and beautiful coloring of the masterpieces.

Jennie remembered coming across some large painted panels representing "Ceres" and "Pomona." Her sojourn at Blenheim, among those glorious pictures, she supposed, had educated her eye. The owner wanted some £300 for them, for which they were to be restored and put into good order. Full of her discovery, she rushed home with a glowing tale, in the hopes of persuading Randolph to buy them. She found him with Mr. Balfour and Sir Henry Wolff, discussing the merits of "Elijah's Mantle," which he had just written for the "Fortnightly." The laughter it provoked reached her ears as she subsequently sat in her drawing-room looking at its bareness, which, alas! had to remain so. "Three hundred pounds , preposterous! Besides, we cannot afford it" , so Randolph settled the question. She reluctantly gave up the panels, which were sold shortly afterward, and turned out to be Morland's, worth at the time of her writing perhaps £7000 or £8000!

London was very animated that season. Randolph's growing prominence in the political world was attracting considerable attention in the social, and they were bombarded with invitations of every kind. The fashionable world, which had held aloof, now began to smile upon them once more. Most people in the course of a lifetime get to know the real value of "the Mammon of Unrighteousness," but few learn their lesson so early. They both profited by it. Personally Jennie would never give up anything by which she really set store for the sake of its unsatisfactory approbation.

A curious phase had come over society. Publicity became the fashion, although it was mild in comparison with what existed in later times. People lived much more before the public than they did. Privacy seemed a luxury no one was allowed to indulge in , even the most uninteresting must be interviewed; their houses, their tastes, their habits, photographs of themselves in their sanctum, all were given to the "man in the street." The craze for exhibiting the photographs of "Ladies of Quality," as they would have been called in the eighteenth century, was a novelty which brought forth much comment. The first time Jennie's found its way into a shop, she was severely censured by her friends, and told she ought to prosecute the photographer.

So great was the license allowed to the public that some ladies who had taken London by storm were publicly mentioned as "Professional Beauties." Conspicuous among them were Mrs. Langtry and Mrs. Wheeler. A fierce war of opinion as to their rival merits raged about them.

Artists extolled Mrs. Langtry's classical Greek profile, golden hair, and wonderful columnlike throat, graced with the three "plis de Venus" [English Translation: "folds of Venus" - referring to three elegant lines around the neck], which made her an ideal subject for their brushes and chisels. So great was the enthusiasm created by the beauty of the "Jersey Lily," as she was called, that in the height of the season Jennie had seen people standing on chairs in the Row to get a peep at her. Professor Newton on one occasion lectured at King's College on Greek art. Mrs. Langtry, as a living exponent of the classical type which the professor was describing, sat in a prominent place facing the audience.

In one of his letters to Jennie while she was in Ireland, Randolph had written: "I dined with Lord Wharncliffe last night, and took in to dinner a Mrs. Langtry, a most beautiful creature , quite unknown, very poor, and they say has but one black dress."

Mrs. Wheeler was quite different with dark hair and deep gray-blue eyes, which held you by their gentle, appealing expression. She was very fascinating.

For a time no party was considered complete or successful without these ladies. People would receive invitations with "Do come; the P. Bs. will be there." This meant the certain attendance of society. On which a poet (saving the mark!) of the day wrote verses celebrating the various beauties of the era, including Lady Dudley, Lady Mandeville, Miss Yznaga, Lady Castlereagh, Lady Florence Chaplin, Mrs. Murietta, Violet Lindsay, Princess Louise, Mrs. Sassoon, and of course, Lady Randolph Churchill herself, who was described as having "sweet tones" that "Make her the Saint Cecilia of the day."

Although London had always been famous for the beautiful women of all nationalities that one could see there, Jennie doubted their having been surpassed since the eighties. To pick and choose among such a bevy was somewhat of an invidious task. She could think of few in her present day who could really compare with the Duchess of Leinster and her sister Lady Helen Vincent, Lady Londonderry, Lady Dalhousie, Lady Lonsdale (better known as Lady de Grey), Lady Ormonde who had the cameo-like features of her mother, the beautiful Duchess of Westminster, Lady Mary Mills, and Lady Gerard.

Mrs. Cornwallis-West, whose daughters had inherited her beauty, held her own with the best of them. It was difficult to find a fault in her bright, sparkling face, as full of animation as her brown eyes were of Irish wit and fun. She had a lovely complexion, curly brown hair, and a perfect figure. Undoubtedly, however, the one who would be handed down to posterity as the most beautiful woman of her generation was Georgiana Lady Dudley, whose imposing presence and small aristocratic head still commanded admiration. Among royal ladies no one could dispute the palm being given to Her Majesty Queen Alexandra.

Snow and Russia

Chartwell, 1964

"Russia in winter," Churchill murmured, settling back into his chair with visible effort. "Not many English ladies would have undertaken such a journey in 1881, particularly not to a country most viewed with suspicion and fear." He reached for a small silver frame on the table beside him, a photograph of his parents in formal dress. "But my mother was curious about the world in a way that transcended politics or prejudice."

Sophia studied the photograph. "What did she discover there?"

"That the enemies we create in our minds are often quite different from the people we meet in reality." Churchill's fingers traced the edge of the frame. "She expected to find the grinding despotism everyone warned her about. Instead, she found warmth, culture, intelligence, a society far more sophisticated than London credited." He looked up at Sophia. "That lesson proved invaluable to me decades later, when I had to navigate relationships with Stalin and the Soviet Union."

"She taught you to see beyond stereotypes."

"She taught me that understanding one's supposed enemies might be the key to eventual cooperation, or at least coexistence." Churchill replaced the photograph carefully. "The Russian aristocrats who entertained her so graciously would be dead within forty years, swept away by revolution. But the human connections she made, the insights she gained about Russian character and culture, those informed my own diplomatic efforts when the fate of the world hung in the balance."

ST. PETERSBURG, 1881

During the winter of 1881, Jennie traveled to Russia with her husband Lord Randolph, the Marquis de Breteuil (whose ancestor had been French Ambassador to the court of Catherine the Great), and Mr. Trafford. They spent an interesting and delightful month there.

Everything they encountered was new and attractive. The people were charming and hospitable, full of good nature. Jennie saw no signs of the grinding despotism and tyranny that was supposedly synonymous with Russian life. Her first impression of the scenery was one of disappointment. The country between Berlin and St. Petersburg, particularly beyond the Russian frontier, was flat and uninteresting. The waste and dreary expanse, covered with snow, inspired a feeling of deep melancholy. Jennie thought that living for months every year buried in that cold, monotonous silence would be enough to account for the vein of sadness that seemed to be the basis of the Russian character, betraying itself in all Russian music and painting.

As their snow-laden train arrived at the station in St. Petersburg, Jennie and her companions stepped out joyfully and stretched their cramped and tired limbs. The broad streets, full of life and animation, and as bright as day with electricity, seemed a delightful contrast. She hadn't known what to expect, but the city disappointed her with its modern appearance. Looking at the houses of rather mean exterior, with their small double windows and tiny doors, Jennie had no idea of the splendor within. Space, however, seemed immaterial, which struck her forcibly, accustomed as she was to London with its narrow streets.

The French system of apartments was common in St. Petersburg, although not as prevalent as in Paris. Where it existed, the entrances and staircases were much more decorated and cared for than was usual where several families lived under the same roof, giving the appearance of a private dwelling. In the great houses, Jennie was struck by the very large number of servants. She was told that in some rich noblemen's homes, whole families of useless dependents, mujiks, with their wives and children, were installed in the lower regions. If this was the case in town, she wondered what it must have been like in the country. Such generosity, combined with the utter absence of real supervision in the financial management of the establishment, must have been a heavy tax on even the largest fortune. It wasn't surprising that Russian nobility of Jennie's day, with the added burden of war and internal dissension, were in an impoverished state.

However, they saw nothing of this poverty during their visit. All the entertainments and functions they attended, whether private or public, were extremely well done. Russians loved light, and on these occasions made their houses as bright as day, with a profusion of candles as well as electric light. Masses of flowers, despite their rarity in such a rigorous climate, decorated every available place, and the staircases were lined with footmen in gorgeous liveries.

Although many of the houses were very smartly furnished with all that money could buy and modern art could suggest, they struck Jennie as lacking in the real refinement and true artistic taste that one saw in Paris. The French, she noted, were born connoisseurs and thought of little else than artistic comfort.

In those days, Jennie found the average Russian drawing room superior to the ordinary English one. If there was a lack of imagination, there was also an absence of tawdriness, which contrasted favorably with the overcrowded London room. At that time in London, the aesthetic and Japanese craze reigned supreme, with evenly balanced structures of paper fans, Liberty silks, and photographs thought decorative, not to mention labyrinths of tiny tables, chairs, and screens.

Jennie had been prepared to suffer greatly from the cold but found, as in most Northern countries, that the houses were heated to suffocation. Windows were rarely opened, with a small ventilator being considered quite sufficient. Russians claimed that foreigners brought so much heat with them that they didn't feel the cold at first. This may have been true, but there was no doubt that visitors felt the want of air and the stuffiness of the rooms, which dried up the skin and took away the appetite.

On the other hand, Jennie thoroughly enjoyed the outdoor life of sleighing and skating. Comfortably seated in a sleigh, behind a good, fat coachman to keep the wind off, she never tired of driving about. The rapidity with which one dashed noiselessly along was most exhilarating, despite a biting wind or blinding snow. The ordinary Russian sleigh, smaller than the American cutter, barely held two, but the thick fur rug, even in a common droshky or cab, was so well fastened down that it helped to keep one from falling out, besides protecting from the cold.

The troikas, wide sleighs with three horses (the middle one trotting while the other two galloped), had become rather rare and were used principally for traveling or for expeditions in the country. Nothing was prettier than a really smart sleigh with two horses, one trotting and the other galloping, covered with a large net of dark blue cord fastened to the front of the sleigh to keep the snow from being kicked into the face of the occupant. The coachman, with his fur-lined coat gathered in at the waist, and his bright red or blue octagonal cap with gold braid, drove with his arms extended to preserve his circulation. Jennie was impressed by the fact that the coachmen hardly ever seemed to use their short, thick whips, which they kept carefully hidden. A footman stood on a small step behind, his tall hat and ordinary great coat looking a little incongruous and marring an otherwise picturesque sight.

The horses were so beautifully trained that a word would stop them. The whole time Jennie was in Russia, she never saw a horse ill-used. There was no need for a "Society for the Prevention of Cruelty to Animals" there. The Isvoshnik who owned his cab-horse looked upon him as his friend, and very often shared the animal's stall at night.

Among the many acquaintances they made were M. and Mme. Polovstow, who showed them great hospitality. He was President of the Council, a very important post, and was high in the favor of the Czar. His early history was rather romantic. As private secretary to the millionaire Steiglitz, Polovstow won the affections and the hand of his adopted daughter, to whom Steiglitz left the whole of his fortune.

Among many institutions founded by her adopted father, Mme. Polovstow took Jennie to see the "Steiglitz School of Art," which was kept up at her own expense. Jennie was much interested to find in the museum a certain Italian cabinet which the late Duke of Marlborough had sold from Blenheim, and the destination of which had always been a mystery.

One night they went to the opera with the Polovstows to hear "La vie pour le Czar" by Glinka, charming music imprinted with all the national characteristics of sadness and wild, boisterous gaiety, though the orchestration seemed rather feeble. All the ladies wore high dresses, which took away from the brilliant appearance one was accustomed to in other opera houses. Sometimes the performance was entirely ballet, no singing, and one night Jennie had the opportunity of seeing the famous dancer Zucchi in "Esmeralda." She was then in her prime, and she certainly was a marvelous dancer of the old school.

After the opera, enveloped in great fur coats and caps, they drove in troikas to the islands in the Neva, where the Polovstows had a charming pavilion. They were ushered into a large conservatory brilliantly lighted and full of orchids and rare flowers, a dazzling and wonderful contrast to the snow-clad scenery outside, on which "the cold, round moon shone deeply down," turning everything to silver. Hidden by palms, a band of Tziganes was playing inspiriting melodies, while in the dining room an excellent supper was served on genuine Louis XV plate. They didn't get back to their hotel until the small hours of the morning. Russians, Jennie found to her cost, loved late hours and seemed never to go to bed, the evening generally beginning for them at midnight.

On one occasion, Jennie was taken for a spin on the Neva with a fast trotter, which she didn't enjoy quite as much, owing to the end of her nose being nearly frozen. When they returned, her host rushed up to her and rubbed it violently with snow, as it looked ominously white. As long as your nose kept a glorious red, you were safe.

While in St. Petersburg, Jennie was able to indulge to her heart's content in her favorite pastime of skating, which she did on the lake of the Palais de la Tauride, a royal palace where Russian society congregated. But great was her disappointment to find that the Russians did not care for figure skating and, in fact, did not skate well. She was told that had it not been for the Czarina (Marie), who was an adept in the art, people would not have appreciated skating at all. As it was, they much preferred tobogganing down the ice-hills, half a dozen or more persons in a sleigh. It was in one of these that Jennie had her first experience of this sport, and was duly "blooded" (if one may call it so) by being placed in the front seat of the sleigh and shot into a bank of snow.

The ice-hills, which were built on the lake, were merely blocks of ice placed on a wooden path raised to a platform at a steep angle, which one ascended by a staircase. To go down one of these hills on skates for the first time gave the same delightful feeling of satisfaction and pleasure which in hunting is experienced in getting over a big fence, leaving the field a bit behind. It was not an easy matter, as the pace was terrific, and coming to the level again at the foot of the hill made it difficult to keep one's feet; but if successful, one shot across the whole lake. Many were the accidents, and Jennie saw one poor lady break her arm.

Sir Robert Morier, the British Ambassador, was away when they first arrived, but later he and his family showed them great kindness and hospitality. Meanwhile, they were bidden to Gatchina to have an audience with the Czar and the Czarina. Gatchina, about an hour by train from St. Petersburg, was the Windsor of Russia. It was a curious mixture of splendor and unpretentiousness and was approached from the station through a series of small parks, which must have been lovely in summer. Jennie was surprised to see so few sentries; to all appearances, the Czar was not more guarded than the King at Windsor. The entrance to Gatchina on the public road had only one sentry.

The palace had no great architectural merits, but its six hundred rooms and endless corridors were filled with priceless Oriental china, and the walls were adorned with tapestries and treasures of art. Coureurs in black and orange liveries, their caps embellished by tossing black, white, and orange feathers, gave a slightly barbaric appearance to the scene, which was added to by the mass of bowing attendants, and by two Nubians dressed in white, with turbans and scimitars, standing outside the Czarina's audience chamber.

While waiting to be received, they were shown into an apartment which had an early Victorian style, with paintings of mediocre quality. Here a dejeuner was served, and afterward they went to their respective audiences. Randolph stayed quite an hour with the Czar, who discussed all the political questions of the day. The Czarina, whom Jennie had had the honor of knowing as Czarevna at Cowes some years before, was most gracious and charming, reminding her of her sister, Queen Alexandra, although not so beautiful. She asked endless questions about England and all that was going on politically and socially, and finally, having arrived "au bout de notre Latin" (English Translation: at the end of our Latin [i.e., having exhausted our conversation]) and Randolph not appearing, Jennie was taken to see the palace.

Among many rooms, Jennie remembered a large hall worthy of an old English country house, full of comfortable armchairs and writing tables, games, and toys. She even spied a swing. In that room their Majesties often dined, she was told, even when they had guests, and after dinner the table would be removed, and they would spend the remainder of the evening there. This seemed strange to Jennie when she thought of the many hundred rooms in the enormous building. But their tastes were of the simplest, and the Czar particularly favored tiny rooms, though they were much at variance with his towering frame and majestic bearing. His manner impressed Jennie with a conviction of sincerity and earnestness.

Before leaving St. Petersburg, they were invited once more to Gatchina. This time it was in the evening; a special train conveyed about one hundred and fifty guests. On arriving, they were met by a long stream of royal carriages, which took them to the palace, where they witnessed an entertainment consisting of three short plays in three languages, after which supper was served. Jennie had been given a seat in the third row, but when the Royalties came in, she was bidden to sit behind the Empress, who every now and then would turn round and make some pleasant remark.

There were some curious customs at the Russian court which did not harmonize with one's idea of a despotic and autocratic sovereign. While they were sitting at small tables, the Czar walked about talking to his guests, all of whom, including officers, remained seated. It appeared that that was the habit of Peter the Great, who disliked ceremony of any kind; and as tradition was everything in Russia, this custom was religiously kept. There was no doubt that the etiquette of the Russian court was much less rigid than it was in England or Germany. For instance, it was not the custom to treat the members of the Imperial Family with so much deference as in other European courts; Jennie noticed that the ladies did not think of courtseying to a young Grand Duke and would rise only when the Czarina did, or at the entrance of the Czar. So too, in making their obeisance, they bowed stiffly from the waist, which was even more ungraceful than the English bob, their apology for a courtesy. The men, on the other hand, were very deferential, particularly to the ladies.

At private dinners, when they were announced, the host would rush forward, seize Jennie's hand, and kiss it, and then proceed to introduce all the men present. She then had to ask to be presented to every lady and duly call on them personally the next day. This she found very irksome and wearying, as it interfered with her sight-seeing.

One of the most interesting sights they were privileged to see was the New Year's Reception at the Winter Palace. At eleven o'clock in the morning, the whole court attended, and society paid its respects to the sovereign. The Czar, dressed on this particular occasion in the uniform of the Gardes du Corps, gave his arm to the Czarina and was followed by the imperial family.

The train of each Grand Duchess was carried by four young officers. Jennie remembered that the train of the Grand Duchess Vladimir was of silver brocade, with a sable border half a yard in depth. These were followed by long files of ladies-in-waiting, dressed in green and gold, and maids-of-honor in red and gold. The procession ended when all the court officials, resplendent in gorgeous uniforms and covered with decorations, walked with measured steps through the long suite of rooms, and lined up on each side with officers in the red, white, or blue of their regiments. To these, the Czar spoke as he passed, saying, "Good morning, my children," to which they replied in unison, "We are happy to salute you."

In other rooms, ladies were assembled, dressed in the national costume of every hue, and covered with jewels, mostly cabochon sapphires and emeralds. All wore that most becoming of head-dresses, the "Kakoshnik," made of various materials from diamonds to plain velvet. The Czarina, with her graceful figure and small head, looked very stately in a magnificent tiara, and a blue velvet and ermine train, as the cortege passed on to the chapel to hear mass. This lasted an hour, everyone remaining standing, an art which Royalty alone seemed to have the gift of practicing without breaking down, and without apparent effort.

Jennie could not adequately describe the scene in the chapel, which, if it had been less perfect in detail, might have appeared somewhat theatrical. On the right, the dresses of the women formed a sea of warm color, the soft red and green velvets of the ladies-in-waiting predominating, their long, white tulle veils looking like halos round their heads, touched here and there by iridescent rays from the rich stained-glass windows. On the left, the men presented a scarcely less brilliant group, the dark velvet cassock of a Lutheran pastor standing out in effective contrast to the vivid red of a Cardinal close by.

The royal choir, which followed the Czar wherever he went, was the finest Jennie had ever heard. Composed of male voices alone, without the aid of any instrument (none being allowed in the Greek Church), it was perfection. The character of the music she found rather monotonous and thought to herself how they would have rendered one of Handel's grand anthems.

A story was told to Jennie about this celebrated choir. Clad originally in funereal black, they offended the eyes of a certain maid-of-honor, a favorite of the Czar, who, remonstrating with her for not attending mass, asked the reason. The lady pleaded that she was suffering from melancholy, and that the sight of the black choir would aggravate it. The next day her excuse was gone, for the choir appeared in crimson surplices braided with gold, and they had continued to do so ever since.

Mass over in the chapel, the procession reformed, a pause being made in the room reserved for the ambassadors and diplomatic corps. His Majesty entered into conversation with a favored few, who improved the shining hour, since, with the exception of some court balls, this was the only occasion they had of speaking to him during the year. Finally, the ladies passed before the Czar and kissed hands, holding on to each other's trains, a sight which was more quaint than imposing. When all was over, they sat down to luncheon, reaching home about three o'clock. Not having any such sumptuous day gowns as Jennie found were worn, she was reduced on this occasion to a blue-and-gold tea-gown, which did quite well, although it seemed a strange garment in which to go to court. On their way out, she saw a sentry guarding a magnificent sable cape, which she was told belonged to the Czarina. It was nearly black, and it had taken years to collect the skins at a cost of £12,000.

Most Russian ladies smoked cigarettes, and at all the parties to which Jennie went, one of the reception rooms was set apart for the purpose, which caused a continual movement to and fro, taking off the stiffness of a formal party and enabling people to circulate more freely. This in itself would ensure a pleasant evening; for who hasn't seen with despair the only chair at hand triumphantly seized by a bore, whom nothing but a final "Good night" will move?

Russians, as a rule, had enormous appetites and were very fond of good living, eating, not to mention drinking, often to excess. Drinking in Russian society was not considered a heinous offense. The night they went to Gatchina, the officer in charge, the Colonel of the Preobejensky Guards, the smartest regiment in Russia, who was responsible that night for the safety of the Czar, was so drunk that he fell heavily on Jennie's shoulder when presented to her. Those near laughingly propped him up, evidently thinking nothing of it.

They lunched several times at the celebrated restaurant kept by Cubat, where their plates were piled with enormous helpings fit for a regiment of soldiers. Cubat was a most interesting person, late head chef to the Czar, whose service he had only just left. When asked the reason, he said that the supervision in the kitchen of the royal palace was so irksome and stringent, dozens of detectives watching his every gesture and pouncing on every pinch of salt, that the salary of £2000 a year did not compensate him. He later bought the hotel Paiva in the Champs-Elysees and started the Cubat Restaurant; but the prices were so high that it soon came to an end.

One night they dined with the Grand Duke and Duchess Serge at the beautiful old "Beloselski" palace. It was built in the reign of the great Catherine, whose hand was found in everything of real taste in Russia. Decorated and furnished by the best French artists of the day, to whom the Empress was a generous patron, with its lovely Bouchers and carved white panelings, Jennie thought it quite the finest house they saw while in Russia.

They waited some time for a belated guest, Mme. X., who finally appeared, looking regal, with the most magnificent jewels Jennie had ever seen on any private person; but on her bare arm, as distinct as possible, was the black-and-blue imprint, fingers and thumb, of a brutal hand. No one could help noticing it, and the Grand Duchess pointed at it in dismay. "No, no," cried Mme. X., laughingly, "X. is at Moscow." "Quelque jaloux!" (English Translation: "Some jealous man!") said Jennie's neighbor.

At dinner, Jennie sat between the Grand Duke Serge and the Grand Duke Paul, who was quite the best-looking man she saw in Russia. She found an old friend there in Count Schouwalow, who had been Ambassador in London; also M. de Giers and his wife, at whose house she afterward met the redoubtable Pobiedonostzeff, Head of the Synod, with whom she had a long talk, a tall, gaunt man, whose strange yellow teeth, seemingly all in one, impressed her more than anything else. Other interesting people dining there that evening were Count and Countess Ignatieff, Prince and Princess Solytzkow, and Prince and Princess Worouzow.

No politics nor anything of that nature, whether internal or external, were discussed; reticence as regards public affairs in Russia was only equaled by discretion as regards the affairs of other nations.

Much to Jennie's chagrin, they did not stay in St. Petersburg for the court balls but, time passing, went on to Moscow. Before leaving, however, they visited the Winter Palace, Prince Troubetsky, the Lord Chamberlain, being deputized to take them over it. He had evidently been asked to "do the civil," but was dreadfully bored and hustled them smartly through the immense number of rooms and interminable corridors. Even then it took them two good hours to get round.

They also visited the School for Naval Cadets, the admiral and his staff receiving them with much ceremony. The cadets looked pale and rather hunted. Jennie felt so sorry for them, penned in small rooms, with only a strip of yard, surrounded by tall brick walls, in which to exercise.

Their friend M. de Breteuil did not go to Moscow with them, as he was invited by the Grand Duke Vladimir to join an expedition to shoot bears. It was significant that on the day they started, the Czar, who was setting out on some journey at the same hour, had three trains kept in readiness, and not even the Grand Duke knew in which his brother was traveling!

For the tourist, there was no comparison between St. Petersburg and Moscow; the latter was so much more striking and so full of local color. Everything was a source of interest, from the narrow streets filled with a motley crowd of fur-clad people, the markets with their frozen fish or blocks of milk, from which slabs would be chopped off, and carcasses of beasts propped up in rows against the stalls, to the Kremlin with its palaces and churches. "La ville des marchands," (English Translation: "The city of merchants") as it was called, was full of riches and rich people.

They visited the Trichiakoff picture gallery, belonging to a retired merchant, where Jennie was amazed to see depicted all the grimmest and most gruesome historical incidents of Russian tyranny and cruelty: Ivan the Terrible murdering his son, or receiving on the red staircase of the Kremlin a hapless envoy whose foot he transfixed to the floor with the spiked ferule of his walking stick, while he read some unwelcome message; Siberian prisoners; horrible deeds perpetrated in the fortress of Peter and Paul; and many other atrocities.

Shortly after their arrival, they received a visit from Prince Dolgorouki, the Governor General of Moscow. A charming old man of eighty, a grand seigneur of the old school, he looked very smart and upright in the uniform of the Chevalier Gardes. He told Jennie that he had been twenty-two years Governor of Moscow and had served fifty-six in the army, under three Czars. He showed them much civility during their stay and did all he could to make it pleasant. His aide-de-camp, Prince Ourousow, went about with them, and as he spoke excellent French, they found him most agreeable.

Every morning Prince Ourousow came to inquire what places of interest they should like to visit, and expeditions of all kinds were arranged for them. One day they drove to the Sparrow Hills, the spot where Napoleon stood when he first looked upon the city which preferred destruction to his rule. The marble statue of himself crowned with laurels which he brought with him was carefully preserved in the Kremlin; but, by the irony of fate, it was a trophy of war, instead of representing, as Napoleon intended, the Conqueror of all the Russias. It stood there as a reproof to the overweening ambition and vanity of the greatest of men.

With the Kremlin, they were naturally enchanted. The old Organaya Palace, and the church, with its mosaics and Byzantine decorations, mellowed by centuries to a wonderful hue, had a mysterious and haunting effect. Could those walls have spoken, Jennie had no doubt she would have fled in terror. As it was, they were so interested and fascinated that they returned again, and this time without an escort. She was amazed to find the whole place full of beggars and cripples of every description, who pestered them for alms; on their previous visit, they had not seen one. They heard afterward that the Governor had issued an order bidding them all to leave the precincts, that the visitors might not be annoyed by them. During their stay in Russia, the authorities were everywhere anxious that Randolph should have a good impression, and while in St. Petersburg, they were followed about by two detectives, not, as they at first imagined, to spy upon them, but to see that as distinguished strangers they were not molested in any way.

Prince Dolgorouki was an absolute autocrat in Moscow. Upon their expressing a wish one night when they were dining with him to hear some Tziganes who were giving a performance some distance off, a messenger was dispatched forthwith, and they were ordered to come to the Governor's house. They gave them a very good representation of wild national songs and dances. What happened to the spectators from whom their performers had been snatched they never heard.

Before leaving, they attended the "Bal de la Noblesse" in the Assembly Rooms. It was a fine sight, the floor excellent, and the music most inspiriting. There was a "Marshal of the Ceremonies," who reminded Jennie of the descriptions of Beau Nash, strutting about, full of airs and graces, introducing people, arranging and ruling with great precision the intricacies of the various dances. Officers would be brought up to her, clicking their spurs together and saluting; then they would seize her waist without a word and whisk her round the enormous room at a furious pace, her feet scarcely touching the ground. Before she had recovered, breathless and bewildered, she would be handed over to the next, until she had to stop from sheer exhaustion.

Jennie learned that when the Court went to Moscow, which it did every four or five years, it was the occasion of the appearance of families bearing the finest old names of the country, who generally lived buried in the provinces, people who looked upon society in St. Petersburg very much as the Faubourg St. Germain looked on the heterogeneous mass of which society in Paris was composed under the Empire; and who were so Russian that even the Mazurka, since it was Polish, must not be danced too well.

The day they left Moscow, their friend the Governor came to see them off and presented Jennie with a lovely bouquet of orchids, which was produced from a band-box at the last moment. But before she had had time to sit down, the poor flowers were shriveled as though they had been scorched, one instant of the twenty-two degrees below zero proving too much for them. She left Moscow with great regret, as, apart from the delights of the place, she met some charming women, whose society she found most agreeable.

Jennie gathered from them that Russian ladies, not indulging in any sport and taking little or no exercise, stayed a great deal indoors, and in consequence had much time to educate themselves, to read, and to cultivate the fine arts. Speaking many languages and reading widely, they formed a most attractive society. It was said that Russians were not given to intimacy, and that foreigners never got to know them well. She thought that this was so, but she saw no reason to credit them with less warmth of heart and faculty for lasting friendship than other nations possessed.

It was, however, a matter of surprise to Jennie that women so eminently fitted by nature and education to influence and help those struggling in the higher vocations of life, should have seemingly but one ambition, to efface themselves, to attract no attention, to arouse no jealousies. Yet she doubted not that their influence was felt, though it may not have been open and fearless as in England or America. As a refutation of the supposed insincerity of Russian character, it was an undisputed fact that a succes d'estime was unknown, and the stranger or diplomatist, however well recommended, or however good his position, was not by any means invited to the fetes as a matter of course. After the first introduction, he was asked only according to his host's appreciation of him. Jennie was not speaking of official circles, where policy was the master of ceremonies. The same could be said of the London society of her day. Although formerly all foreigners and the staff of the Embassies were personae gratae, by then English society had become too large, and a hostess had to pick and choose.

This picture of Jennie with her two sons was taken in the mid-1880s, probably while Lord Randolph was in India.

Jack (left) and Winston (right.)

Randolph in India

Chartwell, 1964

Churchill's afternoon medication sat untouched on the table as he became more animated. "While my father was touring the Raj, writing letters about tiger hunts and elephant rides, my mother was doing something far more significant here in London." He struggled to lean forward, his voice dropping to a conspirator's whisper. "She was building the foundation of my entire political career."

Sophia set down her pen. "At age thirty?"

"She understood something that escaped most political wives of her generation, that influence isn't just about who you know, but about when and how you deploy those connections." Churchill's eyes gleamed with admiration. "Every dinner party she hosted, every introduction she arranged, every letter of recommendation she wrote was calculated to position our family advantageously for the future."

"She was thinking ahead," Sophie said as more of a statement than a question.

"Years ahead, decades ahead. While other mothers were content to see their children safely settled, she was imagining what I might become and systematically removing obstacles from my path." Churchill paused, emotion flickering across his weathered features. "When my father died young, leaving us with little money and uncertain prospects, her network became my lifeline. Every door that opened for me in those early years had been unlocked by her long before I reached it."

LONDON, 1883

In July 1883, an otherwise pleasant season was suddenly turned into grief and mourning for Jennie by the death of her father-in-law. Randolph had dined with him the previous night, when he appeared quite in his usual health. At eight o'clock the next morning they heard a knock at their bedroom door, and a footman stammered out "His Grace is dead!"

It was naturally a great shock to Randolph, who was much attached to his father, and saw him constantly. Jennie regretted the Duke very much; he had always been most kind and charming to her. If he seemed rather cold and reserved, he really had an affectionate nature. Although his children were somewhat in awe of him, having been brought up in the old-fashioned way which precluded any real intimacy, they were devoted to him. The Duke was greatly interested in politics, and was a Tory of the old type, holding in abhorrence anything approaching change. He was one of the strongest opponents of the "Deceased Wife's Sister" Bill, and only a few days before his death, owing to his efforts, the Third Reading of the Bill had been defeated by a narrow majority.

After a few days spent at Blenheim, they left for Gastein, taking their boy Winston with them. There they led the "simple life" with a vengeance, but after the rush of London, and the gloom of the preceding weeks, the peace and quiet were not unpleasant.

In their walks they frequently met Bismarck with his big boar-hound, two detectives following him closely. One day as he was walking rather slowly they tried to pass him, whereupon, much to Jennie's annoyance, the detectives rushed forward in a most threatening manner. She had no idea they looked like anarchists.

Beyond climbing the mountains and taking the baths, there was little to do. They made the acquaintance of Count Lehndorff, who introduced them to an old Grafin, who lived in a villa called "La Solitude." This lady was a great friend of the Emperor William I, and invited them one day to tea to meet him. The Emperor was a fine-looking man, notwithstanding his age, and he had that old-world manner which is as attractive as it is rare. He was full of gaiety, and chaffed some of the young people present. It was a mystery to Jennie how he survived what he ate and drank, although he was doing a cure. He began with poached eggs, and went on to potted meats and various strange German dishes, added many cups of strong tea, and ended with strawberries, ices, and sweet, tepid champagne. They talked banalities; it was not very exciting.

They spent the winter following the Duke's death more or less at Blenheim under the new regime. Jennie's brother-in-law, who had now succeeded to the family honors, was most kind and hospitable, and insisted that nothing should be altered as regarded them. He even persuaded Randolph to revive his harriers. Jennie thoroughly enjoyed the hunting, and was given the proud post of whipper-in. But she owned to her discomfiture that she could never remember the names of the hounds; to her they all looked alike. Randolph, on the contrary, knew not only their names, but their characteristics, and spent many hours at the kennels.

In November 1884, wanting a rest from the arduous political work he had been indulging in, Randolph decided to go to India for a few months. He had been speaking at a good many meetings all over the country, at Edinburgh, at Blackpool, to his own constituents at Woodstock, and finally in a regular campaign in Birmingham, where on one occasion occurred the celebrated Aston Riots, which were organized by Mr. Chamberlain's agent, a Mr. Schnadhorst. How the meeting was broken up, the speakers (Sir Stafford Northcote, Colonel Burnaby, Lord Randolph, and others) fleeing for their lives, is a matter of history. Notwithstanding Randolph's righteous indignation at such treatment, particularly from a friend, even though a political opponent, he made it up with Mr. Chamberlain before leaving for India. Amiable letters passed between them, and they shook hands.

While Randolph was on the high seas, the Aston Riots question, which had already been discussed at length in the House of Commons, came up again. In view of the reconciliation which had just taken place, Jennie was rather disappointed to hear Mr. Chamberlain warmly backing up his constituents. It may have been necessary from his point of view, but she agreed with M. de Camors, "La politique desseche le coeur." (English Translation: "Politics dries up the heart.") Sometimes, indeed, she thought politics a "sorry game." Too often its attributes are callousness and ingratitude, tricks and treachery. In any other "walk of life" these things would not be tolerated for a moment.

The press in those days attacked Randolph most viciously on every possible opportunity. Mr. Buckle, the editor of the "Times," who was by way of being a friend of theirs, often, if not invariably, wrote slating articles on him. One night Jennie met him at the Speaker's after a particularly poisonous leader had appeared in the morning "Times." Coming up, he half-chaffingly asked her if she intended to speak to him, or if she was too angry. "Angry? Not a bit," she replied. "I have ten volumes of press-cuttings about Randolph, all abusive. This will only be added to them."

Jennie sometimes wondered if the power of the press is not greatly exaggerated. She had always observed that it has to follow a popular movement, not lead it, and great abuse of a public man only seems to help him to office. At the last General Election in 1906, with few exceptions the whole press of England preached protection, and yet free trade won all along the line. In all political matters indeed one may say with Omar Khayyam:

"I heard great argument About it and about: but evermore Came out by the same door where in I went."

Randolph remained in India four months, enjoying himself immensely. He wrote Jennie glowing accounts of his travels and all that he was seeing. These letters made her greatly regret that she had not been able to accompany him.

January 1, 1885 - Government House, Bombay Randolph wrote about his pleasant voyage across the Indian Ocean and warm reception by Sir James Fergusson, who sent his carriage to meet them at the dock. He was captivated by Bombay, writing to Jennie: "The complete novelty and originality of everything is remarkable, and one is never tired of staring and wondering. I cannot tell you how much I am enjoying myself or how much I wish you were with me." Though invited to dinner by the Bombay Club, he declined as it would have been seen as a political demonstration against Lord Ripon's administration, and as he explained, "I did not come out to India to pursue politics or to make speeches."

January 9, 1885 - Bombay Randolph described being taken by Sir Jamsetjee Jeejeebhoy, "a great Parsee," to visit the Towers of Silence where Parsee dead were placed to be consumed by vultures. Asked to write his impression in their guest book, he "composed a highly qualified and ambiguous impression which would have done credit to Gladstone." He mentioned dining at the Byculla Club where an American lady gave "very dull recitations from Tennyson" that bored everyone. He also described a lengthy interview with eight leading native politicians who "set forth with great ability their various grievances."

January 14, 1885 - The Residency, Indore Randolph detailed his ceremonial meeting with Holkar, who though ill, came specially to meet their train. "We had an interview of about half an hour, while the other unfortunate passengers were kept waiting. He was most gracious and very intelligent, and when we left he embraced me!" At Indore, they were treated to elaborate entertainments including "fireworks, Hindu drama, Nautch, conjurers, &c. All very Hindu and delightful the first time one sees it," though Randolph admitted "I can quite imagine that after a time it would pall." He described a cheetah hunt for black buck that proved unsuccessful when "the cheetah was sulky and would not run well," though he managed to shoot three black buck himself.

February 1, 1885 - In Camp, Dudna Randolph described their idyllic camp life in a forest at the foot of the Himalayas: "We have been leading a very enjoyable life... Out all day careering round on elephants after game, sleeping in tents at night, always at a different place, always hungry for breakfast, very hungry for dinner, two sensations to me which have the attraction of novelty." He wrote enthusiastically about their elephants: "I think an elephant is the best mode of conveyance I know. He cannot come to grief; he never tumbles down nor runs away... nothing stops him." He marveled at their abilities: "If a tree is in the way, and not too large a one, they pull it down; if a branch hangs too low for the howdah to go under, they break it off."

February 8, 1885 - Government House, Calcutta Randolph excitedly recounted his tiger hunt, which he called "the acme of sport." When others in his party went to shoot ducks, he and a Mr. Hersey chose to hunt for deer instead. They discovered a freshly killed hog carcass, and soon after, the tiger appeared. "All of a sudden out bundled this huge creature, right under the nose of Hersey's elephant, and made off across some ground which was slightly open." After several shots from both men, the wounded tiger took refuge in a patch of grass. "Heavens, how he growled and what a rage he was in!" Randolph wrote. "He would have charged us but that he was disabled by Hersey's last shot." The tiger eventually expired after several more shots. Randolph measured it at "nine feet seven inches in length, and a splendid skin, which will, I think, look very well in Grosvenor Square."

February 10, 1885 - Government House, Calcutta Randolph mentioned his plans to leave Bombay by March 20th and return via Marseilles, expecting to reach London by April 11-12. He described the pleasant atmosphere at Government House: "The Dufferins are very kind and easy-going; the Staff, too, are amiable; and Bill Beresford does everything he can for one." He witnessed a telling political incident when the Government telegraphed Lord Dufferin to send troops and railway equipment to Suakim, only to countermand the order hours later. "Dufferin, diplomatist as he is, could not conceal his disgust at this vacillation when they handed him the telegram on our return from dinner," Randolph observed.

February 17, 1885 - Rewah Randolph mentioned receiving an urgent telegram from his political ally Wolff saying "that affairs were pressing and a crisis impending" and inquiring when he would return. Randolph dismissed this with wry humor: "Mais je connaismon Wolff; he has crisis on the brain and, in any case, no political contingency will hasten my return by an hour. I expect the Government will try and get put out and the Tories will try to come in; I wish them joy of it." He wrote enthusiastically about meeting General Roberts: "The General is all I had imagined him to be." Roberts offered to take him to the frontier areas of Peshawar and Quetta to learn about "the dangers of the Russian advance," though Randolph doubted this would be possible.

February 24, 1885 - Benares Randolph described Benares as "the most distinctly Hindu city I have yet seen; old and curious in every part." They stayed at one of the Maharajah's palaces with "a retinue of servants and carriages at all times ready." Their guide was "an old Rajah, Siva Prasad, an interesting and experienced old man" who spoke "English perfectly though at the top of his voice." At the Maharajah's royal palace of Ramnugger, they received a formal welcome with "all the retainers, elephants, horses, &c., together with army, the latter about 100 strong, drawn up in a long avenue from the gates to the door." Randolph wrote:

"The army gave a royal salute, and the band played 'God save the Queen,' which I had to receive with dignity and gravity; rather difficult!" He described in detail the bathing ghats on the Ganges where thousands performed religious ablutions, and the burning ghats with "five bodies burning, each on its own little pile of fagots." He noted with irony: "Any Hindu who dies at Benares, and whose ashes are thrown into the Ganges, goes right bang up to heaven without stopping, no matter how great a rascal he may have been. I think the G. O. M. [Gladstone] ought to come here; it is his best chance."

March 3, 1885 - Jaipur Randolph wrote that they stayed only briefly in Delhi as "the hotel was piggy," and moved to "the Club at Agra, which is very comfortable, with excellent food and wine." This allowed them to see "the 'Taj' by moonlight, which we were not able to do last time, and which is an unequalled sight." He described dining at the house of a native judge, "a very interesting and clever man", where they met "a most curious collection of native notabilities." Randolph observed critically: "The natives are much pleased when one goes to their houses, for the officials out here hold themselves much too high and never seek any intercourse with the native out of official lines; they are very foolish."

Resignation

Chartwell, 1964

The light was beginning to fade outside, casting long shadows across Churchill's studio. He sat quietly for a moment, his hands folded in his lap, before speaking. "My father's resignation from Salisbury's government was the defining catastrophe of our family's political life. One night he was Chancellor of the Exchequer and Leader of the House of Commons. The next morning, he was finished."

Sophia could hear the old pain in his voice. "How did your mother handle it?"

"With the kind of grace under pressure that would later serve me well in my own political disasters." Churchill's voice grew steadier. "She could have retreated from society, nursed her wounds, played the victim. Instead, she doubled down. If the Conservative Party establishment was going to shun us, she would create her own establishment."

"The Fourth Party?"

"That, and so much more. She turned our drawing room into an alternative center of power, gathering around her everyone who had been overlooked or underestimated by the official hierarchy." Churchill managed a small smile. "She taught me that political setbacks are only permanent if you accept them as such. Every time I faced my own wilderness years, and there were several, I remembered her example."

LONDON, 1885

With the absence of Lord Randolph in India, the political horizon had grown very dark for the Liberal Government, which fell shortly after his return in 1885. The triumphant Fourth Party now reaped the reward of their labors, all being included in the new Administration. Great was the excitement and many the discussions at Connaught Place. Randolph was offered the post of Secretary of State for India by Lord Salisbury and accepted it, but on the understanding that Sir Henry Wolff and Mr. Gorst, who had "borne the burden and heat of the day" with him, should be included. Lord Salisbury demurred, but finally gave way under pressure.

Having joined the Government, Randolph was now obliged to seek reelection at Woodstock. His new office giving him an enormous amount of work, he made up his mind not to contest it personally. Jennie was therefore pressed into service. Of nine elections in which she had taken a more or less active part (Woodstock twice, Birmingham three times, Paddington twice, Oldham and Manchester once each), if Birmingham was the most laborious, Woodstock was the one which left the pleasantest memories.

Accompanied by her sister-in-law, the late Lady Howe, then Lady Georgiana Curzon, they stayed at Blenheim, but had their Committee rooms at the Bear Hotel in Woodstock. There they held daily consultations with friends and Members of Parliament who had come to help. They were most important, and felt that the eyes of the world were upon them. Reveling in the hustle and bustle of the Committee rooms, marshaling their forces, and hearing the hourly reports of how the campaign was progressing, Jennie felt like a general holding a council-of-war with his staff in the heat of a battle. A was doubtful, B obdurate, while C's wife, a wicked, abominable Radical, was trying to influence her husband whom they thought secure, to vote the wrong way. At once they must be visited and their arsenal of arguments brought to bear on them.

Sometimes with these simple country folk a pleading look, and an imploring "Oh, please vote for my husband; I shall be so unhappy if he does not get in," or "If you want to be on the winning side, vote for us; as of course we are going to win," would be as effective as the election agent's longest speeches on the iniquity of Mr. Chamberlain's unauthorized program or Mr. Gladstone's "disgraceful" attitude at the death of Gordon. In some ways the work was arduous enough.

The Primrose League was still in an embryonic state in Woodstock, and there was no Habitation to furnish them with the Primrose Dames, who for the last twenty years have taken a prominent part at every election. The distances to cover were great, and motors were not in existence. Luckily, Lady Georgiana Curzon, who was a beautiful driver, brought down her well-known tandem, and they scoured the country with their smart turnout, the horses gaily decorated with ribbons of pink and brown, Randolph's racing colors.

Sometimes they would drive into the fields, and getting down, climb the hayricks, falling upon their unwary prey at his work. There was no escaping them. Many of the voters of those days went no further than their colors. "I votes red" or "blue," as the case might be, and no talking, however forcible or subtle could move them. Party feeling ran high, and in outlying districts they would frequently be pursued by their opponents, jeering and shouting at them; but this they rather enjoyed. They were treated to jingling rhymes, celebrating the American lady's campaign efforts.

At the end of a tiring fortnight, Randolph was returned at the head of the poll. From the window of the Bear Hotel, Jennie made a little speech to the crowd, and thanked them "from the bottom of her heart" for returning her husband for the third time. She surpassed the fondest hopes of the Suffragettes, and thought she was duly elected, and certainly experienced all the pleasure and gratification of being a successful candidate. She returned to London feeling that she had done a very big thing, and was surprised and astonished that the crowds in the streets looked at her with indifference.

After the election, Jennie received a letter from Lord James of Hereford (then Sir Henry James) dated January 1885, congratulating her on the result and praising her personal exertions. He joked that he would need to introduce a new Corrupt Practices Act to deal with tandems, arch looks, and handkerchief waving, calling these her campaign tactics.

Of a very different order from Woodstock was the contest for Birmingham at the General Election of 1885, when Randolph and Colonel Burnaby opposed Mr. John Bright and Mr. Chamberlain. During the election Jennie had occasion to see a good deal of Colonel Burnaby, whose "Ride to Khiva" gave one an idea of his adventurous spirit. He was a gentle voiced, amiable man, notwithstanding an enormous frame and gigantic strength. She remembered one night in Birmingham, while walking back after a meeting to the hotel where they were staying, they encountered a crowd of opponents who were inclined to be hostile, jostling them in such an alarming manner that she became nervous; but seemingly with the wave of his arm, Colonel Burnaby scattered them.

Innumerable were the stories told about Burnaby. Once at Windsor Barracks, for a bet, he walked up a narrow staircase with a fair-sized pony under each arm. The dumb-bells he exercised with weighed two hundred pounds, and on one occasion, hearing a brother-officer make some disparaging remark about him, he took him up and flung him across the room. A few months after the election Colonel Burnaby was killed in action at Abu Klea.

The Duchess of Marlborough, Jennie's mother-in-law, came down to help her. It was the first time that women had ever indulged in any personal canvassing in Birmingham, and they did it thoroughly. Every house in the constituency was visited. The Duchess would go in one direction, and Jennie in another; the constituency was large, and the work arduous. The voters were much more enlightened than the agricultural laborers of Oxfordshire; the men particularly were very argumentative and were well up in the questions of the day. The wives of the Radicals were also admirably informed, and on more than one occasion routed Jennie completely.

Sometimes she invaded a factory addressing a few words to the men in their dinner-hour. On one occasion she was received in sullen silence; when she inquired why, one, speaking for the rest, said they did not like being asked for their vote. "But you have something I want," she cried; "how am I to get it if I do not ask for it?" This struck them as quite reasonable and when she left they cheered her.

The excitements and amusing incidents repaid one for the fatigue. During the whole of the election she never encountered a disagreeable incident or any rudeness, however poor the slum into which she went. Only once did she come across a Philistine, a publican who was in the cellar when she called. "Lady Churchill wants to see you," said the wife through the trap-door. "Oh, does she?" came in guttural tones from behind the barrels of beer. "Well, tell Mrs. Churchill to go to , ," at which she beat a hasty retreat. On the other hand she had a great success with a butcher, with whom she exchanged flowers; he gave her his vote and some time after the election she was the proud recipient of half a sheep, sent by her useful admirer.

The election, alas! It was not won, but to have brought down the great Mr. Bright's majority to 400 was a virtual triumph. The

Radical Caucus and Mr. Chamberlain's stronghold were shaken to their foundation. In spite of his defeat, Randolph did not give up hope of contesting Birmingham again. He kept in touch with the constituency, and often held meetings there.

Jennie remembered one particular electioneering experience: Being asked to help canvass for Mr. Burdett-Coutts, she was pleading with a waverer for his vote. Waggishly and with a sly look he said, "If I could get the same price as was once paid by the Duchess of Devonshire for a vote, I think I could promise." "Thank you very much," she replied, "I'll let the Baroness Burdett-Coutts know at once."

About this time Sir Henry James, of whom they saw a good deal, although politically he was of the "other way of thinking," being a Liberal, was instrumental in bringing about a reconciliation between the Prince of Wales and Randolph. Friendly messages had already been conveyed from his Royal Highness, and the matter finally culminated in their giving a dinner for the Prince and Princess of Wales. Lord Rosebery, Mr. and Mrs. Gladstone, Mr. Henry Chaplin, and Mr. and Mrs. Chauncey Depew were among the guests. The dinner was animated, Mr. Gladstone and Mr. Chauncey Depew keeping the ball rolling. This reconciliation was a lasting one, all old wounds being healed.

A few days later the peacemaker, delighted with his success, went off with Randolph for a little jaunt abroad. Sir Henry James wrote Jennie a humorous letter about their journey, describing how Randolph had boasted about the Channel crossing being smooth but then became terribly seasick, to the point of being washed off the bridge of the ship. The letter detailed his gradual recovery and their enjoyable time in Paris.

Among the many political meetings Jennie attended with Randolph during those two years, she thought the biggest and most imposing was that held in the Manchester Drill Hall. Eighteen thousand people filled the place to suffocation, no singer that ever lived could command the audience of a popular politician. If the building had held 40,000 or 50,000, it would still have been crowded. Most of the people had been standing for two hours before they arrived. Manchester gave Randolph a magnificent reception, thousands lined the streets and covered the roofs of the houses as they slowly drove through the town in a carriage drawn by four horses. Over 200,000 people were said to have turned out that day. Jennie felt very proud. Randolph's speech lasted for over two hours. The heat was great, and on leaving the building the crowd pressed round the carriage to such an extent that two men were killed.

Jennie was also with Randolph at Sheffield, and heard the famous speech in which he asked Lord Hartington to abandon Gladstone and Home Rule and "come over and help us." This phrase led her later into trouble. Happening to meet Lord Hartington at dinner while he was still making up his mind as to whether he would join the Liberal Unionists or not, she asked him if he intended responding to Randolph's invitation. "I have not yet decided; but when I do, I suppose I shall be thought either a man or a mouse." "Or a rat," said she. Lord Hartington laughed, as the French say, "d'un rire jaune." [English Translation: "with a forced laugh"] Very pleased with what she considered her "bon-mot," she repeated it to Randolph, who, to her discomfiture, gave her a severe lecture on the iniquity of ill-timed jests. "Those are the sort of remarks which upset a coach," he said.

Many of their Liberal friends were in great trepidation at that time, torn between their hatred of Home Rule and their reluctance to leave the "Grand Old Man." Sir Henry James wrote expressing his low spirits about the political situation, seeing no way out of the "breakers" they had drifted into. He later wrote thanking Jennie for her sympathy regarding his Tuesday night vote, mentioning he was receiving "rough usage" from candid friends but felt he had done right. This referred to the division on Mr. Jesse Collings's amendment to the address on January 26, 1886, when seventeen Liberals including Lord Hartington, Mr. Goschen, and Sir Henry James voted with the Government against Mr. Gladstone, laying the foundation of the Liberal Unionist Party.

While Randolph was at the India Office, Jennie was told that the Order of the Crown of India would be given to her if he recommended her for it. This decoration, instituted by Queen Victoria and designed by the Duke of Albany, had a pretty pearl and turquoise cipher attached to a pale-blue ribbon edged with white. She thought it would be nice to have it, but Randolph demurred at recommending his own wife, and she sorrowfully gave up the idea. A few months later, however, much to her delight, a letter arrived from Windsor Castle inviting her to receive the insignia personally from the Queen.

On the appointed day she went to Windsor, having been instructed to wear "bonnet and morning dress, gray gloves." The Queen, with one of the princesses and a lady-in-waiting, received her in a small room. The Queen stood with her back to the window, wearing a long white veil which made an aureole round her against the light. After addressing a few kind words to her, the Queen proceeded to pin the order on her left shoulder. Her black velvet dress was thickly embroidered with jet, so much so that the pin could find no hold, and unwittingly the Queen stuck it straight into her. Although like the Spartan boy she tried to hide what she felt, she gave a start, and the Queen realizing what she had done was much concerned. Eventually the pin was put right and she courtesied herself out of the Royal Presence. As she reached the door, the Queen suddenly stepped forward saying with a smile, "Oh! you have forgotten the case," holding it out to her at the same time. This little touch of nature relieved an otherwise somewhat formal ceremony.

Shortly after this they were commanded to Windsor to dine and sleep. They dined in rather a small room with walls hung with family portraits by Winterhalter. Conversation was carried on in whispers, which Jennie thought exceedingly oppressive and conducive to shyness. When the Queen spoke, even the whispers ceased. If she addressed a remark to you, the answer was given while the whole company listened.

The night they were there, the household seemed slightly agitated, and the Queen retired earlier than usual. The next morning they understood the reason when they were told that a young Prince of Battenberg had been born that night in the Castle. Following the ancient custom which prescribes that a Cabinet Minister should be in attendance in the royal residence on such occasions, the Home Secretary, Mr. Henry Matthews, had been hastily sent for from London, in preference to Randolph, whom the Queen thought "too young," although he was a married man and the father of a family, as well as a Cabinet Minister at the time, besides being actually in the house.

India and things Indian loomed largely in Jennie's eyes that winter, and she acquired more knowledge of the country and its history than she had ever possessed before. The Far East, although she had never been there, always had a great fascination for her, and Randolph's graphic descriptions of his travels made her very envious.

While he was at the India Office she was called upon to help Lady Dufferin with the fund she was getting up in aid of the National Association for Supplying Female Medical Aid to the Women of India. This was the beginning of a remarkable institution. Besides giving employment to numbers of English female doctors, it opened a career for native women, and alleviated some of the terrible sufferings of others. The Lord Mayor agreed to hold a meeting at the Mansion House in aid of the fund. Already

Jennie had collected a goodly sum. Randolph was delighted with her activity and wrote to her from Scotland praising her letter to Lady Dufferin and her plans for the fund.

At the meeting at the Mansion House a handsome sum was subscribed. Among the many speeches, Jennie remembered thinking that Mrs. Fawcett's was by far the most eloquent, perhaps on account of its simplicity, free from any attempt at rhetorical effect. She noted that a woman's high pitched voice carries very far in comparison with that of a man, and when the manner is slightly deprecatory, it becomes very effective, particularly to the male sex.

Lady Dufferin, who was watching the progress of her fund from afar, wrote Jennie a letter dated January 4, 1886 from Government House, Calcutta. She congratulated Jennie on receiving the Crown of India decoration and updated her on the fund's progress, mentioning that the Queen had contributed £100 and various donors in India were supporting the cause. She noted that they were getting on very well with little initiatives starting in unexpected places.

The political events which led to Lord Randolph Churchill's resignation of the post of Chancellor of the Exchequer and Leader of the House of Commons, which he held in Lord Salisbury's second administration, were a turning point. Although the recipient of many confidences, so little did Jennie realize the grave step Randolph was contemplating, that she was at that moment occupied with the details of a reception they were going to give at the Foreign Office, which was to be lent to them for the occasion. Already the cards had been printed.

The night before his resignation they went to the play with Sir Henry Wolff. Questioning Randolph as to the list of guests for the party, she remembered being puzzled at his saying: "Oh! I shouldn't worry about it if I were you; it probably will never take place." She could get no explanation of his meaning, and shortly after the first act he left them ostensibly to go to the club, but in reality to go to the "Times" office and give them the letter he had written at Windsor Castle three nights before. In it he resigned all he had worked for for years, and, if he had but known it, signed his political death warrant.

When Jennie came down to breakfast, the fatal paper in her hand, she found him calm and smiling. "Quite a surprise for you," he said. He went into no explanation, and she felt too utterly crushed and miserable to ask for any, or even to remonstrate. Mr. Moore (the permanent Under-Secretary at the Treasury), who was devoted to Randolph, rushed in, pale and anxious, and with a faltering voice said to her, "He has thrown himself from the top of the ladder, and will never reach it again!" Alas! he proved too true a prophet.

Sandringham

Chartwell, 1964

Churchill reached for a leather-bound photo album, his movements slow but purposeful. "After my father's political fall, the invitations to grand houses might have dried up. But my mother had cultivated relationships that transcended party politics." He opened the album to reveal a formal group photograph. "Here, Sandringham, 1887. The Prince and Princess of Wales, and there, my parents, still very much part of the inner circle."

Sophia studied the photograph. "She maintained her position despite your father's... ahh... decline?"

"More than maintained it, she enhanced it. You see, Miss Carter, she understood that in society, as in politics, being interesting is often more valuable than being officially important." Churchill turned the page slowly. "The Prince of Wales found her conversation stimulating, the Princess genuinely enjoyed her company. They didn't invite her because she was the wife of a Cabinet minister, they invited her because she was herself."

"She had transcended her husband's position."

"Precisely. And in doing so, she preserved options for our family that would have otherwise been lost forever." Churchill closed the album gently. "When I later needed royal support for various ventures, my early military postings, my political advancement, those relationships she had maintained proved invaluable."

SANDRINGHAM, 1887

When Lord Randolph Churchill resigned his position as Chancellor of the Exchequer and Leader of the House of Commons, the political world stood aghast. Friends bemoaned, and the toadies and sycophants fell away and vanished. His action aroused much censure, and every hand seemed against him; yet his only crime was to advocate economy.

Jennie remembered with bitterness her feelings in those days. The political atmosphere around them suddenly seemed full of strife and treachery. It was gall and wormwood to her to hear Randolph abused in every quarter, often, as she thought, by the very men who owed their success, if not their political existence, to him. On every side she heard of the defection of political allies, even of some whom they had every reason to believe would remain loyal. But she supposed the flowing tide was too much for them, and they drifted away with the rest.

It was fated that the first political speech made after Randolph's resignation should be by Sir John Gorst, who criticized him in no measured terms. Well might Randolph have exclaimed with Zechariah, "I was wounded in the house of my friends." In speaking some years later of Sir John at a public meeting, Randolph referred to him as "my honorable friend."

To Jennie, who had resented what she rightly or wrongly considered an unfriendly act on the part of Sir John, this was too much, and she remonstrated warmly. "The fact is," said Randolph, laughing, "it slipped out; I forgot." She remembered hearing Lord Salisbury say that a man who could not be vindictive was not a strong man. She often quoted this without effect to Randolph.

When she looked back at the few preceding months which seemed so triumphant and full of promise, the debacle appeared all the greater. She had been sure that Randolph would enjoy the fruits of office for years to come, and apart from the honor and glory, she regretted those same "fruits." But on this subject he was adamant. "Politics and money do not go together," he would often say to her; "so put the thought away."

How dark those days seemed! In vain she tried to console herself with the thought that happiness does not depend so much on circumstances as on one's inner self. But she had always found in practice that theories are of little comfort. The vicissitudes of life resembled one of those gilded balls seen in a fountain. Thrown up by the force of the water, it flies up and down; now at the top, catching the rays of the sun, now cast into the depths, then again shooting up, sometimes so high that it escapes altogether, and falls to the ground.

It was with pleasure that Jennie turned from these disagreeable reflections to the remembrance of a charming visit they had paid to Sandringham a month previous, in honor of the Prince of Wales's birthday.

Queen Victoria purchased the Sandringham Estate for the Prince of Wales (who later became King Edward VII). By 1885, Sandringham House had been largely rebuilt in a Jacobean style and had become a favored country retreat for the Prince and his wife, Princess Alexandra. They undertook significant improvements to both the house and the estate.

The Prince of Wales was a keen sportsman, and Sandringham was renowned for its excellent shooting. The estate provided opportunities for hunting and other country pursuits, making it an ideal private escape for the royal family. The Prince and Princess of Wales actively developed the gardens and grounds. By 1885, features like lakes and a rock garden were being established, creating a more picturesque and enjoyable environment.

The Prince and Princess dispensed their hospitality with that remarkable simplicity of which English royalty alone has the secret. One felt at home at once; indeed, the life was the same as at any pleasant country house.

Breakfast, which began at nine o'clock, was served at small, round tables in a dining-room decorated with Spanish tapestries given by the late King of Spain. The men were in shooting get-up, and the ladies in any dress they chose to affect, short skirts and thick boots or elaborate day gowns. No one cared or noticed. None of the Royalties appeared before midday, although the Prince of Wales joined the shooters, who made an early start after breakfast.

The feminine contingent, left to their own devices, generally congregated in the large hall, which contained writing-tables, a piano, and masses of books and newspapers. The amount of scribbling which went on in a country house, and in which Englishwomen in particular indulged, was always a source of astonishment and amusement to foreigners. Jennie had heard them exclaim: "Mais qu'est-cequ'ellesecrivent toute la journee?" (English Translation: "But what are they writing all day long?") No foreigner, indeed, could understand the Englishwoman's busy life, full as it was of multitudinous occupations ranging from household duties to political gatherings, and all necessitating correspondence.

Just before luncheon they would sally forth to join the shooters: some driving and others walking to the rendezvous. The Princess of Wales, looking in her neat dress and small felt hat as young as her own daughters, would drive a pair of ponies. The luncheon in a big tent was always very animated and sometimes so prolonged that a gentle reminder was needed of the birds waiting to be shot. At this time the young princesses were unmarried. If their manners in public were perhaps too diffident and shy compared with those of foreign royalties, in private they were full of gaiety and fun, dearly loving a joke, particularly if it was directed against some familiar friend who might be staying there.

The sport was exceedingly good and well-managed, owing to the Prince of Wales, who, an excellent shot himself, took a personal interest in the arrangements instead of leaving them all to the keepers. The ladies stayed out to see the sport, many forming a gallery around Lord de Grey, who was one of the guns on this occasion, and whose wonderful shooting had gained him world-wide reputation among sportsmen. Jennie remembered once at Panshanger, when she was staying with the late Lord Cowper, seeing Lord de Grey shoot in one stand fifty-two birds out of fifty-four, and for a bet this was done with one hand. He had two loaders and three guns.

Five o'clock tea was a feature at Sandringham. The simplicity of the day attire was discarded in favor of elaborate tea-gowns. After tea, Signor Tosti, who was a great favorite with the royal family, would be made to sing some of his charming songs. He would ramble on in his delightful impromptu manner for hours. Besides his musical gifts, he was a most amusing man, and kept them all laughing at his stories and witty sallies. Sometimes Jennie played duets with the Princess, who was particularly fond of Brahms's Hungarian dances, which were just then in vogue. Or it might be that they would go to Princess Victoria's sitting-room, where there were two pianos, and struggle with a concerto of Schumann. The pace set was terrific, and Jennie was rather glad there was no audience.

Although no uniforms were worn at dinner, this was a ceremonious affair, with everyone in full dress and decorations. Rather unpunctual in those days, Jennie was always on the verge of being late. The clocks were put half an hour in advance; but that did not help her, as she traded on the fact, forgetting that it made no difference. When everyone was assembled, Their Royal Highnesses would be announced, each lady in turn having the privilege of being taken in by her royal host, who arranged the list himself, and was very particular that there should be no hitch as to people finding their places at once. An equerry with a plan of the dining-table would explain to each man who was to be his partner and where he was to sit. The dinner, which never lasted more than an hour, was excellent and admirably ordered, which is not always the case in royal households where indiscriminate profusion is often paramount.

Conversation was fairly animated; there was none of that stiffness which pervaded Windsor and made one fear the sound of one's own voice. The evenings were not prolonged, for in those days there was no Gottlieb's band to listen to, as there invariably is now, or bridge to keep one up late. The Prince would have his rubber of whist, while the rest of the company sat about and talked until the Princess made a move to go to bed, when the ladies would troop off together, stopping to laugh and chatter in the passages, which seemed to amuse the young Princesses more than anything else.

Sometimes the Princess would ask one into her dressing-room, which was crowded with objects and souvenirs of all kinds. The dressing-table was so littered with miniatures and photographs of children and friends, besides every conceivable bibelot, that there was no room for brushes or toilet things. On a perch in the center of the room was an old and somewhat ferocious white parrot, which Jennie remembered made disconcerting pecks if you happened to be within his radius.

At other times the Princess might surprise you by coming to your room, ostensibly "to see if you had everything you wanted," but in reality to give a few words of advice, or to offer her sympathy if she thought you needed any. For without people realizing it, few things escaped her observant eyes. To those who have the privilege of coming into contact with her, Queen Alexandra has endeared herself by many such kind acts, as well as by her gentle and tactful sympathy.

Among those who were at Sandringham on that occasion was the Comtesse de Paris, of whom Jennie saw a great deal later, and who was much liked, everyone finding her tres bonne enfant (English Translation: "a very good sport"). She was most unlike a Frenchwoman. Tall and rather thin, with a pleasant smile and a desire to please, she affected sporting clothes and distinguished herself with a gun.

Personally, although Jennie saw no harm in a woman shooting game, she could not say she admired it as an accomplishment. The fact was, she loved life so much that the unnecessary curtailing of any creature's existence was more than distasteful to her. Not long ago, while in Scotland, she had seen a young and charming woman, who was surely not of a bloodthirsty nature, kill two stags in one morning. The first she shot through the heart. With the aid of a powerful pair of field-glasses, Jennie had watched her stalk the second. She described the cruel scene in vivid detail, concluding: "If these things must be done, how can a woman bring herself to do them?"

But this digression had taken her far from the Comtesse de Paris. She cherished ambitious schemes for the Comte de Paris, and at that time was confident that he would eventually become King of France.

They had long conversations about the Primrose League, which interested the Comtesse vastly. So greatly did she admire its organization that she started a league in France on more or less the same lines. "La Ligue de la Rose," as it was called, had for its symbol "la Rose de France," and its object was the restoration of the monarchy. Unlike the Primrose League, Jennie feared it did not make the stir or gain the recruits that the Comtesse hoped. Nevertheless, for some years it flourished in a mild way. The Primrose League was founded in memory of the popular Conservative Prime Minister Benjamin Disraeli, who had died in 1881. The primrose was believed to be his favorite flower, hence the name of the organization.

Her Royal Highness having meanwhile honored Jennie with her friendship, they met frequently, and she constantly sought Jennie's advice as to the details of her scheme. An inspired article on the "Rose League" appeared in the "Primrose League Gazette," which gave the Comtesse great satisfaction.

The Comtesse wrote two significant letters to Jennie about the Rose League:

First Letter - July 25, 1888, from Sheen House, East Sheen, Surrey:

In this letter, the Comtesse thanked Jennie for her interest in their attempts to establish a League in France. She enclosed two circulars that would soon be printed and distributed, hoping Jennie would read them with indulgence and keep them to discuss later if they achieved good results. The Comtesse acknowledged it was Jennie who gave her the idea to create something similar in France, saying "I always think of you while working on this great undertaking, and I already owe you, before we even begin, the firm belief that we will succeed by following your example." She noted that "The Rose will never equal the Primrose; but perhaps later they will often meet." She explained that she didn't mention the Primrose League in the circulars only out of modesty, not daring to compare the immense success of the first flower with the very modest beginnings of the second, but in all her private letters she mentioned it to inspire everyone with the same idea: to succeed like Jennie had.

Second Letter - October 7, 1888, from Sheen House, East Sheen, Surrey:

In this letter, the Comtesse thanked Jennie for a copy of the Primrose League Gazette containing a most kind article about the Rose League. She wrote: "I thank you both for sending it and for the article, as I am quite sure you had a large part in it; if I am mistaken, please convey my thanks to the author." She added that the Primrose League was truly kind in giving such a warm welcome to its younger sister, the Rose League. She mentioned sending Jennie a copy of "Le Soleil" newspaper so she could see their new paper in its entirety, saying "you will no doubt find phrases that you recognize and I hope that you will approve, I believe I have followed your advice." She reported receiving very good news from all sides, saying "it appears that the Rose is working wonderfully," and hoped this fine enthusiasm would last a long time, adding "and it is to you first of all that we will owe our success."

It was sad to think that so much energy and zeal came to nothing. The "Ligue," as well as its object, is a thing of the past. But in France political movements are not furthered by the help of women: the existing form of government and the ridicule attached to their public appearance preclude them from airing their views or promoting a cause on a platform. Besides, the majority of Frenchwomen are too much occupied with the domestic affairs of their homes or with business matters to give much attention to anything outside. How different from the part Englishwomen play in politics, and particularly in London society, where they are more important agents than in any other capital of the world! This is owing to the happy blending of matters social and political which an established order of things has fostered for centuries.

Among the people at Sandringham were Lord and Lady Salisbury. Jennie didn't know Lady Salisbury well, but she impressed her as being a woman of great strength of character and full of common sense. One couldn't help liking her, notwithstanding a rather brusque manner. Jennie fancied she detested affectations of any kind, and her masterly mind must have disdained the ordinary society twaddle to which she was often called upon to listen. Jennie remembered a heated argument on the duties incumbent on a politician's wife, which, according to Lady Salisbury, were rather arduous, involving the necessity of making a study of the various political problems of the day. Jennie confessed she felt no desire to tackle either the Plan of Campaign or the Budget, which were the two prominent questions of the moment, and thought she could help Randolph in other ways.

In looking at the old photograph of the party, Jennie noticed that Lord Salisbury and Randolph were standing side by side. How little did she or anyone else there realize the great and irretrievable breach which was to come so soon and so suddenly between these two! In the midst of delightful people, occupations, and amusements, she was quite happy and far from imagining that the political horizon was not clear.

The celebration of Queen Victoria's Jubilee (1887) was the occasion of every sort of festivity. London was crowded to its utmost, and people came from all parts of the world to see the pageant and the crowning ceremony in Westminster Abbey. The day was blessed with the proverbial "Queen's weather." Rarely had Jennie seen London look so festive, blue sky and bright sunshine, flags everywhere, and an excited yet patient crowd filling the thoroughfares and the route of the procession.

As the wife of an ex-Cabinet Minister, Jennie was given a good place in the Abbey. The magnificent sight impressed her greatly. Gorgeous uniforms and beautiful dresses were enhanced by the "dim religious light," pierced here and there by the rays of the summer sun as it streamed through the ancient stained-glass windows. The Queen, representing the glory and continuity of England's history, sat alone in the middle of the great nave, a small, pathetic figure surrounded by that vast assembly, whose gaze was riveted upon her. A wave of emotion passed over it as silent tears were seen to be dropping one by one upon the Queen's folded hands. Perhaps the fact that the Te Deum which was being played had been composed by the Prince Consort added yet another note of sadness to the burden of her memories.

Once again Jennie had occasion to see Queen Victoria at a great function. This was at the opening of the Imperial Institute. The Queen, with a look of intense anxiety on her face, sat on a throne in the middle of the huge hall, which was filled to overflowing. She had to make a speech, which evidently was a great ordeal; but when she did so, her voice, soft and gentle as it was, never wavered for a moment, and every word could be heard by all.

Many were the public functions of all kinds to which they were bidden that year in honor of the Queen's Jubilee. Among them was an invitation from the White Star Company to cruise for a few days on board one of their ships, and to see the Naval Review, which was to take place in the Solent. In the middle of the London season, suffering from the heat and glare of a big city in the month of June, the prospect was a delightful one.

The trip proved most enjoyable. The Duchess of Manchester (since Duchess of Devonshire), Mr. Chamberlain, Lord Hartington, and a host of well-known and agreeable people, were on board. Great were the political foregatherings; arguments and discussions never ceased. Although Mr. Chamberlain had left Gladstone and the Home-Rule Party, he was not yet prepared to join the Conservatives, notwithstanding the overtures made to him by Lord Salisbury. Tired of inactivity, he was revolving at that time, in conjunction with Randolph, a scheme for a new party which was to be called the National Party, and both were anxious that Lord Hartington should join it.

The moment was thought propitious, and it was settled that Mr. Chamberlain should speak to Lord Hartington. That afternoon Jennie was sitting on the deck with the latter when Mr. Chamberlain joined them. Drawing up a chair, he suddenly plunged into the matter without preliminaries and with his usual directness. Lord Hartington, taken au depourvu (English Translation: "by surprise"), looked uncomfortable and answered very shortly. Mr. Chamberlain, full of his scheme, pressed the points home, taking no notice of the monosyllables he got in answer. But after a time the frozen attitude of Lord Hartington began to take effect, and the conversation languished and died. Jennie believed the subject was never reopened. In any case, nothing came of it. She imagined that Lord Hartington was a difficult person to persuade against his will and most uncompromisingly definite in his likes and dislikes. She had always thought that there existed a gulf between him and Mr. Chamberlain that no political expediency could really bridge. But of course this was only her own opinion.

Jennie had heard Randolph say that in most political questions he considered Lord Hartington's judgment infallible. He was slow, but sure. If an important paper, requiring an early answer, was sent to him to read, it might be pigeonholed for weeks. But when he did read it, he would at once discover any flaw or weakness, and his verdict generally carried the day. In private life no one was pleasanter or easier to get on with than the late Duke of Devonshire. His rather stern countenance belied a mirth-loving soul, and he thoroughly appreciated a joke.

He was rather careless about his clothes and once on his birthday his friends, as a joke, sent him every conceivable sort of head-gear from the ceremonious silk hat to the flannel cricketing cap. Jennie's contribution, she remembered, was a pot hat. For hours they poured in; she believed he received over fifty.

In old days before he succeeded to the dukedom they used to stay with him at Hardwick Hall for shooting-parties. It was a wonderful place, full of thrilling historical associations. Jennie never tired of hearing about them, or of wandering through the beautiful rooms filled with memories of Mary, Queen of Scots, most ill-fated of Queens, and of her gaoler the great "Bess of Hardwick" (Countess of Shrewsbury), ancestress of their host.

During their visit Randolph slept in "Queen Mary's Bedroom" which was of small dimensions, and had a window by the side of the door so that the unfortunate occupant could be spied upon at all times of the day or night. Two centuries later Marie Antoinette was put to the same indignity in the Conciergerie. Bess of Hardwick, when she pulled down the old Hall to build the present house (begun 1576, finished 1599) evidently intended this room for her prisoner, but Queen Mary did not live to occupy it. Beheaded in 1586, all her belongings were subsequently removed to it, including the original bed-hangings and coverlet worked by herself. Hence the name given to this room by tradition. Jennie's imagination ran riot as she gazed upon the screens and cushions worked by the Queen during the long years of her captivity. Who knows? On these very canvases her tears may have been as numerous as were the stitches with which she tried to find solace.

Close by was the Long Gallery which was supposed to be haunted by the restless spirit of the redoubtable Bess, not to speak of Queen Mary and Queen Elizabeth. There are some lines written apropos of this Gallery by the beautiful and celebrated Georgiana, Duchess of Devonshire, who spent long periods after her marriage at Chatsworth and Hardwick, whence she writes in French to her mother, Countess Spencer:

Sept. 3, 1777. "We set out for Hardwicke this morning. . . . Hardwicke looked extremely well. We'd walk all about the house, & paid our compliments to Queen Mary & Queen Elizabeth. I never look at the melancholy picture of Mary which was drawn in the 10th year of her imprisonment, and which has a countenance that looks worn by misfortune without pitying to the greatest degree the misery she must have liv'd in, for even the pomp she was treated with, those melancholy hangings and coffin like beds, must have added to the tristesse of her situation". . .

And again:

(Wednesday, the 14th of Feb. 1780.) ". . . Sachantcommevous le faitesnotre solitude ici, que nous avons pour toute societe, les arbres du Pare, et Les portraits de La Gallerie et Les Ombres des bonnes gens qui y sontpeints, ici . . .

O^ nous avons pour compagnie L'Ombre de La Reine Marie, Qui eut un nombreetonnant De maux, de soucis et d'amants. Ou bien par sabonte extreme La Grande Elisabeth meme Sort quelquesfois du Canevas Pour demander comment I'onva, (Celle qui regnant sur la terre De saVirginitefutfiere Et si Pon croitences temps-la A tort la Reine s'enpiqua)."

(English Translation: "Knowing as you do our solitude here, that we have for our only society the trees of the Park, and the portraits of the Gallery and the Shadows of the good people who are painted there, here, where we have for company The Shadow of Queen Mary, who had an astonishing number of troubles, worries and lovers. Or else through her extreme kindness The Great Elizabeth herself Sometimes comes out of the Canvas To ask how we are, (She who, reigning over the earth Was proud of her Virginity And if one believes in those times Wrongly did the Queen pride herself on it).")

Jennie remembered having a large, tapestries room the door of which had a keyhole big enough to put one's hand through, and which gave on to the Presence Chamber. The first night she thought the arras seemed to move about, so arming herself with a poker, she thrust it here and there, when to her dismay she felt the tapestry give, and on looking behind, saw a small, winding stone staircase disappearing into unknown depths. This made her so nervous that she sat shivering for hours in an arm-chair, surrounded by all the candles she could find, until she fell asleep from sheer fatigue. It was with quite an emotion that she one day put on a puce satin cloak that had belonged to Bess of Hardwick, hoping perhaps that it might have the virtues of Elijah's mantle.

Lord Hartington, in showing them some of the pictures, came across a portrait of one of the Dukes of Devonshire of whom he told rather an amusing story. The agent came to the Duke, complaining that his son, the Lord Hartington of the day, was spending enormous sums of money. "Well," said the Duke, "isn't there plenty of it?"

Sir Henry Wolff, Randolph, and Jennie were once staying at Buxton, and they went over as tourists to visit Chatsworth. When she told Lord Hartington that she had been there, and was much impressed with the grandeur and beauty of the place, all he said was, "Did you break anything?"

Ten years later another naval review was held to celebrate the Diamond Jubilee, at which Jennie was also present, having again accepted an invitation to spend three days on board the Teutonic, H.M. armed cruiser for the nonce. Among the guests she found Mr. John Morley, Lord and Lady Charles Beresford, Sir John and Lady Lister Kaye, Lord and Lady Lonsdale, and many other friends. By the irony of fate the captain had particularly picked out Sir John Gorst to sit next to her at dinner. They had not spoken for several years, but of course she ignored the estrangement.

Everything on this occasion was wonderfully well done, and they had many privileges for seeing all there was to be seen. The fleet in array made a splendid show, and at night the harsh ugly lines and grim realities of the ironclads disappeared in the glare of thousands of electric lights, which made a surprisingly brilliant spectacle. The day of the review Lord Lonsdale interested and amused the fleet in general and the Teutonic in particular by dashing about in a turbine which shot in and out among the battle-ships at great speed. A turbine was a great novelty at that time and they were all greatly excited at seeing it.

In this year (1887), Randolph, having more leisure since he was out of office, became keener about the turf. They had both of them often attended race-meetings, particularly Newmarket, but till then he had not owned any race-horses. In partnership with Lord Dunraven, he now bought a number of horses, which were trained by R. Sherwood. For some years the stable was very successful. They took a small house (Bemstead Manor) on the Chieveley estate, about three miles from the town of Newmarket, where Jennie passed many a pleasant week. They would ride out in the early morning from six to seven to see the horses do their gallops. It was a most healthy and invigorating life, and she became greatly interested, spending hours with Randolph at Sherwood's, when he and the trainer would study the racing calendar and decide upon the entries for the horses.

Newmarket had become very different from what it was in the early eighties, when Jennie first went there. Then only the old stands existed, some of which date back quite two hundred years. The ladies who came were habitues, and did not muster a dozen at the outside. Among them were Caroline Duchess of Montrose, who was a large owner of horses; the Duchess of Manchester (now Duchess of Devonshire); and Lady Cardigan, who would drive up in an old-fashioned, yellow tilbury, in which she sat all day. Lady Bradford and Lady Cadogan were always there; as were Lady

Castlereagh (now Lady Londonderry), Lady Gerard, and a few others. It was the fashion to ride, those who did not appearing in ordinary country clothes. Nowadays velvets and feathers are worn by the mob which throngs the stands, many not knowing a horse from a cow, but coming because it is the fashion. Jennie had heard amusing tales of the ignorance displayed on these occasions. One lady was overheard declaring that as she had not been to Newmarket for years, she had quite "forgotten the names of the horses," and another, that someone had told her the name of "the yearling which was going to win the Derby at the next Newmarket meeting." A charming duchess, who cares only to see her friends at the races, generally brings her needlework, and takes no heed of the strenuous efforts of the horses and jockeys as they race past her.

The shining light of their stable was the "Abbesse de Jouarre," for which Randolph gave £300 at the Doncaster sales, eventually selling her for £7000. Jennie had been reading "L'Abbesse de Jouarre," written by Renan in order, so it is said, to disprove the assertions of his friends that he could not write something imaginative. She suggested the name as a fitting one for the beautiful black mare, which was by "Trappist" out of "Festive." She was a gallant little thing, with a heart bigger than her body, and her size made the public so sceptical that she invariably started at long odds. When she won the Oaks those who backed her got 20 to 1.

Neither Randolph nor Jennie witnessed her triumph. He was fishing in Norway, and she was with some friends who had a house on the Thames. On that day they happened to reach Boulter's Lock shortly after the hour of the race. Asking the lock-keeper which horse had won the big race, he replied, to her great delight and amusement, "The Abcess on the Jaw." The "Abbesse," after winning many races and producing numerous progeny, died in the breeding stables at Welbeck. It was with great satisfaction that

Jennie witnessed that horse's grandson "Land League" win the Cambridgeshire in 1907.

Russia, France and Berlin

Chartwell, 1964

"The late 1880s saw my mother at the height of her social powers," Churchill said, accepting a fresh cup of tea from his secretary with a grateful nod. "While my father's health declined and his political influence waned, she became something unprecedented, an independent force in international society." He sipped carefully before continuing. "Her travels through Russia, France, and Germany weren't pleasure trips. They were diplomatic missions conducted through drawing rooms rather than embassies."

Sophia looked up from her notes. "Unofficial diplomacy?"

"The most effective kind. She could have conversations that formal diplomats couldn't, ask questions that wouldn't be permitted in official channels, form relationships that transcended national boundaries." Churchill's voice grew stronger as he warmed to his subject. "When I later found myself negotiating with foreign leaders, I drew constantly on her insights about European character and culture."

"She was your advance scout."

"My mother mapped the social and political terrain of Europe through personal relationships. She understood that behind every policy position is a human being with fears, ambitions, and vanities." Churchill set down his teacup with satisfaction. "That understanding, that politics is ultimately about people, not abstractions, became the foundation of my own diplomatic approach."

From RUSSIA to BERLIN – Late 1880s

Jennie loved talking about Paris and Russia in her memoirs - and own of her favorite subjects was her privilege to know best; namely, the Dowager Duchess of Saxe-Coburg-Gotha, formerly Duchess of Edinburgh. They used to see her very often when she lived in England. A warm-hearted woman of rare intelligence and exceptional education, her early life as the only daughter of the Czar (Alexander II) was a most interesting one, as, quite apart from the exalted position she held, it was her duty for two hours daily to read her father's correspondence and the secret news of the world, in itself a liberal education. An excellent musician, Rubinstein once said of her, so she told Jennie, "Vous ne jouez pas si mal pour unePrincesse!" (English Translation: "You don't play so badly for a Princess!") They frequently played together duets on two pianos, or quartettes in which Lady Mary Fitzwilliam, Jennie's sister Mrs. Leslie, and Signor Albanesi would join. A fine linguist, speaking fluently several languages, the Duchess wrote them equally well.

The text includes several letters from the Duchess of Edinburgh (later Marie, Duchess of Saxe-Coburg-Gotha) to Lady Randolph Churchill. Here are summaries:

From Stuttgart

The Duchess congratulates Lord Randolph on his parliamentary success and the defeat of Gladstone ("the G.O.M."). She mentions she's visiting her aunt, the Queen of Württemberg, who she describes as "a very charming and amiable old lady, a real grande dame of the past generation." The Duchess expresses shock about the tragic death of the King of Bavaria, whom she knew as a child and described as having "the finest eyes one could dream about." She invites Lady Randolph to visit Coburg in September.

From Peterhof

The Duchess congratulates Lord Randolph on becoming a Minister again while jokingly mentioning she "shed a tear or two over the fall of 'my idol'" (Gladstone). She describes her summer life in Russia, where family members live in separate villas in the park while the palace is used for receptions. She mentions there are "dozens of cousins of every description" including the Queen of Greece with her children. The Duchess notes she no longer dances, as she was "a slim young lady then, a fat matron now." She describes a ballet in the open air, illuminations in the park, and military reviews at the camp where 30,000 troops are assembled.

From Malta

The Duchess thanks Lady Randolph for her letters from Russia and is pleased they had a good experience. She mentions she had recommended them to her relations, noting that two of them "had already been greatly impressed" by Lady Randolph - the Grand Duchess Vladimir in Paris and her brother Serge in London. She refers to an "escapade" by Lord Randolph in Messina that makes her laugh and expresses a wish to have another good talk with him.

The Escapade in Messina

The "escapade" referred to by the Duchess relates to an incident described in letters from Lord Randolph. In March 1887, while in Messina, Sicily, he and his companion Harry T. found themselves trapped by a quarantine imposed due to cholera in Catania. Not wanting to be detained indefinitely, they arranged with local fishermen to smuggle them across the Straits of Messina to the Italian mainland in an open boat at night. After landing, they had to evade authorities who might have put them in quarantine, struggled with a cart that overturned on a rough road, and eventually reached the house of an Englishman who gave them shelter. The next day they slipped onto a train to Naples, arriving without servants or luggage but having successfully escaped the quarantine.

This discussion concludes with Jennie mentioning another Russian friend, M. de Staal, for many years Russian Ambassador in London. He was described as having a delightful personality, charm of conversation, and a kind heart, which made him extremely popular. Before his death, he sent Jennie his photograph with a charming note in French saying: "Here is the very old face of a very old man who is half-dead but loves you well. Do not welcome it too badly." Jennie treasured this note as characteristic of his charming personality.

The visit to Russia left a lasting impression on Jennie. She had entered the country with certain preconceptions based on Western views of Russian tyranny and despotism, but found instead a society of warmth, culture, and surprising informality. The contrast between the harsh, cold landscape and the warmth of the Russian character fascinated her. The opulence of the imperial court, with its elaborate rituals and magnificent displays, coexisted with unexpected simplicity in the personal lives of the royal family.

Jennie was particularly struck by the Russian aristocratic women she met. Their combination of education, artistic accomplishment, and linguistic abilities created a society that was intellectually stimulating in ways different from London or Paris. Though she noted that these women seemed to deliberately efface themselves in public life, she sensed their quiet influence behind the scenes.

Her observations of Russian social customs - from the elaborate etiquette of court functions to the hearty appetites and late-night entertainments of private gatherings - revealed her keen eye for cultural differences. The physical contrasts of Russia also captivated her: the brutally cold weather that could destroy a bouquet of orchids in an instant, the sleigh rides across frozen lakes, the unexpected splendor hidden within modest exteriors.

Throughout her stay, Jennie demonstrated her adaptability and enthusiasm for new experiences, whether participating in tobogganing, admiring the architecture of the Kremlin, or navigating the complex social protocols of imperial audiences.

On their way back from Russia in 1888, Jennie and Randolph stayed for ten days at the British Embassy in Berlin. Sir Edward Malet, who was the Ambassador, was very much in favor with the Imperial Family. A man of small stature, he nevertheless had a commanding presence, with a pleasant and open countenance and the most courteous of manners. He was very well informed and talked agreeably on all subjects. Lady Ermyntrude, his wife, who was equally liked, was a daughter of the late Duke of Bedford, and an extremely cultivated woman. They both showed the Churchills the greatest hospitality, even giving a dinner in their honor.

After ultra-fashionable and brilliant St. Petersburg, Berlin society seemed a little quiet to Jennie. But there were some exceptions, notably Princess Karl Egon Fürstenberg (now Comtesse Jean de Castellane), Princess Antoine Radziwill, and Countess von Hohenau. This lady was renowned for her beautiful figure, which Jennie had seen equaled only by that of Lady Claud Hamilton. Princess Fürstenberg (who was a stepdaughter of the late Duc de Valançay and half-sister of the Prince de Sagan, already mentioned in these reminiscences) held a unique position. To her own vivid personality she added her husband's great name and immense wealth. Well educated, and with a restless and ambitious mind, she had always taken a keen interest in politics. Had her life been spent in England instead of abroad, she would certainly have played a greater part. In Germany there was little scope in that line for a woman, and in France still less. Her dinners and her parties were the most successful entertainments given in Berlin.

Prince Fürstenberg, who has since died, was a very independent man, and some years later he incurred the present Kaiser's wrath in a quarrel which made considerable stir at the time. William II issued an order to the effect that army officers should take precedence of the nobility. The Prince retired from the Court in high dudgeon, after writing a letter to the Kaiser in which, it is said, he expressed his views with more vigor than diplomacy; not hesitating to compare the Hohenzollerns to their detriment with his own high and mighty, not to say much older, family.

Jennie and Randolph spent their days pleasantly in visiting the palaces, galleries, and museums. At one of the galleries they were much interested to see three pictures which used to be at Blenheim, one of them being the famous "Bacchanalia" by Rubens, which had filled one side of the dining-room. Jennie found Sans Souci enchanting and could hardly tear herself away from its lovely rooms, with their Louis XV decorations and delicious Watteaus. How strange, she thought, that those two grim men, Frederick the Great and Voltaire, should have lived in such incongruous surroundings! Visions of beautiful women in powder and patches could alone be associated with these boudoirs, where the panels, adorned with silver tracings, and the soft-colored silk curtains would have made a fitting background for their loveliness.

The bedroom so long occupied by Voltaire, with its priceless Dresden china, and hangings of green damask, looked like a nest for a pink-and-white maid of honor. One note, however, gave an indication of the king's mind in respect to the guest whom he hated and feared as much as he admired him. A large, grinning china monkey did service for a chandelier, holding in its hands the candles which lighted up the sardonic features of its human counterpart. At the end of a cul-de-sac was a small, round room of which the only outlet was a window giving on to the garden. With books to the ceiling, and a huge writing-table in the center, this was Frederick the Great's sanctum. Perhaps it was on this very table that he wrote the verses he was so anxious Voltaire should admire, and which in the hands of the "Patriarch of Ferney" became the weapon with which he ridiculed the King at the time of their famous quarrel.

Among the many festivities to which they were bidden was a gala performance at the opera. A gala night under the auspices of the German Court was a very different thing from the same function in London. In Berlin the boxes and seats were not sold, and only those who received a royal invitation might attend, whereas in London it was a case of the longest purse and the highest bidder. In consequence, the audience in London was anything but representative of London society. Jennie remembered being very much struck by the wonderful ensemble and perfection of the orchestra in Berlin, far surpassing any in London of those days. Sembrich sang in "Les Noces de Figaro," and the whole royal family were present, including the aged Emperor William I.

The prospect of a state concert, preceded by an informal Drawing-room, at which they were to be presented, rather alarmed Jennie, not knowing the rules and etiquette of a court so different from any she had yet seen. Also, not expecting to attend any such function, she had no court train with her, and this added to her embarrassment, for there was no doubt that to be well dressed gave confidence. In the end, however, it all proved quite simple.

Etiquette required that before appearing at court Jennie should visit the Mistress of the Robes. She therefore called with Lady Ermyntrude Malet on Countess Perponcher, a rather formidable lady with an 1830 coiffure and a stiff, rustling silk gown.

The Countess received her with many reverences, which Jennie duly returned. On the night of the concert, they were ushered into a small room where the Emperor William stood surrounded by the royal family, the officials of the court, and the diplomatic corps, and with others they were presented. The Emperor, looking most upright in his smart uniform, welcomed Jennie in a few well-chosen words, also referring to their tea-party at Gastein and the jokes they had had with the children. Little did she or any one else present think that this was to be his last entertainment, and that in a few weeks the kind and noble old monarch would be no more.

Suddenly a side door opened, and the Empress Augusta, sitting in a small bath-chair, was wheeled in. Dressed in pale-blue satin, with jewels to her waist, her venerable head crowned with a magnificent tiara, she made a brave, if somewhat pathetic figure. She asked Jennie many questions in excellent English, addressing her as "Lady Churchill" and inquiring after the Czarina, "whom she understood Jennie had just seen." She also asked so much after her "dear Queen Victoria" that Jennie came to the conclusion she was mistaking her for Queen Victoria's lady-in-waiting, Jane. Her remarks were almost inaudible, and Jennie had to answer in a very loud voice, as the Empress did not hear well. Jennie did not recollect ever having felt more embarrassed or uncomfortable than during this conversation at cross purposes, carried on before the whole court, which was listening in respectful silence.

Presently they all moved into an adjoining room, at the end of which was a small platform. Round tables were dotted about, the places being arranged beforehand. Randolph sat at the table of the Princess while Jennie sat at Prince William's. After listening to an excellent concert, at which Sembrich sang, supper was served, the whole function being over by eleven o'clock. Much to her delight, in the course of the evening Jennie made the acquaintance of the great Moltke, who, notwithstanding his stern and ascetic countenance, surprised her agreeably by his sunny smile and pleasant voice.

There is no doubt it would be difficult to find a greater contrast than the Russian and German courts presented at that time; the one, brilliant, imposing, lavish in its extravagance, barbaric in its splendor; the other, unpretentious and, perhaps, a little dull, but full of traditions and etiquette. In Berlin, and particularly at the court, signs of the all-conquering and victorious army were everywhere apparent; everything military was in the ascendant. Jennie remembered Prince William visiting her at the Embassy, and their having a great discussion on German and Russian uniforms, the gorgeousness of which had impressed her while in St. Petersburg.

If the Court of the Emperor William I was somewhat depressing, the magnificence of the existing regime was a great contrast. William II rightly wished to maintain a proper standard, and while condemning extravagance, liked to see a dignified display. It had been reported that he once said, apropos of his court balls, that "men came for discipline, and women for deportment." Permission to dance was given only by royal order, and the privileged had for many days to rehearse the intricate steps of the stately minuets prescribed. Woe be it if they made any mistakes, for a dancing-master sat aloft in a gallery recording the faux pas of his pupils. This may sound arbitrary, but there is no doubt that if something similar could be introduced at the Court of St. James the proceedings would gain in dignity, as it is with difficulty that the majority of people can go through an ordinary quadrille.

Before leaving, the Churchills dined one night with Count Herbert Bismarck. At the end of the dinner he produced, as a bonne bouche, a sort of paste, made principally, as far as Jennie could gather, of lard and garlic, of which he spoke with pride as having been made by his mother. Count Herbert was a kindly man, and although to English ideas he may perhaps have seemed a little rough and uncouth, he was really very popular in England, and left many friends to deplore his premature death. He was greatly interested in English politics, and Jennie remembered that at this dinner he had an argument on the subject of Mr. Gladstone, whom he cordially hated, remarking, much to their amusement, that his father always said "Gladstone would drag England to the lowest ground of hell."

Randolph and Jennie were disappointed in not seeing Prince Bismarck, who was then in the country; but some years later, when at Kissengen, they were fortunate enough to make the "Iron Chancellor's" acquaintance. They dined with him at the old schloss where he was living, its picturesque red roof making a landmark in the flat Bavarian scenery. They were only a party of six: the Prince and Princess, Count Herbert Bismarck and his wife (who was of English origin), and themselves. They dined in a large room which had a vaulted ceiling, and seemed to be used as a general living-room. At dinner Jennie sat on one side of the Prince, and Randolph on the other, the huge boar hound, their host's constant companion, lying on the ground between them. Conversation was animated. Bismarck spoke excellent English, but very slowly; and if he could not find the word he wanted, he would pause and think until he did. His family looked up to him with awe and admiration, and listened with the greatest attention to every word he uttered. The old Princess, who seemed very feeble, did not take much part in the conversation.

After dinner they adjourned to another part of the room, where they sat round a long table covered with books and newspapers. There were a great many illustrated papers, full of caricatures of Bismarck, which, in answer to a question, he assured Jennie he did not mind in the least. Later, however, Count Herbert contradicted this, saying that his father was really very sensitive and disliked being caricatured.

Speaking of the country and the long walks he took daily, Bismarck said he loved nature, but the amount of life he saw awed him, and that it took a great deal of faith to believe that an "all-seeing Eye" could notice every living atom when one realized what that meant. "Have you ever sat on the grass and examined it closely? There is enough life in one square yard to appal you," he said. When they were about to leave, his great dog fixed his fierce eyes on Jennie's in so persistent a manner that she became alarmed and thought he was going to spring upon her; but the Prince reassured her, saying, "He is looking at your eyes, because he has not seen any like them." This was said in a grave voice and without a smile, leaving it doubtful if he intended to pay her a compliment.

Quitting Berlin with much regret and with gratitude to their kind hosts the Malets, the Churchills proceeded to Paris, where they remained for some time. Their friend the Marquis de Breteuil helped to make their visit delightful, for at his charming house, where they often dined, they met every one of note and interest. It was at one of these dinners that Jennie saw General Boulanger for the first time. M. de Breteuil was a believer at that moment in Boulangism, and, in common with many Royalists, thought he saw in the General, faute de mieux, the preserver of the French monarchy, through a Restoration which was to follow a Republic under which all Frenchmen could rally.

The Duchesse d'Uzes, the Comtesse Greffhule, the General, Randolph and Jennie, made up the party. The duchess, who kept a pack of hounds in the vicinity of Paris, and hunted the stag with all the pomp and picturesqueness foreigners display in matters connected with the chase, had, it appears, been hunting that day, and in consequence arrived late, breathless, and somewhat untidy, but covered with magnificent jewels. Granddaughter of the Veuve Clicquot of champagne fame, Mme. d'Uzes had inherited a large fortune, and with this "fruit of the vine" was able to regild the shield of the Duc d'Uzes, who bore one of the oldest names of France. The

Duchess, who was then a widow, had espoused the cause of the "brav' General" with all the ardor of an energetic enthusiast, and she emphasized her support by giving him three million francs.

Mme. Greffhule, who was a Belgian by birth and came of the historic house of Chimay, had a European reputation for grace, charm, and esthetic tastes. Although she was very young, her salon had already acquired the name for artistic and literary prominence which it bears to-day, and people were eager to be counted among its habitues.

Boulanger, notwithstanding a military bearing, a fierce mustache, and, to French ideas, a handsome face, gave Jennie the impression of a man not quite sure of himself. At that moment his popularity was great, and the eyes of France, not to say of Europe, were turned upon him; yet he seemed unable to rise above his middle-class origin and early surroundings. He talked little, and preferred answering questions to putting them. Later, when he came to London he dined with the Churchills several times, but even on better acquaintance his diffidence did not vanish. He was banal in conversation, and Jennie cannot recall anything of interest he said to her.

As the General had no political mission in England, the Prince of Wales honored them with his company on one of these occasions. Among those who came, besides General Boulanger and General Dillon who accompanied him, were the Duchess of Manchester (now the Dowager Duchess of Devonshire), Lady Norreys, Lord Hardwicke, Lord Hartington, Sir George Lewis, and Mr. and Mrs. Leopold de Rothschild, who got into great trouble with their French relatives for having been there. So confident of success were Boulanger and those about him at that time, that General Dillon, who sat next to Mrs. de Rothschild, invited her in the General's name to stay at the Tuileries, "where we shall be in a few months," quoth he.

There was in England a very strong opinion against Boulanger, and the Churchills were much taken to task for receiving and entertaining him; but Randolph was rather fond of exotic specimens of mankind, and liked to study them without regard to public opinion. Although undoubtedly a brave man morally, Boulanger was not sufficiently courageous to risk everything for a cause in which he undoubtedly was, as he perhaps suspected, a cat's-paw. The extraordinary rise and popularity of the man seems incredible, unless one takes into consideration not only the French character, which made such delirious enthusiasm possible, but also the state of France at that time.

Perhaps it will not come amiss here to recapitulate some of the salient points of this strange and eventful career. The malcontents of every shade of politics, Royalist and Bonapartist, each thought that Boulanger, having gained the confidence of the masses, would, once Dictator or President, pave the way to a Royalist or Bonapartist monarchy. Boulanger himself had vast ambitions, of which, it appears, he showed signs when a boy at college. Although a good officer, he had not attained his rank of general by prominence in the field, but, according to his enemies, by lobbying for many years in public offices and anterooms. Politically he coquetted with all parties, and it was probably for this reason that he was made Minister of War in the Freycinet Government of 1885, as he was on fairly good terms with both Radicals and Moderates.

It was while he was in the Government that he began to show his true colors, and some of his Royalist supporters fell away when they found him becoming more radical and voting with the advanced party for the exile of the Bourbon Princes. Jennie was in Paris at the time of the publication of the Due d'Aumale's letter from Boulanger, and well remembers the great sensation it made. It revealed the fulsomeness of the court he paid to the Duke, to whom he owed his rank of general, and his ingratitude in joining those concerned in voting for a cruel and unnecessary law against harmless princes, not to say French citizens. Notwithstanding this revelation of his character, his prestige, shortly after the Fete Nationale on the 14th of July, seemed untarnished, and M. de Breteuil, in writing to Jennie, said at that time, "Son étoile est plus brillante que jamais." English Translation: "His star is more brilliant than ever."

Like a comet, Boulanger traversed the skies, "an empty-headed thing with a fiery tail," which, to continue the simile, fell to earth in the flash of a pistol report on the tomb of his one true friend, Marguerite Bonnemain.

Like Parnell, Boulanger, ambitious as some may have thought him, put the love of woman above that of power. All his thoughts were centered in and controlled by her who was the mainspring of his life. After the plebiscite of February, 1889, he had a majority of 70,000 votes in Paris alone, and his popularity rose to fever heat; but instead of going straight to the Elysee, where he might have challenged his fate and, who knows? been acclaimed President, he rushed off to Mme. Bonnemain's house, and could not be found. This was the turning-point in his career. He disgusted his followers and those who believed in him; and the opportunity never returned.

Randolph, writing to Jennie from Paris, February 5, 1889, said:

"...Boulanger does not seem to me to have made as much out of his victory as he ought. If he does not do something soon, the effect of it will be forgotten."

And again in September:

"It is evidently all up with Boulanger. I suppose we shall have him now en permanence in London. People won't run after him quite so much."

Life in Paris was most attractive to Jennie. She sought out all her old friends, and made many new ones. Society was then, as it is now, very cosmopolitan, but it was reinforced by a certain section of the "Noble Faubourg" who were not averse to being entertained by the foreign element. They did not feel it compromising to meet their own compatriots, were they Bonapartists or Republicans, on such neutral grounds. A number of Mexicans, Peruvians, Chilians, etc., "rastaquouères," as they were dubbed, were much to the fore; and as they seemed to have millions, and entertained lavishly, the gay young Parisians flocked to their houses en masse.

Exclusiveness is so much a thing of the past that one is astonished nowadays to meet it, Jennie reflected, individual merit being far more an open sesame to society than formerly. Those who travel and mix perforce with their fellow-creatures forget that people still exist in this world who cannot understand or tolerate anything or anybody beyond their immediate entourage. Is it to be wondered at that these people become narrow-minded, prejudiced, and self-centered? Personally Jennie felt her acquaintance could never be too large. When she reflected that there are thousands of delightful and interesting people one may be missing, no opportunity ought to be lost of cultivating as many as possible. Friends are in another category. Time alone can prove friendships. The friends who stand by you through all vicissitudes are more precious and rare than "les amis des beaux jours." English Translation: "fair-weather friends"

To lose one of them is indeed a calamity. To find a cold heart where you were certain of a warm one, to find mistrust and indifference where you hoped for trust and faith, is the greatest of disillusions and the saddest. "La lampe de l'amitié a besoind'huile," but if the lamp is faulty, no amount of oil will keep it alight. English Translation: "The lamp of friendship needs oil"

Speaking of exclusiveness, Jennie was reminded of an amusing illustration of it which she came across in Paris. Having made the acquaintance of the Duchesse de la Tremoille, she dined with her one night. The Duke, who belongs to one of the oldest families in France, and owns Serrant, a sixteenth-century chateau on the Loire, also possesses a charming house in the Avenue Gabriel. Before leaving for England, Jennie went to call on the Duchess and asked if she was at home. Hearing that she was, Jennie walked through the courtyard to the front door, where, to her surprise, notwithstanding a bell announcing her arrival, no one came forward to meet her. She waited; still no one. There were two doors. She chose one, and found herself at the foot of a large staircase embellished with palms and statues. Making her way up, she saw a suite of three or four rooms. In vain she waited for a footman or some one to announce her. At last dimly perceiving a figure at the far end, she went toward it, and found the Duchess, who expressed her surprise that Jennie had taken so long to appear.

Presently the timbre sounded again; this time it was the Grand Duke Vladimir of Russia who arrived unannounced. It was amusing to see the man before whom Russia trembles dropping on one knee with mock solemnity, kissing the Duchess's hand, and thanking her in exaggerated language for some "divine turkeys" she had sent him. More visitors appearing, Jennie departed, finding her way out as she had come.

Having heard that the Duchess was supposed to be very exclusive, Jennie confessed she thought this a free-and-easy way of receiving, and said as much to a Frenchman. "You don't understand," he said. "During certain months of the year the

Duchess receives her own particular coterie of intimate friends every day from four to six. They know they are sure to find her and be welcome. As habitues there is no need for them to be announced, and the appearance of servants would detract from the delightful sans gene and intimacy of the visit." "But what about the casual caller, or possibly an unwelcome visitor?" "Oh," replied her friend, "none of these would dream of asking if Madame la Duchesse was at home unless they were on her particular list." This explanation somewhat disturbed Jennie, and she felt herself, for the nonce, a trespasser.

M. de Breteuil would sometimes, for the Churchills' delectation, invite strange people to meet them. Among them was a certain M. de Meyrenna, a young and good-looking man, who interested and amused them for a whole evening by relating the adventures of his extraordinary and thrilling life. He had a few months previously been proclaimed King of the Sedangs (a tribe somewhere in Indo-China) and called himself "Marie I." Although in a wild and distant country, his subjects did exist, which is more than can be said for the "Emperor of Sahara," a would-be monarch of the same type. Marie I invited Jennie to pay him a visit. She was to be met by a caravan with elephants and camels and escorted to his capital, where he promised she should be treated royally. Jennie believed he died a year or two later, an adventurer to the last.

Another eccentric person was King Milan, father of Alexander late King of Servia, who, with his wife Draga, was treacherously murdered by his subjects. When Jennie first met Milan in Paris he had just abdicated in favor of his son after a fierce quarrel with his wife, Natalie, a Princess of Stourdza. He certainly was one of the most uncivilized beings she had ever encountered. A short, thick-set man with inky black hair and mustache, of little or no education save what his natural intelligence helped him to pick up, he was notwithstanding an agreeable personality. Later he came to London, where he was not persona grata either at the English Court or in general society, into which, however, he never attempted to penetrate.

Jennie remembered once at a small dinner party he was induced to describe his early life before he became, in 1868, Prince of Servia on the assassination of his cousin Michael. Up to that time, barefoot and clad in rags, he had lived the life of a goatherd in the mountains, where he often went without food, sleeping in caverns. In relating these past experiences, his encounters with wild beasts, and narrow escapes from those who for their own ends wanted his life, he became so excited that, suddenly forgetting he was not in his native wilds, he began to eat with his fingers, tearing the meat on his plate.

His life on the whole was a sad one, and he really deserved something better, although totally unfitted by his early bringing up to govern any country, far less a semibarbaric one like Servia. Jennie dined with him again, this time at the Amphitryon, a restaurant which was half a club, and was much in vogue in London at the moment. They were a party of eight or ten. In a private room, the walls of which were entirely covered with orchids, they had a most fantastic repast. Although nightingales' tongues and peacocks' brains did not figure on the menu, Jennie has no doubt the bill was equally extravagant, for Milan had absolutely no sense of the value of money.

A few months later he went back to Servia, whether in the hope of helping his son or to intrigue against him Jennie did not know. Disgusted at Alexander's marriage, which took place shortly after his arrival, with Mme. Draga Maschin, who had been lady-in-waiting to Queen Natalie, Milan left Servia in haste, never to return. Writing to Jennie from some Austrian Baths, he poured forth his troubles in his impulsive manner:

"Chere Madame: Depuislongtempsj'ai voulu vousécrire. Cette lettrevousparviendra-t-elle? Je ne le saurai que sivousvoulez bien me répondre deux mots pour me dire que vousl'avez reçue. Je n'ai rien de bon à vous dire sur moncompte. Après m'êtredévoué corps et âme à monfils, il m'ajoué le tour d'épouserunepersonne plus qu'impossible et ayant quatorze ans de plus que lui au grand scandale du pays et de l'Europeentière.

Je n'ai pas voulu accepter cette situation, et me revoilà de par les grands chemins sans savoir ce que jeferai. Pardon si je vous parle de ces choses, mais dans mes vieux jours, et avec mescheveux plus que poivre et sel, c'est dur. J'aimieuxmérité que cela.

Milan."

English Translation and Summary: This is a letter from King Milan to Lady Randolph Churchill, written from an Austrian spa. In it, he expresses his distress at his son Alexander's marriage to Draga Maschin, who was fourteen years older than Alexander and whom Milan considered "more than impossible." He laments that after devoting "body and soul" to his son, Alexander has rewarded him with this scandal that shocked the country and all of Europe. Milan writes that he refused to accept the situation and has now left Serbia, wandering without knowing what he will do next. He apologizes for burdening Jennie with these troubles, but says "in my old age, with my more than pepper-and-salt hair, it's hard. I deserved better than this."

One of the most interesting incidents in Paris in 1889 was the great Secretan sale, which took place in July. Among the art collectors and connoisseurs who flocked to it was H.R.H. the Due d'Aumale. His vast knowledge and exquisite taste made all who knew him desirous of obtaining his opinions. The catalogue, which consisted of two large volumes, was admirably got up, and so largely sought for that, much to Jennie's chagrin, she was unable to procure a copy. The Due d'Aumale, hearing of this, presented her with one of his, writing in it a charming inscription. These books, beautifully bound, are among the treasures of her library.

The duke, with his military prestige and martial bearing, was besides a man of great culture, and fitly described as "un gentilhomme au bout des ongles." English Translation: "a gentleman to his fingertips"

He was, moreover, an ardent sportsman, and the magnificent Chateau of Chantilly which he presented in 1886 to the Institut de France is filled with his hunting trophies. During his exile in England, Jennie remembered dining with him at his house in Rutland Gate, and being impressed by his charming and gentle manner. He talked much about France, and his love for his country seemed in no way impaired by the cruel measure which had been passed against him by his own countrymen.

One of the houses Jennie frequented in Paris was that of Mrs. Ferdinand Bischoffsheim, a clever and beautiful American who died a few years ago. She had a salon in Paris which was quite literary. It was there that Jennie first met M. Bourget, then unmarried, and began a friendship which has lasted unimpaired to this day. He had just written "Mensonges," which added greatly to his reputation as a novelist, although it was freely criticized. An animated and amusing correspondence was being carried on in the press, mainly by the fair sex, who were irate at his description of a mondaine, his heroine.

Jennie recollected his being chaffed by a compatriot, who asked him why he did not depict a real woman of the world in his books? Bourget, who thought he had accurately done so, was naturally annoyed but, unlike most Frenchmen, he could stand chaff. Perhaps his long stay in England had inured him to it. Now, one of the Forty Immortals, wearing "les palmesacadémiques" and happily married to a most attractive and talented woman, his books are more serious; but to Jennie the delightful "Sensations d'Oxford," which he wrote years ago, and which for literary style and charm of description he has in her estimation never surpassed, is quite staid enough. They often discussed his literary projects, and she has many pleasant letters from him, from which she quotes at random the following:

"...Ma vie à moiestattristéepar la difficultéd'écrire 'Une IdylleTragique.' C'est un beau sujet sur lequel je devraisvousécrirevingt pages. Avec de la patience j'enviendrai à bout, maisc'estterriblement dur. Arrivé à un certain point de la vie, on ensait trop, on veut trop mettre, et on ne peut pas dire ce que l'on a à dire... Savez vous que Tourguéniew a résumé le dernier mot de tout quand il a dit 'La vie estune affaire brutale.'"

English Translation: "My own life is saddened by the difficulty of writing 'A Tragic Idyll.' It's a beautiful subject about which I should write you twenty pages. With patience I will manage it, but it's terribly hard. Having reached a certain point in life, one knows too much, wants to include too much, and cannot say what one has to say... Do you know that Turgenev summarized the last word on everything when he said 'Life is a brutal business.'"

Lord Randolph and Birmingham

Chartwell, 1964

The shadows had lengthened considerably as Churchill shifted uncomfortably in his chair. "Birmingham," he said with a mixture of fondness and regret. "My mother's greatest political campaign, and perhaps my father's greatest missed opportunity." His voice carried the weight of decades of reflection. "She threw herself into that constituency with a passion that amazed even seasoned political operators."

"But your father didn't win the seat."

"No, but that wasn't really the point. What mattered was watching her discover her own political gifts, the ability to connect with working-class voters, to organize complex campaigns, to inspire loyalty in people who had every reason to be cynical about aristocratic politicians." Churchill paused, his breathing slightly labored. "She proved that an American woman could understand British politics better than most British men."

Sophia waited as he gathered his strength. "Did that influence your own political style?"

"Enormously. She taught me that authenticity resonates more than breeding, that genuine interest in people's lives matters more than polished speeches." Churchill's eyes brightened briefly. "Every time I campaigned in working-class constituencies, I heard her voice reminding me that voters respond to respect, not condescension."

BIRMINGHAM, 1889

Lord Randolph Churchill's interest in politics remained as strong as ever in 1889, although he was out of office. It was during this time that he made some of his best speeches. His followers in Birmingham had never ceased working on his behalf since he had stood for the constituency in 1885, and when John Bright died, their greatest desire was for Randolph to represent them in Parliament.

Jennie observed that Randolph himself was very keen about it and would probably have won the seat eventually had he not listened to the over-scrupulous advice of the Unionist Party. Great discussions and controversies took place in their councils about whether he ought to stand. The decision was finally left to Lord Hartington and Mr. Chamberlain, who, quite naturally from their perspective, persuaded him to withdraw his candidature.

This was a tremendous blow to his friends and supporters in Birmingham, who felt they had been sacrificed to Mr. Chamberlain's ambitions. Remembering the political campaign of 1885 and all the hard work she had participated in, which now seemed a waste of time and energy, Jennie felt extremely incensed. On the day Randolph returned from the House of Commons and informed her of the pressure brought upon him and how he had given in, she accused him of showing the white feather for the first time in his life. He said he had made up his mind to abide by the opinion of the Party leaders. "But not when those leaders are your political enemies," she exclaimed. Her arguments, however, proved useless. Even if he was right in his decision, he received no appreciation for it, and a great opportunity for him to demonstrate his strength and power was lost.

After Randolph left the Government, their relations with Lord and Lady Salisbury gradually became more and more strained. They maintained outward appearances, such as still being invited to political gatherings at Arlington Street, but all genuine cordiality ceased. Mutual friends tried to facilitate a reconciliation, and eventually they were invited to dinner. Much against his inclination, Randolph was persuaded to accept. The dinner, which was a large one, was a failure as far as the purpose of their attendance was concerned, because beyond a bare greeting, neither Lord nor Lady Salisbury exchanged a word with Randolph. He resented this greatly and regretted having gone.

Jennie did not believe this was intended as a slight, for shortly afterward she received a letter from Lady Salisbury:

Letter from Lady Salisbury Date: April 24, Hatfield House, Hatfield Sender: Lady Salisbury Summary: An invitation for Lord and Lady Randolph to dine and sleep at Hatfield House on Sunday the 22nd, and to help receive Irish delegates on Monday. Lady Salisbury noted that Sunday train schedules were poor, but offered to meet them at either the 1 p.m. or 6:30 p.m. train from Kings Cross. She expressed that they would be "much pleased" if the Churchills would come.

There was to be a garden party on the Monday featuring political speeches, with Mr. Chamberlain and Randolph advertised as the principal speakers. A large gathering of Unionists was expected, and presenting a united front was highly desired. At the last moment, however, Randolph flatly refused to go. No arguments moved him; he insisted that Jennie keep the engagement alone.

As she drove up to the historic Elizabethan house, an ideal residence for the Prime Minister of England, Jennie's feelings were anything but enviable. She would never forget the look of dismay and the ominous silence with which her feeble excuses for Randolph's absence were greeted. That night at dinner in the splendid banqueting hall, she sat next to Lord Salisbury. Courteous as ever, he talked pleasantly with her but made no allusion to the subject uppermost in her mind.

The next day was fine, and crowds of people brought by special trains from London filled the beautiful gardens, gathering around the various speakers. Calls for Randolph were heard everywhere; many had come expressly to hear him, and bitter was their disappointment when they realized he was not present. No adequate explanation could be given for his absence, and the "rift within the lute" was made more apparent than ever. Jennie confessed she was very glad when she could slip away, as she had rarely felt so uncomfortable or experienced anything more disagreeable.

London rejoiced in Jubilee functions that year and was very animated. A diversion was created by the arrival of the Shah of Persia, Nasr-ed-din, whose eccentricities kept society amused and interested. A true barbarian, he was induced with difficulty to conform to Western customs. Many stories circulated about him.

One night at a banquet at Buckingham Palace, he was asked to escort Queen Victoria. He refused, having decided to accompany a lady whose voluminous proportions had caught his attention. Considerable pressure had to be applied before he was persuaded to change his mind. With reluctance and a cross expression, he dragged the Queen along as he strode into the dining room.

Another evening at the opera, he sat with a glum countenance, evidently quite bored, to the despair of his entourage, until the orchestra during the intermission began tuning their instruments. At these discordant sounds, the Persian monarch brightened up and requested an encore, applauding vigorously.

At one of the Court balls which the Shah attended, Jennie and Randolph were commanded, much to their embarrassment and the annoyance of Lord Chamberlain (as it violated royal etiquette), to approach the dais and be presented to His Majesty. Sir Henry Wolff, who was then Ambassador to Teheran, had often spoken to the Shah about Randolph, which probably explained his desire to meet him.

Muttering something that sounded like "Lady Churchillias," he grasped Jennie's hand with tremendous force, then with a peremptory gesture, waved her away to make room for Randolph, who, like her, understood not a word spoken by the fierce old man. As she descended the steps of the dais feeling acutely self-conscious, the Prince of Wales, with his customary kindness, came forward and shook her hand, saying, "This presentation is contrary to all precedent, but the Shah insisted," adding with a laugh, "You had better go quickly as I see you are getting black looks from the Duchesses' bench."

Many foreigners came to London that season, attracted by the unusual sights and festivities. Jennie met many at Lady de Grey's, who had always been one of the most cosmopolitan hostesses. Her well-known artistic and musical appreciation made her house then, as now, the meeting place for all gifted artists and intellectual foreigners who visited London. She was indeed their Mecca, and many artists owed their success to her timely assistance and good advice. With her personal charm and beauty, thorough knowledge of the world, and mastery of the difficult art of entertaining, it was no surprise that invitations to her small but delightful gatherings were highly prized.

Considering the abnormal size of London society at that time, being a popular hostess was no easy feat. As for "salons", they were nearly extinct twenty years before. It was obvious that none could exist without selection, which naturally led to excluding those who lacked wit or talent. The passport to the famous Parisian salons of the eighteenth century, those of Mme. du Deffand, Mme.

Geoffrin, Mlle. de Lespinasse and others, consisted of intellectual ability; no other credential was necessary. If the rooms of these celebrated women were crowded, it was with the genius and talent of Europe, and newcomers were only admitted after thorough scrutiny; to be accepted was itself a guarantee of excellence and was as eagerly sought as Academic honors.

Conversation in these salons covered a vast range of subjects, from formulating new government policies to discussing the latest sonnet or the most recent scandal, and success depended on the decision of these arbiters of merit. How remote these brilliant discussions seemed from the gatherings of the "Mrs. Leo Hunters" of the day, where crowds jostled each other on the staircase, often not getting any further, and where card games replaced conversation. Fortunately, there were exceptions, and then as now, it was possible to find people who preferred more stimulating company.

At a particularly pleasant luncheon party given by Lady de Grey, Jennie once met M. Jules Claretie of the Comédie-Française, the gifted actress Mlle. Bartet, Lord Ribblesdale, and Mr. Oscar Wilde, than whom no more brilliant conversationalist existed, when he was in the mood. An argument arose between Wilde and Lord Ribblesdale about after-dinner speeches, with Wilde declaring there was no subject on which he could not speak at a moment's notice. Taking him at his word, Lord Ribblesdale, raising his glass, said "The Queen." "She is not a subject," answered Wilde, quick as lightning.

Once, having been accused of misquoting from "The Importance of Being Earnest," Jennie appealed to Mr. Wilde, telling him she had wagered on her accuracy and that if she was right, he would receive a beautiful pen-holder from her. This was his response:

Letter from Oscar Wilde Date: Undated, from The Cottage, Goring-on-Thames Sender: Oscar Wilde Summary: Wilde confirmed Jennie's quotation as correct: "The only difference between the saint and the sinner is that every saint has a past and that every sinner has a future." He playfully chided men for not listening to "brilliant women" and looking at "beautiful ones," noting that when a woman is both beautiful and brilliant (implying Lady Randolph was both), men should admit she is "verbally inspired." He mentioned needing the pen to begin writing his new comedy.

As Jennie had won her bet, the pen was duly sent to him.

Around this time, she made the acquaintance of two financiers who had come prominently to the forefront. One was Colonel North, the "Nitrate King," and the other Baron Hirsch, who eventually made many friends in England. Colonel North was what might be called a "rough diamond." He owned a large estate near London, furnished regardless of expense, where he kept open house and entertained in the most lavish manner the hordes of hangers-on and sycophants who, like all wealthy men of that type, invariably surrounded him.

When dining with the Churchills once, Jennie was greatly amused by his description of his picture gallery. That very day he had purchased a "grand picture" for which he had paid the large sum of £8000. When she asked who it was by, he couldn't remember, nor even the subject. "But," he added, "it is twelve feet by eight!" He was, however, a kind man and very charitable.

Baron Hirsch, whose generosity to his co-religionists would long preserve his name, was one of the few millionaires Jennie had met who thoroughly knew how to enjoy himself. He possessed a genuine "joie de vivre" and delighted in seeing people amusing themselves. His shooting parties in England and Austria were most pleasant. An accomplished sportsman himself, he had the knack of gathering congenial people and the best marksmen. On one occasion at his estate, St. Johann in Hungary, when the Prince of Wales, Lord de Grey, Mr. H. Stoner, and Lord Ashburton were present, the total bag of partridges for a single day reached 3000.

Life at St. Johann was simple and healthy. Shortly after breakfast, eight or ten victorias would appear at the door, the horses in colorful harnesses and the postilions in hussar-like blue jackets, Hessian boots, and shiny, high-crowned hats. They would then drive to the meeting point where an army of beaters, six hundred or more, waited. Arranged in a line, they started at the sound of a bugle and the cry of "Vorwärts" ("Forward" in German), advancing in formation, walking for miles over the sandy plains, dotted with tufts of stubble which provided cover for the enormous blue hares common in that region.

Occasionally they came across woods where roe deer, blackcock, and pheasants abounded. Luncheon was always served outdoors, regardless of weather. Some days were devoted solely to partridge shooting. Jennie remembered laughing heartily at one shooter in whose blind she was standing. As huge coveys flew over him seemingly from every direction, he kept calling out in his excitement, "For Heaven's sake, stop! Oh, do wait one moment!"

On her way back from one of these parties, Jennie stopped in Vienna for a few days. The late Colonel Kodolitch, who was well known in London, invited her to review his Hungarian regiment. He provided her with a charger, and on this prancing steed she galloped down the line with him, afterward watching the various maneuvers and the mass charging over hurdles and fences, a very pretty and unusual sight. As she was leaving, escorted to the station by Colonel Kodolitch and some of his officers, he said to her, "Please say 'Ich dankesehr' to the officers." She did so, much to their amusement, as she later discovered it was the customary remark of a general after inspecting a regiment. She was thoroughly teased about the joke played on her.

Once while passing through Paris, Jennie had a strange and unpleasant experience. She was planning to take the midday train and happened to be standing in one of the archways in the Gare du Nord, which presented its usual busy and animated scene, when she suddenly heard a shot, followed by two or three more in rapid succession. A man with his hand on his hip and an agonized expression on his face ran, or rather hobbled, past her from behind one of the pillars of the archway.

He was closely pursued by another man holding a revolver, which he fired again, this time so close to Jennie that she fled in terror, seeing as she ran the victim fall to the ground while his assailant continued shooting at him. A large crowd, which had scattered in every direction at the first shots, now rushed to the scene.

Meanwhile, fearing the gunman might be firing indiscriminately and that she could be the next target, Jennie ran down the platform as fast as her heavy fur coat and various encumbrances allowed. Unfortunately, she dropped her muff, a sable one adorned with tails, containing her purse and ticket. Before she could retrieve it, a man seized it and raced toward the swinging glass doors leading out of the station.

As she followed, calling out, she saw him disappear through one door and reappear through another like a clown in a pantomime. Calm and unconcerned, he was swinging a cane with no muff visible. While she stared in amazement, she noticed one of the tails of the muff protruding from his coat, which he was trying to keep closed. At that moment, the departure bell for her train began to ring.

There was no time for words; it was a case of "Do or die." She rushed at the thief, grabbed the visible tail of the muff, and jumped onto the train, which she barely caught, leaving the man standing with his mouth agape, still staring as the train pulled out of the station.

Regarding the unfortunate victim of the shooting, Jennie later learned that the assassin had shot him seven times before being overpowered, and then tried to beat him with the butt of the revolver, so determined was he to kill his target. A bystander was hit by a stray bullet in the leg, creating a scene of wild excitement and confusion. From newspaper accounts of the incident, it appeared both men were Americans, with the assailant having stalked his prey for over a year before catching him as he was leaving France for America. The trial revealed that love and money were the motives for the crime. With the usual delays of French justice, the case dragged on for so many months that Jennie lost track of it in the newspapers.

In 1891, Jennie paid her first, and to her, memorable, visit to Bayreuth. Wagner's music was not as popular then as it later became, at least in England. The "Ring des Nibelungen," which had been performed for years with great success in New York, had not yet been produced in London. The average opera-goer considered himself quite advanced if he could sit through "Lohengrin"; as for "Die Meistersinger" or "Tristan und Isolde," most people found them merely a series of discordant sounds.

The public's ignorance was vast. Jennie herself once heard a couple sitting behind her during a performance of "Tristan" sympathize with Isolde for her "long wait" for Tristan in the third act. Van Dyck, singing the role of Tristan, had been performing for more than half an hour, and while he might conceivably have been mistaken for a woman while lying covered with a rug, they should have been able to distinguish between a tenor and a soprano voice.

Even aspiring Wagnerians were sometimes led astray. A friend of Jennie's, who was not at all musical, was persuaded by an enthusiastic acquaintance to attend "Lohengrin." "But I don't think I care about music," the reluctant one had protested, "and I know I shall not understand anything." "Nonsense, of course you will," his friend had replied, and so they went. As the violins began the long sustained A note that opens the overture, the two looked uneasily at each other. "What is that noise?" asked the unmusical one. "I can't think," said the other as the note continued, "unless it's the gas escaping."

Jennie's sister Mrs. Leslie, who planned to accompany her to Bayreuth, had the excellent idea of arranging lectures on the "Ring" at her home to familiarize them with the work. A German musician, a well-known Wagner expert, was enlisted, bringing a female vocalist who sang the different leitmotifs. The lectures became quite popular and were attended by all their musical friends.

The professor's knowledge of English was, at that time, as limited as his accent was strong, adding an unintended hilarity to the proceedings. With young ladies present, he was often greatly challenged in explaining the story of the "Ring." "Siegfried" particularly troubled him. "Dee ladeesmus not mind dis bad bisness of Sigmund und Sieglinde; it is schrecklich, but it is only zee lofs of zee gods, vich do not count... Und here we have zee lofe motif illustrated by 'triolets' or triplets as you say in English." Amid suppressed laughter, the lecturer would play the motif and the lady would sing.

A few years saw Wagner's popularity in England increase tremendously. Soon no concert could be given without one or more Wagnerian selections, and at Covent Garden Opera House, the "Cycle," performed two or three times every season, attracted huge audiences. The public even enthusiastically supported a very creditable performance in English by an English company in the winter of 1908. It must be added that Dr. Richter conducted, which largely accounted for its excellence.

Contemporary music seemed imbued with a Wagnerian spirit, and orchestration had undoubtedly gained what had been lost in originality. This reminded Jennie of a music critic seated next to her during the Leeds Festival of 1907. An ardent admirer of Elgar, whose "Kingdom" was being performed, he noticed her making notes on her score and asked afterward what she had been recording. "Only my recollections of 'Tristan' and 'Parsifal' as they recur to my memory in this work," she mischievously answered. Looking at her with a somewhat dubious expression, "Oh, yes, quite so," he murmured; "I do not deny that Wagner came first, but," with a comprehensive gesture, "Elgar has gone on." Such enthusiasm was refreshing.

Speaking of the Leeds Festival, Jennie found it curious that these musical celebrations flourished better in England than anywhere else, considering that the English were not generally thought to be musical. Perhaps this was due to the excellence of the Leeds, Birmingham, and Huddersfield choirs which, according to Dr. Richter, were the finest in the world. Whatever the reason, only an English audience would endure a week of oratorios.

Even opera was taken much more seriously than in the past. With "all lights out" and "no talking," it had become a solemn affair, not to be treated lightly. In Paris, the opposite prevailed. People were invited to the opera to "see so-and-so dance," and it was generally treated as a venue for social interaction and conversation.

One night at a dinner in London, Jennie sat next to the Duc de G, , who had just arrived from Paris. "Délicieuse soirée à l'Opérahier," he remarked, "il y avait foule." ("Delightful evening at the Opera yesterday, it was crowded." - English Translation: "What was performed?" Jennie inquired. "Oh, je n'ensais rien, mais nous avonsreçuscinquante-quatre visites dans notre loge!" ("Oh, I have no idea, but we received fifty-four visitors in our box!" - English Translation). This was one approach to opera, but the person who insisted on explaining everything or humming the melodies being sung was equally annoying.

A story was told of the late Lord L, , a regular opera-goer who supposedly had this bad habit. One night in the omnibus box, he began whistling and humming as usual. "What a bore that Jean de Reszke is!" remarked a wit who was present. "Why?" asked Lord L, in astonishment. "Because the fellow is preventing me from hearing you properly."

But this digression had taken Jennie far from Bayreuth. Her party consisted of Lady de Grey, her sister Mrs. Leslie, Mr. Evan Charteris, and one or two others. Bayreuth was not as luxurious then as it later became. It was frequented only by true music lovers who were prepared, for art's sake, to endure as much discomfort as German notions of hospitality could inflict. Everyone was billeted with different hosts, who in some cases could accommodate only one lodger. Jennie and her sister were fortunate enough to secure rooms at a banker's home, where they lived quite comfortably compared to others.

They devoted themselves entirely to the music, taking it very seriously and thinking only of what they were about to hear or had just experienced. Jennie's first impression of "Parsifal" was, as the Germans would say, "colossal." The pilgrimage to Bayreuth, the "low living and high thinking," combined with the musical atmosphere they were immersed in, undoubtedly contributed to the rapture they felt, but its existence was undeniable.

Their small group had arranged to meet between acts to exchange opinions, but so powerful were their emotions that they all fled in different directions, avoiding one another until the performance concluded and they could be more composed. The audience was so serious that they weren't even disturbed when Parsifal's wig fell off during the Flower Maidens' scene in the third act. Not a single laugh was heard.

They spent a delightful week, although Jennie personally suffered terribly with toothache until she found an unexpected Good Samaritan in the lady seated behind her, who produced cocaine. This lady was none other than Mrs. Sam Lewis, wife of the well-known money-lender, an excellent musician who was a godsend to countless artists. At her death she left many legacies to musicians, besides £10,000 annually to a Consumptive Hospital, from the immense fortune inherited from her husband. Mr. Lewis, unlike his wife, was not artistic. It was said of him that, having once spent a fortnight in Rome, when asked how he liked it, his laconic answer was, "You can 'ave Rome."

They varied their activities with excursions on days when there were no performances, and by attending Frau Cosima Wagner's receptions, which were charming and informal.

Later, in Paris and London, Jennie had occasion to meet Cosima's son, Siegfried Wagner. At a dinner given in his honor, the question arose as to which composers one would choose if limited to only two. Of the twelve people at the table, Jennie was the only one who did not name Wagner. Partly out of contrariness and partly because she truly believed it, she mentioned Bach and Beethoven. "My father would also have chosen them," said Siegfried, to the embarrassment of the flatterers!

Jennie met him once or twice afterward in Paris at the home of Countess Wolkenstein, the Austrian Ambassadress at that time.

This distinguished lady, who as Countess Stieglitz had maintained a salon in Berlin, was reportedly the only woman whose influence Bismarck feared. A lifelong friend and patron of Wagner, she had supported him during his difficult periods and later shared in his triumphs. Mme. Wolkenstein never missed her annual visit to Bayreuth, where she usually stayed with Mme. Wagner.

When in Paris, Jennie and the Countess often went sightseeing together, accompanied by Widor, the celebrated organist of St. Sulpice. A wonderful pianist herself, Mme. de Wolkenstein was rather hypercritical and positively dreaded hearing mediocre music. Once when Jennie invited her to dinner to meet a young and talented amateur who was also very amusing, the Countess hesitantly asked, "Est-cequ'il pratique?" ("Does he practice?" - English Translation). After being assured he would not play, she accepted. In the end, however, he did perform, much to Jennie's delight and the Countess's appreciation.

Jennie was once invited to meet the Abbé Liszt at the Russian Embassy in London when M. de Staal was Ambassador. She sat next to the great man, whose strong and distinctive face, so often captured in paintings and sculptures, seemed strangely familiar. He was so visually impaired that he ate his asparagus by the wrong end until she pointed out his error. "Ah!" he exclaimed, "merci bien, il me semblait tout de même que celan'était pas très bon!" ("Thank you very much, I did think it didn't taste very good!" - English Translation). After luncheon, despite his arthritic fingers, he was persuaded to play. "Hélas," he said, "le moindre de mesélèvesjouentmieux que moimaintenant." ("Alas, the least of my students plays better than I do now." - English Translation). And it was sadly true. Jennie never heard him at his best.

She well remembered Rubinstein with his long hair flying about, perspiration streaming down his face as his large hands thundered up and down the piano. Full of mannerisms, to which many artists become addicted, when he reached the culminating fortissimo, wild with excitement, he would strike as many notes as possible with his palms or forearms, until he seemed to reach the very limits of the instrument, making the strings snap and the wood resonate. When Jennie was in Russia, she was told that the headmistress of a well-known girls' school in St. Petersburg once asked him how many hours a day her pupils should practice the piano. "None," Rubinstein replied.

Many musicians had honored Jennie by performing at her home, and apart from the pleasure they brought her, she always felt great sympathy for them in their demanding and precarious careers. "So many are called and so few chosen," and their success rested on such fragile foundations! A cold, an illness, and their voice and fortune might vanish; and consider the grinding slavery that instrumental mastery required! Planté the pianist, that master of technique, told her that if for some reason he was unable to practice for three months, he would never have the courage to resume. Then there were the empty concert halls and negative reviews during the struggling early days that tested the resolve of even the strongest.

When Paderewski first came to London, he brought Jennie a letter from a mutual friend. She invited a select few whom she knew could appreciate and evaluate him. Their admiration and enthusiasm were, predictably, boundless. A few days later, he gave his first concert in St. James's Hall. The venue was only half full, and behind Jennie sat two music critics taking notes for their papers. "There's not much in this fellow," said one. "He would be all right," said the other, "if he would leave Chopin alone, which he plays against all traditions."

Stephen Heller, one of Chopin's friends and Jennie's first music teacher, had told her that the great composer never played his works twice the same way, so much for the musical critics! The following year, Paderewski, having achieved enormous success in Paris and elsewhere, returned to London, where he received an ovation from an excited and enthusiastic audience who stormed the platform to kiss his hands!

Personally, Jennie had never been able to overcome the nervousness she felt when playing before an audience, whether in ensemble pieces or solo. What musician, good, bad, or indifferent, had not at some point felt their confidence failing as they approached a difficult passage? Merely thinking about it was fatal!

Once, at a charity concert, she was performing a classical piece, the first movement of which contained a few challenging measures. The first time through the da capo, she managed well, but to transition to the next movement, it had to be repeated with variations in another key. To her dismay, she found herself beginning the same passage, which of course led her back to repeating the first movement. Again, as she approached the difficult section, she faltered and made the same mistake. Three times she repeated that movement until the audience was becoming quite familiar with the tune. She felt trapped in a horrible nightmare and was about to jump up from the piano and flee the stage when, mercifully, the fourth time she mechanically played the correct bars and eventually brought the piece to its conclusion. Hans von Bülow reportedly did the same thing once with a Beethoven sonata until, in desperation, he had to send for the sheet music.

On another occasion, Jennie was brought to confusion, but this time through no fault of her own. It was at a concert at the Mansion House before a large audience. She and Mademoiselle , were to play a Chopin Polonaise on two pianos. As their turn came, Mademoiselle, a professional with considerable experience and skill, said hurriedly to her, "At the eleventh bar on the sixth page, when I signal you, stop, as I intend to insert a little cadenza of my own." Before Jennie could protest or point out that this would be an unnecessary addition to one of Chopin's masterpieces, the lady had seated herself at the piano, forcing Jennie to do likewise.

When they reached the eleventh bar of the sixth page, she nodded vigorously to Jennie, then proceeded to dazzle the audience with arpeggios, runs, and trills, until Jennie began to wonder if she would ever find the right moment to rejoin. She eventually did, only to hear people in the front row comment as she left, "Poor Lady Randolph, what a pity she lost her place for so long!"

To read music well and to accompany were all that should be required of amateurs. In an age of virtuosos and mechanical instruments, even the poorest judge was becoming hypercritical. There was no doubt that the days had passed when people would patiently listen after dinner to the "Moonlight Sonata" or the "Prièred'une Vierge" performed by the daughter of the house. Previously in England, every girl was taught to sing whether she had a voice or not, but the intelligent mother of Jennie's time realized that her daughters were better employed listening to good music than performing badly.

Jennie thought it fitting to end this chapter, which had somehow evolved into one about music, by mentioning the late Sir Arthur Sullivan, one of the kindest and gentlest of men and a great friend of hers. She had the good fortune to attend most of the "first nights" of his productions, and those who weren't present couldn't imagine the boundless enthusiasm with which they were received, or the excitement with which the public anticipated each new work. It was truly a national event. Gilbert's delicate and subtle humor combined with Sullivan's melodies and exquisite orchestration created such a perfect partnership that Jennie couldn't imagine time would ever diminish their appeal.

Churchill's Mum

When the South African War broke out, Sullivan composed the music for Rudyard Kipling's "The Absent-Minded Beggar." Sales of this song raised £75,000 for the war fund. Happening to visit Sir Arthur one day just after he had completed it, Jennie asked him to play it, which he did. She confessed she didn't care for it. "Well, what is your opinion?" he asked. She answered cautiously, "I'm afraid I think the words are rather vulgar: 'Cook's son, duke's son, son of a belted earl!'"

"And so is the music," Sir Arthur replied.

Jennie's World Tour

Chartwell, 1964

Churchill struggled to his feet again, moving slowly to examine a world map hanging on his studio wall. His finger traced a route across continents with trembling precision. "1894," he said simply. "While I was a young subaltern learning the basics of military life, my mother embarked on the adventure that would define her later years." He turned to face Sophia, leaning heavily on his walking stick. "Around the world in an era when such journeys were still genuinely perilous."

"What drove her to undertake such a trip?"

"Restlessness, I suppose. Curiosity. The American wanderlust that never quite left her system." Churchill's voice carried a note of admiration. "But also, I think, a recognition that my father's health was failing and she needed to see the world while she still could, with him."

Sophia studied the map, noting the penciled route marks. "It must have been quite an undertaking."

"Eight months, Miss Carter. Eight months of steamships and trains, hotels and private cars, meeting maharajas and mining magnates, Japanese nobility and American industrialists." Churchill returned slowly to his chair. "She came back with a global perspective that few British politicians of her generation possessed. That worldview, the understanding that Britain was part of a larger, interconnected world, shaped how she raised me to think about empire and international relations."

EUSTON STATION, 1894

On the morning of June 27, 1894, Jennie embarked on a tour around the world with her husband, Lord Randolph Churchill. They departed from Euston Station amid a gathering of friends and family, including Lord and Lady Londonderry, Lady Jeune, Lord Rosebery, and Mr. Goschen. Randolph was particularly touched that his old friend Lord Rosebery had come to see them off, a gesture he mentioned frequently afterward.

At Liverpool, Mr. Ismay met them aboard the Majestic, reminding Jennie of the Jubilee trip on the Teutonic, which already seemed like the distant past. The voyage across the Atlantic was uneventful, with rough seas and uninteresting passengers. Jennie remembered only the obligatory concert, in which she was pressed to perform, and the excitement one night when they nearly ran down another vessel.

They stayed just two days in New York, as the thermometer registered 81 degrees in the shade. Mr. Chauncey Depew, one of the few people they met, kindly placed his private car at their disposal for their journey to Bar Harbor. Jennie asked him if he had indeed telegraphed to Lord Rosebery when "Ladas" won the Derby, "Nothing left but Heaven," and he confirmed he had.

This was Jennie's first experience with a private rail car, which proved as well-appointed as a small yacht and made for a most enjoyable mode of traveling. The colored cook prepared an excellent dinner, and they slept as comfortably as they might have in their own beds.

After the dust and heat of New York, Bar Harbor seemed a haven of rest with its fresh sea breezes, lovely drives, and mountain walks. Jennie gathered that life there was very much like Newport, consisting of perpetual dressing, dinners, dances, and the dreaded ritual of leaving calling cards. Nevertheless, it was pleasant, and they indulged in all the amusements of the place.

They were invited to a dance at the Kebo Valley Club, a charming house perfectly suited to the countryside. Jennie took real joy in dancing the "Boston," which she felt only Americans knew properly. There they met many pretty girls whom Jennie often saw driving or playing lawn tennis, invariably without hats, which she was told was to bleach their hair. These girls were forerunners of what would later be called the "hatless brigade."

Jennie made the acquaintance of some delightful women with whom she found herself in perfect sympathy, the kind that can only exist among compatriots. Mr. George Vanderbilt, a very cultivated young man who was then unmarried, had a steam yacht in which he took them to see East Harbor, where they enjoyed a fine view. Close to his house, which faced the sea, was an open-air swimming bath through which salt water constantly flowed. Here Vanderbilt and his friends of both sexes swam and dived without shyness, though Jennie noted, without vanity either, as women did not look their best under such circumstances. While in the water, there was no hilarity or banter; everything was conducted with the greatest decorum, almost ceremony, which added to the ludicrous effect for spectators.

One night Jennie dined with Mrs. Van Rensselaer Jones to meet Marion Crawford, who was staying with her. Jennie found Mr. Crawford to be excellent company, tall, dark, with piercing blue eyes, a decisive chin, and a kind mouth adorned with a small mustache. She considered him the very best type of good-looking American. He had a pleasant voice, modulated by his constant use of Italian, and conversed agreeably on all subjects. At that time, he took a very gloomy view of America's political outlook, declaring that the problem of socialism would be solved there. When someone accused him of being idle and loving the "dolce far niente" (sweet doing nothing), his eyes sparkled with indignation as he exclaimed, "Idle! For sixteen years I have worked and made a living by my pen, and have produced twenty-five novels!"

At the same dinner, Jennie met for the first time Mr. Courtland Palmer, a young amateur pianist inspired with the real "feu sacré" (sacred fire), who could hold his own with professionals. During her stay at Bar Harbor, they met frequently and played the piano together.

One of their many expeditions was a sail in the Mayflower, the yacht that had won the International Yacht Race against the Galatea. There was a Bishop on board described to Jennie as a "bully Bishop," but they thought his appearance somewhat disreputable and did not cultivate his acquaintance. Mr. C, , commonly called the "Greek god", a nickname which Jennie thought suited him admirably, was also there. When she told Randolph his nickname, he declared he "could have nothing to do with a Greek god." But he did, and liked him.

Before leaving Bar Harbor, the Nourmahal, a large steam yacht belonging to the John Jacob Astors, came into the harbor. Mrs. Astor's beauty and grace, not to mention the charming simplicity of her nature, commanded admiration; but Jennie observed that had she been the Empress of Russia, her arrival could not have caused more commotion.

It was with regret that they left Bar Harbor and its bright, hospitable inhabitants to embark on their Canadian journey. With some difficulty they procured a private car from the Pullman Company, as the president of the Canadian Pacific Railway, despite their letters to him, proved unhelpful. The officials were persuaded to place them at the end of the train so they could use the observation room of their car, the "Iolanthe," which proved a great boon. They sat there all day, or on the platform, regardless of dust and cinders.

The scenery at first was disappointing, an endless straight track bordered on either side by a small pink flower that never left them until they reached Vancouver. The station names seemed to represent all the nations of the world: Portage la Prairie, Winnipeg, MacGregor, Medicine Hat, and so on. At Medicine Hat, they stopped for an hour and visited the hospital, where the superintendent proudly showed them the signatures of the Duke and Duchess of Connaught in the visitors' book.

On average, their train stopped every half hour, with much whistling, ringing of bells, and exchange of greetings between the engine driver and the inhabitants. Every log cabin was a station, and every platform served as the social club for these isolated people, whose only excitement was the daily arrival of the train.

After Winnipeg came two days of prairies which Jennie would have liked to ride across. Occasionally in the distance, she caught sight of a ranch surrounded by trees, looking like an oasis in the desert. Before reaching the Rockies, they spotted some prairie dogs, strange little animals like hairless squirrels with rat tails. Jennie reflected that life on one of these prairies, although probably monotonous, must have the compensations that come with peace and the close study of nature.

At Banff, they had their car put on a siding and spent two days there, which well repaid them. For the first time, they saw the Rockies in all their grandeur. Unfortunately, a prairie fire they had passed some thirty or forty miles from Banff had filled the air with smoke, making the mountains appear misty. Still, they could see enough to appreciate the magnificence of the scenery.

The heat and mosquitoes ("skeeters") were rather a drawback to expeditions, but they could not resist the "call of the wild" and drove about all day in uncomfortable buckboards and "cutunders." On one drive, Jennie insisted on getting down to touch some "Hoodoos" for luck. These curious natural monuments, half earth and half stone, were regarded with great superstition and awe by the Indians, "hoodoo" being the Indian word for "spook." They were indeed uncanny objects. One over seventy feet high looked exactly like a half-formed figure of a man seated on a pedestal.

Their driver was a very intelligent, well-educated young man. Jennie was amused when he told her that the last Englishman he had driven thought "it was a mistake to plant the trees so close together"!

The Vermilion Lakes (so called because the reeds that filled them turned bright red in autumn) enchanted them with their marvelous beauty. They were rowed the entire length of the two lakes, eight miles. The enormous snow-clad mountains created a vivid contrast to the fresh green vegetation around them, brilliant with mauve, pink, and yellow flowers, while the blue water was so clear they could see the bottom of the lake, over which two eagles circled.

On the journey to Vancouver, they couldn't tear themselves away from the observation room and platform, the scenery was so glorious. Among those stupendous heights, Jennie expected to see the Valkyries rushing from peak to peak and Wotan on the war path. Again, however, they lost much of the view due to smoke that sometimes hung for miles between them and everything else. Great forest fires seemed to be raging everywhere, and at times they traveled through burning trees on either side. It was a melancholy sight to see miles of black stumps and leafless skeletons, their twisted and tortured branches standing out against the background of snow, while bright green ferns and variegated flowers made a carpet at their feet. Jennie thought the destruction rather wanton, as in some places they saw trees burning close to stations on the railway track, but no one attempted to extinguish the fires.

Twenty-four hours of Vancouver was enough for them, and they left for Victoria in a small steamer filled with a motley crowd. The weather was so cold they could only view the scenery through their cabin windows. They found Victoria far more attractive than Vancouver, even though it was possibly being "left behind," as the rival city asserted.

Jennie lunched one day with the Bishop of Columbia and suddenly realized she was in a British dependency when a group of healthy-looking girls arrived from playing in a lawn tennis tournament, escorted by a couple of curates. While there, they received a visit from Colonel Baker, a brother of Valentine Baker of Egyptian fame. Being in the British Columbian government, he was full of information. Jennie was somewhat startled when he said, "Now that I am in the Cabinet." Her ignorance was so great that she learned for the first time that British Columbia had its own constitution and Parliament, Home Rule with a vengeance! Colonel Baker enlightened her, explaining that their Parliament lasted for four years, and their parties were not divided into Liberals and Conservatives but were called the "Ins" and the "Outs." Their policy was merely that of a Local Government Board or County Council, with interest in foreign questions only as they might affect them. The "Ins" wanted to stay in, and the "Outs" strived to get in, which struck Jennie as describing the feelings of politicians of all countries and parties.

At Victoria, Jennie had her first experience with a male Chinese housemaid whom she mistook (despite his trousers) for a comfortable old woman. She found an excellent Steinway piano in the hotel and played to her heart's content, to the evident delight of some old ladies who gathered to hear her. On one occasion, however, she scattered them like frightened wood pigeons when, in response to an inquiry about what "sweetly pretty" tune she was playing, she answered "Götterdämmerung," emphasizing the third syllable. With one look of pained surprise, they gathered up their skirts and fled.

H.M.S. Royal Arthur, with Admiral Stephenson aboard, was anchored off Esquimault (pronounced "Squimalt" by the locals). They lunched with him one day and saw the sights. It was very pleasant to meet an old friend again, and he took them back to Victoria on his barge. On the way, they came across many canoes filled with Indian families, the old squaws paddling vigorously. A large log with two men astride it and a dog sitting solemnly between them formed a strange-looking craft. They paddled with great skill, as the slightest movement would have upset them, a tightrope was security compared to it. From a distance, they looked as if they were sitting in the water.

Continuing their journey, they embarked for San Francisco on a steamer rejoicing in the name Walla Walla. After three days of cold, comfortless sea travel, about which Jennie drew a veil, they arrived in San Francisco to find the weather windy and sunless. Walking was unpleasant due to the innumerable electric tramways that seemed to approach from every direction.

They visited Chinatown with a detective. The joss houses, opium dens, and gambling establishments were very stuffy and astonishingly small. The opium smokers lay on bare boards in such uncomfortable positions that Jennie wondered how they could find enjoyment in the pernicious practice. She was looking with amazement at a fat old Chinaman who had contorted himself into a true lover's knot, which ought to have caused agonizing cramps to anyone human, when he half-opened his eyes and, with an expression of beatitude, said, "It makee me feel good." The combined smell of the Chinaman and the opium, half sour, half sweet, was revolting. Jennie was eager to see the theaters, but their guide thought it might be unwise.

Jennie received many beautifully arranged flower baskets, white, pink, and mauve sweet peas, roses of all kinds with long stems, and magnolia blossoms in profusion. She noted, however, that although California flowers were lovely, they had little fragrance, and the fruit, while gorgeous, lacked taste, like a beautiful woman devoid of brains.

At a dinner at the University Club (which had a room prettily paneled in oak where ladies could dine), Jennie was introduced to an "oyster cocktail," which she took to kindly, and to a "fancy roast," also made with oysters.

Despairing of seeing the sun, they departed for Monterey. They had heard much of its beauty and were not disappointed; indeed, the gardens surpassed all Jennie had imagined. She never tired of walking about and admiring the splendid trees, shrubs, and plants of all kinds, while the flowers grew in a profusion she had never seen equaled anywhere. The Arizona Garden with its tropical plants was new to her.

They took what was known as the "Seventeen-mile Drive" along the coast. The charm of this road was in its variety. As they drove through Monterey, which resembled a small Spanish town and which California regarded as extremely ancient, being over one hundred years old, their driver pointed out several buildings, gravely noting they dated from 1830 or 1850! After several miles of forest, the ocean suddenly came into view, and they saw many seals disporting themselves on the rocks, with an exciting fight taking place between two of them. They watched for a long while, sometimes the seals would tumble off into the water but quickly scrambled back up to have a few more rounds. Jennie proposed waiting to see the outcome, but their driver informed them the fight might continue for a couple of hours.

On their way back, they passed through the celebrated Cypress Grove, a very entrancing spot, full of mystery and charm. These ancient trees, so old that generations had lost count of them, twisted their gnarled trunks away from the sea, their dark green heads embellished by long pale strands of the feathery moss that eventually strangled them.

The Del Monte Hotel at Monterey was alive with the most energetic young people Jennie had ever seen. They swam in the early morning, rode, drove, played lawn tennis, and danced all night. While observing a ball one evening, Jennie happened to relate to a gentleman whose acquaintance she had just made an anecdote about a Frenchman with whom she had once danced. "C'est terrible," he had said, as, panting and puffing, he tried to catch his breath. "Well, why do you dance if you hate it?" she had inquired. "C'est pour l'hygiène, Mon médecin me le recommande." (English Translation: "It's for health reasons, My doctor recommends it.") Jennie was rather startled to see her story appear twenty-four hours later in a newspaper, wonderfully embellished under the heading "Lady Randolph Tells Good Stories in the Porch of Del Monte!"

While in America, they managed to evade reporters fairly successfully. At San Francisco, however, an enterprising journalist, having been denied an interview with Randolph, published an imaginary one that was so comical Jennie couldn't be angry. A female reporter, having pursued Jennie without success, invaded her bedroom one morning as she was emerging from her bath. When Jennie gently but firmly pushed her out, the woman burst into tears. Her weeping softened Jennie, and she saw her later.

Poor thing! Jennie suspected that, if the truth were known, the reporter hated the interview as much as she did.

Leaving San Francisco on the Umatilla, they repeated their somewhat uncomfortable journey, returning to Victoria on their way to the Far East.

The Empress of Japan, in which they sailed for Yokohama, proved to be an ocean palace, clean and comfortable. To Jennie's delight, the saloons were decorated with quantities of Japanese plants and shrubs. The Chinese waiters, dressed in butcher-blue or white, looked picturesque. Among the passengers were Baron Speck von Sternburg, later German Ambassador at Washington, and Mr. Villiers, the war correspondent of "The Graphic."

They were excited at the prospect of finding Japan in a martial state, as the Chinese-Japanese War was then at its height. Not knowing Japan, they anticipated stirring scenes. Great were to be the doings of Mr. Villiers, who expected to go directly to the front.

Upon arrival, they discovered that Yokohama harbor was laid with torpedoes and submarines, requiring the captain to obtain a government boat to pilot them in. Jennie was glad to leave the ship, as the Pacific had been anything but peaceful, rough seas, gray and leaden skies, constant rolling and pitching, and the monotony had begun to weary them.

Anchoring in the harbor, they immediately found themselves surrounded by vessels of all sizes and shapes, from steam launches to sampans, with Japanese junks hovering on the outskirts. Jennie watched the motley crew, amused by their various costumes, or lack thereof. On a government launch were some diminutive military men, "dorés sur toutes les coutures" (gilded on all the seams), coming to greet the Japanese officers aboard their ship. Much bowing and scraping ensued.

They were surrounded by sampans trying to avoid collision, manned by coolies dressed only in white cotton Eton jackets and bright blue headbands, a stark contrast to the gorgeous uniforms. They were not sorry to disembark and proceed to their hotel.

There they found many war correspondents who looked dejected, as they were not permitted to join the army. Mr. Villiers eventually managed to get to the front, but with such restrictions that Jennie imagined his reports could have been of little value, as he was denied use of the telegraph, and everything he wrote had to be submitted to the minister of war for supervision.

A great Japanese victory had occurred the day before, making the war even more popular, although they saw few signs of celebration. Jennie gathered from different people she met that the government was forcing the situation to create a diversion from internal troubles. She was told that the English in Japan rather sympathized with the Chinese, whereas later, in China, they found the opposite to be true. Although the Chinese had the men and the money, they hated fighting, as proven by the campaign's outcome. Jennie always felt that the Japanese were very badly treated by Europe in general and England in particular in not being allowed to reap the fruits of their victory. Even in the recent Russian war, though victorious, they were not given a free hand.

After the cold of the Pacific, Yokohama's damp heat was very trying, and they stayed only a few days before going to Myanoshita in the hills.

Before leaving Yokohama, Jennie went to the theater, which was unlike anything she had ever seen. They sat on the floor of their so-called box and had tea like the crowd, and what a crowd! It was an endless source of interest and amusement to watch them: whole families, mothers-in-law and daughters-in-law, children of all ages, and parents of different generations, fathers, sons, and grandsons. All had brought their dinners. Little trays appeared with tiny boxes of rice, bowls of strange foodstuffs, pink, white, and green, seaweed on rice cakes, raw fish, and nameless yellow condiments, accompanied by tea in microscopic cups, naturally without milk or sugar. The Japanese couldn't understand Europeans putting milk in their tea, as they found it had a strong smell.

Children were dressed and undressed during the intermissions, and people smoked, slept, ate, talked, and fanned themselves. It was certainly a contrast to see a little "musme" such as Pierre Loti described, daintily dressed in the gayest of kimonos and smartest of obis, sitting between a coolie wearing nothing but a loose cotton jacket and an old hag nursing a baby. Although most of the men wore very little, and the thermometer read 85 degrees, the atmosphere wasn't impossible, as Jennie was sure would have been the case in a European theater under similar circumstances.

The plays usually comprised fourteen or fifteen acts and lasted all day, sometimes two. This particular one, lacking an actress like Sadi Yacco to interpret it, was quite unintelligible to Jennie, but she admired the grace of the actresses, their easy movements when dancing, and how they managed their tight clothes. Imagine her surprise when she later discovered they were all men! Until recently, men and women did not act together in Japan; theatrical companies consisted of either one sex or the other. But change had come, and there were now mixed companies.

One afternoon Jennie visited Bohmer's nursery gardens, where she saw many of the stunted shrubs and trees so cherished by the Japanese, with which they decorated their miniature gardens. She purchased several, including a century-old maple about ten or twelve inches high, with tiny leaves that were bright red at that moment. Upon returning to England, she gave this little tree to the Princess of Wales, who was delighted with it; for all Jennie knew, it might still have been alive.

The entire place was perfumed by gold and white "moxa," and Jennie longed to take some away, along with the huge gardenia and daphne plants, which were as large as ordinary lilac bushes. Baron Sternburg, who accompanied her, suggested they walk back from the gardens, but they soon lost their way. Hot and dusty, they took refuge in an inviting tea house while sending for a jinrikisha.

The establishment was evidently not frequented by Europeans, as the little maids who waited on them hovered around Jennie with the greatest curiosity. Before she could stop them, one had put on her gloves, another had seized her hat and placed it on her own greasy black locks, and a third was strutting about with her parasol. Eventually, they became quite obstreperous, and only when her companion promised them sake did they leave the visitors in peace.

Leaving Yokohama, they said goodbye to their steamer friends and traveled by train to Myanoshita.

At the station was a great crowd: naked coolies; merchants in flowing kimonos carrying Mrs. Gamp umbrellas and topped with monstrous pot hats; artisans in blue cotton tunics with their trade's description and badge printed on their backs in white or enclosed in a black circle on a red ground; and masses of women. The married ones were easily recognizable by their shaved eyebrows and blackened teeth, a hideous custom they practiced to demonstrate fidelity to their husbands, though Jennie thought it might conceivably produce the opposite effect on the husbands themselves.

Among them were numerous girls, their shiny hair stiffened with camellia oil and adorned with combs, tiny chrysanthemums, and coral beads, their painted faces breaking into smiles when looked at. The motley crowd, which grew at every station, walked, stumped, and toddled into the train, which consisted of a few diminutive carriages more like a glorified toy than anything else. Most people wore clogs, making a loud and curious noise.

After two hours of slow winding between soft green hills covered with feathery vegetation, they arrived at Kodga, where they boarded a tramway (made in Birmingham) and rattled for an hour through one long street comprising endless villages. Due to the hot weather, the inhabitants, including babies, were carrying on their various activities in front of their open houses, minus their clothes. All seemed hardworking and good-humored.

The Japanese are proverbially fond of children, who, to prevent them from getting lost, each wore a little metal identification tag with name and address attached. Attractive as they undoubtedly were, Jennie noted it was a mistake to say they never cried, just as it was untrue that Japan was free of unpleasant odors. Defective drainage and stale fish did not remind one of the "perfumes of Araby."

They stopped occasionally to change the wretched horses. Japanese horses had no quarters and were sorry-looking quadrupeds; Chinese horses, on the other hand, had no shoulders. At Yumoto, they all transferred to jinrikishas, each with two men, one to pull and the other to push, and proceeded at a trot up the stoniest road Jennie had ever traveled.

Once they stopped at a tea house, where the landlady, with much in-drawing of breath (to show her civility by not breathing in visitors' faces) and with much bowing and rubbing of knees, served Japanese tea in the usual handleless cups, accompanied by the pink-and-white cakes seen everywhere, impossible, dry, musty horrors. Their jinrikisha men, perspiration pouring from their brown bodies, removed their white jackets (their only garment) and washed themselves at the nearby pump. The pump was pretty and picturesque, consisting of two bamboos, one brown, the other dark green; one held a large bunch of wild flowers, while from the other poured a clear mountain stream into a delightful big Japanese tub. The face of Jennie's maid (a prim, highly respectable person) was a study as the men resumed their mushroom hats and girded up their loins afresh. Having treated them to sake at the tea house, Jennie and her party were trotted briskly up to the Fujiyya Hotel.

The place looked pretty and quaint, and the calm and peace were welcome, but it was disappointing to find the hotel full of Europeans, mostly pale, jaded people from Hong Kong, Shanghai, and even Singapore, come to recover in Myanoshita's fresh air, 3,000 feet above sea level.

They spent a pleasant fortnight there. Jennie never tired of the mountains, with their changing shadows, deep gorges, rushing streams and cascades, and occasional glimpses of the distant sea. The vegetation was a great source of interest and pleasure, all so new and attractive. On their journey up, Jennie had counted fifty-five different kinds of agricultural products and shrubs. The numerous villages and houses dotted about afforded a good view of Japanese peasant life. All seemed hardworking, contented, and good-humored.

One day they went to Lake Hakone, carried in straw chairs supported by bamboo poles borne by four men, not a very comfortable mode of transport. The carriers had a remarkable way of changing positions with one another to relieve the weight on their shoulders without causing the slightest disturbance to their passengers.

At a bend in the mountain path, they suddenly came upon a large Buddha carved into the rock face. Countless prayers in the form of paper slips on sticks were planted before him. His legs were crossed, and the soles of his feet turned upward to show he never sullied them with earthly contact. The look of eternal peace characterizing all Buddha effigies was due, Jennie thought, to the closed eyes being set far apart, with the serene, slightly smiling mouth adding to the unfathomable expression.

Japanese photographers, being excellent artists, always managed to find the most picturesque viewpoints. If one didn't follow in their footsteps when visiting a place, one might be disappointed and think they must have idealized it. Such were Jennie's feelings about Lake Hakone, although she appreciated its beauty. They crossed the lake in two sampans, gazing skyward in search of Japan's focal point, Fuji-yama, the great, the sacred. But as usual, she had veiled herself in mist, and not having yet seen her, Jennie had to be content with her image on the new kimono she found upon returning to the hotel.

They walked back part of the way over very rough ground steaming with sulfurous springs.

Mr. Le Poer Trench, the English Minister, had arrived, and they were delighted to make his acquaintance, as well as that of Professor Basil Hall Chamberlain, whose book "Things Japanese," over which Jennie had been enthusiastically poring, was a standard work for all English speakers. They brought news of the great battle of Pyong-yang, where the Japanese claimed to have killed 20,000 Chinese, and of a naval engagement where six Chinese and three Japanese ships had been sunk or blown up.

Mr. Trench, who was unmarried, had not been in Japan very long at that time. His health was not the best, as the climate of Mexico, his previous diplomatic post, had not agreed with him. A thin, pleasant man of about forty-five, Jennie found him a great addition to their circle. They took long walks together, climbing the most precipitous hills.

The three weeks of absolute rest at Myanoshita did Randolph much good. Everything was so reposeful, from the quiet Japanese landscape with its soft grays and greens to the bevy of little "musmes" who waited upon them, moving silently and swiftly about in their stocking feet, always smiling and gentle.

Intending to go to Tokyo, they retraced their steps to Yokohama, where they stayed two nights. There they found considerable excitement in the harbor over the arrival of four large German ironclads on their way to Korea to "watch" the war's progress. Jennie couldn't help thinking it a pity that the British seemed so apathetic and unrepresented. The Japanese were becoming very proud, and the English government had rather yielded to them over the last commercial treaty, or so thought the English residents and merchants.

The war was the only topic in town. Jennie went to a popular theater to see a play depicting the battle of Pyong-yang. It was densely crowded, and with difficulty they secured places in the gallery. In the last act, the Chinese troops, represented by three men, were repeatedly killed by twenty Japanese soldiers who rushed about constantly blowing bugles, brandishing swords, firing rifles, and thoroughly enjoying themselves. In the center of the revolving stage stood a cardboard town eventually illuminated with red lights. The climax came when a small, yellow general in a smart European uniform emerged from the smoke and, in a high-pitched voice, addressed a speech to his army of twenty, all present and accounted for. This sent the audience into such a frenzy of excitement that Jennie and her party fled. Wata, her jinrikisha man, asked her if it wasn't a "good big play."

Although Tokyo was only eighteen miles away, it took nearly two hours to reach. They met a train full of soldiers going to the front, with much cheering and many "sayonaras" exchanged. Fujiyama, or "Fuji" as the Japanese affectionately called her, showed herself for the first time. Only the top was visible, and that just for a few moments, before the "Peerless One" retreated again behind the clouds. The expedition to the summit was, Jennie understood, very tiring but thrilling. When descending, one "tobogganed" on one's feet through the ashes. This had been done by Sir Harry Parkes and his wife forty years earlier, they being the first Europeans permitted to ascend the mountain, which until then had been sacred and closed to Westerners.

Jennie was astonished to find Tokyo such a vast place, covering an area as large as London. The distances were enormous, and she pitied the poor jinrikisha boys who often trotted for miles for minimal payment. They visited the Shiba Temples and saw the tombs of the shoguns. The inner temple was filled with large stone and bronze lanterns, offerings and tributes to the dead from their royal relatives.

To enter the temple, they had to remove their boots while an apathetic priest looked on, his shaven head shaped like an emu's egg, his somewhat tawdry kimono making him appear anything but prepossessing. Matsuda, their guide, prostrated himself, beating his head repeatedly against the floor. The shrine was a rather small but beautifully decorated room with a lacquered ceiling, containing only a few glass cases on the floor holding the swords and armor of Ieyasu, the deified shogun. A fourth door of beautiful gold lacquer opened into the innermost shrine, shown only to the Emperor and the chief priest, which contained the effigy of Ieyasu.

Through Matsuda, they conveyed their thanks to the chief priest, a venerable old man with a pleasant smile, dressed in a pale-blue net garment over white, with a conical black hat secured by two cords under his chin.

The inner shrine of the Ieyemitsu temple, which they also visited, was much larger, with gold columns around the room. On a low table in the center were sacred missals, incense burners, and vases with gold lotus flowers, all beneath a fine canopy. This being a Buddhist temple, it contained more objects than the Shinto temple of Ieyasu, which was simpler. Nearby, the sacred white pony "Jimme" was kept "for the god's use" in a sumptuous stable in one of the courts.

On their way back, they encountered a family of three struggling up the steps in pouring rain, their traditional dress proving thoroughly impractical. The man wore a brown kimono with a hint of white petticoat showing above his socks and high wooden pattens, topped with a huge square hat, spectacles, and carrying a voluminous Japanese umbrella. The woman, with not a hair out of place, had an artificial camellia standing upright in front of her shiny black topknot, a mauve tassel hanging near her left ear, some green cord, coral beads, and a couple of combs completing her coiffure. She wore a light gray kimono with her family crest embroidered in coral on the sleeves, a pale mauve collar, a black satin obi with gold characters, and extra-high pattens. But oh, the blackened teeth proclaiming her respectability! Jennie wondered why virtue must be so ugly. The baby, strapped to its mother's back, was fast asleep, its tiny tuft of hair falling backward as though about to drop off, its bright red crepe kimono with green flowers making it look exactly like a Japanese doll.

Deluges of rain drove them away from weird, mystical Nikko. It wasn't possible to resist the elements, and after changing their clothes and boots three times in one day, they surrendered.

They fittingly ended their visit to Japan by staying at the best place last: Kyoto, the ancient capital considered the art center of Japan. Jennie was enchanted with its quaintness and local color. The view from their rooms at Yaami's Hotel was most pleasing, and the first evening of their arrival, she gazed for a long time at the thousand twinkling lights of the city lying in the valley below, with mountains forming the background in the twilight.

Within ten days, they saw all of Kyoto's sights, visiting numerous curiosity shops that Jennie found enticing, and spending many hours at the cloisonné, satsuma, and silk factories. There she was shown beautiful modern productions that equaled any ancient Chinese or Japanese work. Although it was said that all truly fine art objects had left Japan and China for America or London, Jennie still found many attractive pieces.

The nighttime streets were a captivating sight, particularly Theater Street, where jinrikishas were prohibited. It was crowded with people and illuminated with Chinese lanterns. Outside each theater, wonderful paintings displayed the blood-curdling dramas being performed within. They entered a playhouse of actresses and watched two acts of the usual incomprehensible Japanese play: magnificent costumes, daimyos in full war regalia, distressed females, tears and sobs echoed by the audience, and of course ritual suicide, performed in detail and at great length.

The Mikado's palace, which they visited, had endless reception rooms with the usual screens and fine matting. Jennie learned that the Emperor sat on the floor when receiving Japanese visitors but used a chair for European audiences. Some of the ceilings were highly decorated. His private study faced south, overlooking a garden and small artificial lake; its absolute quietness seemed very peaceful.

The castle, being older and having belonged to the shoguns, was more ornate, with the golden Tokugawa crest, gorgeous ceilings, and highly lacquered screens everywhere. In the two or three audience chambers, the Mikado's chrysanthemum replaced the three lotus leaves. One particularly nice room had a small raised platform where the Emperor would sit when receiving visitors, arriving from a side room. On the left was a recess containing lacquered shelves adorned with bits of old cloisonné in a lovely blue that seemed impossible to reproduce in modern times. A few unusual screens completed the rooms.

After Nikko, Jennie was too jaded with temples to visit many in Kyoto, but she did see one containing thirteen hundred and thirty-three gold-lacquered life-size images of Kwannon, the Goddess of Mercy. She also visited the new, unfinished, colossal temple of Shokonsha, where great stacks of rope made from women's hair were displayed as offerings from Japan's women. Nearby stood a hideous mound that made them shudder, containing Korean ears and noses, trophies of war.

The Governor of Kyoto, Nakai by name, died during their visit. He had formed part of Sir Harry Parkes' escort when the latter, on his way to an audience with the Mikado, was attacked by sword-wielding men, causing a great stir in Japan at the time. Jennie witnessed the funeral procession from a curio dealer's shop on a main street lined by a quiet throng dressed in blue (the mourning color). Large baskets of flowers preceded the hearse, which resembled a Noah's Ark carried on men's shoulders. Through the open sliding panels, Jennie glimpsed a cocked hat and feathers. Immediately behind came a jinrikisha carrying the deceased's daughter, entirely in white, with her face enameled to match. An enormous crowd followed, dressed in kimonos and wearing pot hats of every conceivable shape, many with white cotton gloves. The effect was ludicrous, and Jennie reflected that if people wondered what became of all the old hats, they need only visit Japan.

One of their final expeditions was to Lake Biwa. The journey was long and dusty, and Jennie found the jinrikisha exhausting. The sights along the way were distressing, masses of toiling peasants doing the work of beasts, dragging and pushing heavily loaded carts up and down hills. All looked exhausted, and in most cases, a woman was harnessed at the front with a rope across her chest. Jennie noticed one poor creature spitting blood upon reaching a hilltop.

The lake itself was splendid, and they enjoyed a fine view from a temple. They were shown the street where the Cesarewitch (the future Russian Emperor) had been attacked. The two jinrikisha boys who saved his life were pensioned and, it was said, given so much money that they led idle lives and were ruined by drink. They saw the largest pine tree in Japan at Biwa, which, although curious with its innumerable gnarled roots and branches growing into the ground, was so propped up with poles that its symmetry was lost and one could hardly distinguish the actual tree.

They also experienced the rapids of Katsuregawa, being skillfully navigated upstream in a sampan. The hills on either side were lovely with autumn colors, the red maple leaves just beginning to turn. Their long drive back was enlivened by a beautiful sunset, with the moon rising while the sky remained bright pink with glimpses of turquoise blue, the trees and quaint cottages silhouetted in deep brown against it.

They rejoined their ship, the Ancona, at Kobe, more than sorry to leave Japan, a restful country of enchantment, land of courteous men and soft-voiced women. For months afterward, Jennie's ears still listened for the two most characteristic sounds of Japan: the tap-tap of little pipes being emptied before refilling, and the mournful notes of the reed lutes played by blind masseurs walking through village streets.

Aboard the Ancona, they found Mr. de Bunsen, the future English Ambassador to Spain, and a young officer returning to India after wasting his leave trying unsuccessfully to witness the war, thwarted by Japanese authorities. Mr. de Bunsen was an old friend whom Jennie had known in Paris when he worked at the embassy there. At this time, he was military attaché in Bangkok, and he shared many interesting details about Siam and his life there, trying to persuade them to visit.

Three days were sufficient to exhaust the sights of Hong Kong, with its magnificent view being the main attraction. Jennie amused herself by riding the steep tramway to the peak several times daily. Many buildings were in disrepair due to the recent typhoon.

They made a brief visit to Canton, traveling up the Pearl River on a large steamer with an English captain. Upon boarding, Jennie noticed stacks of rifles in the saloon, with printed instructions for passengers to use them if necessary. This was unsettling, as these river steamers were known to be attacked by pirates occasionally. In Hong Kong, they had been advised against visiting Canton, as the Chinese, following their defeat, were in a turbulent state. However, they thought they would be safe enough during a day trip.

The steamer anchored at the river mouth due to torpedoes laid across it, with Chinese pilots uncertain of their exact locations. It was a lovely moonlight night, and Jennie remembered the ghostly effect of a searchlight from a nearby fort repeatedly sweeping over them, illuminating strange craft and lumbering Chinese junks with square sails hovering nearby.

At Canton, they were immediately surrounded by sampans and junks. Their guide, A. Cum, had arranged everything, and they found a row of palanquins waiting, each with three bearers. Jennie's was bright green lined with pale blue, with transparent blinds that she insisted on keeping raised, not being a Chinese lady.

Their carriers moved at a swinging pace through the labyrinth of narrow, crowded streets, shouting loudly for people to clear the way. The streets were filled with open shops, banners, Chinese lanterns, and gaudy signs, with a continuous stream of people creating an animated scene. The locals scowled at them as they passed, calling them "Frank-wei" ("foreign devils"). They spat at one member of their party and struck another, who fortunately didn't retaliate, or they might have faced serious trouble.

The shops were very attractive, and Randolph bought Jennie a green jade bangle that later became fashionable. It was supposed to ward off the devil, and she continued to wear it.

A visit to the execution ground proved less appealing. Eight men had been decapitated a few days earlier, and blood still stained the ground. They declined an offer to view the heads, which had been placed in jars.

Warned by the ship's officers that their expedition was somewhat dangerous unless they were prepared to "turn the other cheek" to any insult, some of their party persuaded them to return to the ship quickly. After lunch at an old palace called "The Garden of Flowers," they hurried back through more streets, occasionally encountering a "towkee" or mandarin surrounded by attendants, resulting in competing criers trying to outshout each other.

Returning to Hong Kong, they departed the next day for Singapore. Mr. de Bunsen accompanied them. Sir John and Lady Mitchell invited them to Government House, where they stayed a week. For the first time, Jennie found the heat nearly unbearable, like a vapor bath and so enervating that any activity seemed impossible. Nevertheless, she was delighted by the tropical plants, especially the traveler's palm, its height and symmetry a revelation.

The Malay villages built on poles were picturesque, particularly those in coconut plantations near the sea. In town, every nationality seemed represented, Malays, Chinese, Hindus, Klings, Japanese, and Europeans of all countries, with the Chinese, who owned the best houses, predominating.

The Sultan of Johore gave them a sumptuous luncheon at his palace that lasted as long as a lord mayor's feast. The house displayed a curious mixture of good and bad taste; a few genuine art objects, such as old lacquered cabinets and fine Satsuma vases, were lost amid tawdriness and vulgarity. In one room, tables and chairs made of cut glass were upholstered in bright blue velvet with glass buttons!

After lunch, the Sultan, a charming and courteous old man, summoned his Sultana to meet them. She was a very pretty Circassian of about twenty-five, a gift from the Sultan of Turkey. Enormously fat, they were told she was fed every two hours, the Sultan admiring large proportions. Her outfit was peculiar: a Malay silk sarong, a blouse with huge diamond buttons, diamond and sapphire rivieres around her neck, and on her short black curls, a velvet glengarry cap with an eagle's feather and diamond aigrette, cocked over one ear. The Sultan, apparently deciding she had been displayed long enough, pointed sternly toward the door. Casting a frightened glance at him, she fled as quickly as her fat little feet could carry her.

After a week, they departed for Rangoon accompanied by Sir Frank Swettenham, Resident of Perak and future Governor of Singapore. He traveled only as far as Penang with them, which they regretted, finding him an entertaining companion. A man of exceptional intelligence, he was effectively the ruler of the Straits Settlements, and no one better understood the natives or how to manage them. His books "Malay Sketches" and "Unaddressed Letters" were deservedly popular.

Rangoon was a pleasant surprise; although the heat was intense, it was dry and therefore tolerable. The Governor, Sir Charles Mackenzie, and Lady Mackenzie were away, but they had offered Government House for their use. To Jennie's surprise, she found a pleasant company of English people who entertained them hospitably and energetically played golf and polo despite the heat.

Jennie visited the Royal Lakes, which were gorgeous and beautifully maintained, with abundant tropical plants and colorful flowers. Great bushes of alamanders grew wild at the lakeshores, bougainvilleas climbed everywhere, and a tree with dark green foliage and large clusters of red flowers like grapes (whose name she didn't learn) caught her eye. Passing by, she saw half a dozen priests in yellow robes standing on marble steps leading to the lake. Behind them in the setting sun, the great golden dome of the Schwe Dagon Pagoda shone in the distance, forming a superb picture.

The pagoda itself was endlessly interesting, and they spent pleasant hours among its many shrines. Two enormous white stone dragons guarded the entrance, standing out against the deep blue sky, with waving palms and tall coconut trees in the background creating a quintessentially Eastern scene. The only drawback was the lepers and beggars infesting the steps.

Inside, everything glittered; temples inlaid with colored glass and mirror fragments shone like jewels in the sunlight, their graceful minarets and domes exquisitely carved. Before every shrine were piled offerings from the faithful, with gaudy umbrellas fringed in gold or beads particularly noticeable. Jennie revisited the pagoda by moonlight and found it even more appealing, having lost the garishness apparent in daylight. A spell of silence enveloped the scene, broken only by the melodious voice of a fanatic reciting verses as he solemnly circled his favorite shrine.

One day, Jennie was amused to receive a visit from relatives of the late King Thebaw, three princesses. Two were young and pretty (by Burmese standards) and swathed in wraps concealing even their hands, while the third, old and ugly, wore minimal clothing as was customary in the country. They presented Jennie with artificial flowers they had made themselves and some cheroots they "hoped she would smoke," then departed in a bullock cart, a mode of transportation unchanged in Burma for thousands of years. Jennie reflected that perhaps they wouldn't have been so gracious had they realized her husband had helped destroy their dynasty and annex their country.

Cholera was raging in Mandalay, preventing them from visiting to their disappointment. Randolph particularly wanted to see more of the country, being proud of his role in Burma's annexation during his time at the India Office.

Crossing the Bay of Bengal to Madras, they stayed briefly with Lord and Lady Wenlock at Government House, where they were treated with great kindness.

They had intended to travel for several months in India, but Randolph's health, which until then had been good enough to allow him to enjoy the tour, suddenly deteriorated. They were forced to curtail their further travels and, proceeding to Bombay, embarked for England. Jennie does not discuss Lord Randolph's death in her memoirs, probably because Lord Randoph's cause of death has been a subject of much speculation and debate. His death certificate listed the cause as "bronchial pneumonia from paralysis of the brain." However, the prevailing medical opinion at the time, and a widely held belief since, was that he suffered from general paralysis of the insane, a condition now known to be a result of chronic syphilis. The death of her husband, marked the end of Jennie's Act Two of her life.

Jennie herself did not come from immense personal wealth in the European aristocratic sense. Her father, Leonard Jerome, was a wealthy American financier, but her inheritance was not necessarily a vast, secure fortune upon her marriage. Lord Randolph's financial situation was somewhat complicated. While he came from an aristocratic family, he wasn't exceptionally wealthy compared to some of his peers. He had a political career that provided an income, but he wasn't sitting on vast inherited estates. Upon Lord Randolph's death, Jennie would have received whatever financial provisions were made for his widow in his will. The specifics of his will aren't as widely discussed as other aspects of his life, but it's likely she would have been provided for, though perhaps not in a way that made her exceptionally wealthy by the standards of the aristocracy. After Lord Randolph's death, she demonstrated considerable resourcefulness. She became involved in various ventures, including acting, writing and journalism, to support herself and her sons. In the next part of her memoirs she almost makes an excuse of the why and how she became a writer. Jennie possessed a strong resilience and a determination to forge her own path. She was not one to be defined solely by her marital status.

TOWN & COUNTRY

NEW SERIES OF THE HOME JOURNAL

New York, Saturday, February 29, 1908

MRS. GEORGE CORNWALLIS WEST

Jennie – The Writer

Chartwell, 1964

Churchill's hands shook more noticeably now as he reached for a leather portfolio on his desk. Inside were bound volumes of an elegant magazine, their covers elaborate reproductions of historical designs. "My mother's greatest independent achievement," he said with unmistakable pride. "The Anglo-Saxon Review, a literary magazine that lasted only three years but left an indelible mark on both sides of the Atlantic."

Sophia examined one of the volumes. "It's beautiful."

"Beautiful and significant. She convinced some of the finest writers of the age to contribute, Lord Rosebery, Bernard Shaw, Henry James. Each cover was a facsimile of a famous historical binding." Churchill opened one volume carefully. "But more than that, it represented her vision of Anglo-American cultural unity decades before such cooperation became politically essential."

"She was building bridges."

"Intellectual and cultural bridges that would prove crucial when political bridges became necessary." Churchill's voice carried deep satisfaction. "When I stood before Congress in 1941, appealing for American support, I was drawing on relationships and understanding that she had begun building at the turn of the century through this magazine."

LONDON, 1899

It was during one of her many visits to Bradford when Lord Randolph Churchill was holding political meetings there, that Jennie first remembered hearing Lord Curzon of Kedleston (then

Mr. George Nathaniel Curzon) make a speech. Called upon unexpectedly to second a resolution, he spoke with natural eloquence and an astonishing choice of words. Randolph predicted to her then that Curzon would go very far. They knew him well while he was still at Oxford when he used to come over to Blenheim, a distance of only eight miles.

When Curzon was made Viceroy of India, his many friends gave a farewell dinner to him and Lady Curzon. The speeches were most amusing, notwithstanding the note of sadness which prevailed at the prospect of losing such a delightful couple for several years. Mr. George Wyndham contributed verses which were received with great applause, including lines like "So 'Go in and win!' What's five years but a lustre to shine round a name that already shines bright?"

The few brilliant years the Curzons spent in India were too recent and too familiar in people's minds for Jennie to dwell on that time or the tragedy which was so soon to follow their departure. To her great beauty, Mary Curzon added grace of manner and kindness of heart, and her extraordinary and unselfish devotion to her husband made her a paragon among wives. Jennie recalled one other remarkable woman who was equally devoted and absorbed in her husband's career, and whose life was one of sacrifice to duty and care for others - her sister-in-law Fanny, Lady Tweedmouth, without exception the noblest character she had ever met.

It was always a regret to Jennie that she was unable to accept the Viceroy's invitation to attend the great Durbar, that crowning function of a most memorable viceregal reign. She often corresponded with Lady Curzon, and in one of her letters, Lady Curzon wrote:

Letter from Lady Curzon - May 18, 1903, from Viceroy's Camp: Lady Curzon described the success of the Durbar, explaining that the £200,000 expenditure was justified by bringing together people from the frontiers of Tibet, Siam, Burma, Nepal, and many other regions. She noted that chiefs from "the outer fringes of civilization" were astonished by the display of British power, with some remarking they would have remained peaceful had they known what they were fighting against. Lady Curzon praised her husband's organizational skills and mentioned she was "sticking to the sides of the Himalayas like a barnacle with only a three weeks' old copy of the Times." She concluded by asking Jennie to write, calling her "the only person who lives on the crest of the wave and is always full of vitality and success."

On the eve of their departure from England, the Curzons paid a visit to the Duke and Duchess of Portland at Welbeck. Jennie was of the party, and sitting next to Lord Curzon at dinner one night, they approached a subject which, without her knowing it at the time, was fraught with great importance for her. In a despondent mood, she bemoaned the empty life she was leading at that moment. Lord Curzon tried to console her by saying that a woman alone was a godsend in society, and that she might look forward to a long vista of country-house parties, dinners, and balls.

Thinking over their conversation later, Jennie found herself wondering if this indeed was all that the remainder of her life held for her. She determined to do something, and after cogitating for some time over what it should be, decided finally to start a review. Her ideas were of the vaguest, but they soon shaped themselves. She consulted her friend Mrs. Craigie ("John Oliver Hobbes"), whose acquaintance she had made some years before at the Curzons'. At Mrs. Craigie's house she met various people who helped her with their good counsel, notably Mr. Sidney Low, who became much interested in the scheme and assisted her greatly, editing and bringing out two numbers during her subsequent absence in South Africa.

Mr. John Lane, who published the first numbers of the Review, was full of ideas and originated that of having a new cover for each issue. Mr. Cyril Davenport of the British Museum joined the staff and helped in the selection of the bindings, which were to be facsimiles of celebrated books of the sixteenth, seventeenth, and eighteenth centuries, mostly chosen from examples in the British Museum. He also contributed a short article descriptive of each cover. Mr. Lionel Cust of the National Portrait Gallery undertook to supervise the illustrations, which were reproduced as photogravures. The late Mr. Arthur Strong, librarian of the House of Lords and at Chatsworth, was responsible for the historical matter.

A delightful and enthralling period began, which absorbed Jennie from morning till night in the most interesting of occupations. She left no stone unturned to make the Review a success, and her friends helped her enthusiastically. Sometimes she became a little bewildered at the conflicting advice and suggestions that she received, such as including articles in three languages or publishing "New Ideas on Free Love" or "Sidelights on Royal Courts."

Then came the question of a title. Many were offered, from "The New Anthology" to "The Mentor of Mayfair." Sir Edgar Vincent, whose classical and literary education was backed by the most admirable common sense, suggested "Anglo-Saxon." Jennie thought the name most apt, and was enchanted. "The Anglo-Saxon" , how simple! It sounded strong, sensible, and solid. Of course the moment she had settled on the name, some obscure man claimed it as being registered for his still more obscure paper or magazine. However, she found that adding the word "Review" made it quite safe.

Jennie gave a luncheon party to introduce "Maggie," as the Review was affectionately called by some of her friends. The book in its gorgeous cover, the replica of Thevet's "Vie des Hommes Illustres," which was executed about 1604 for James I, presented a brave appearance. If she could only ensure that its "ramage se rapporta a son plumage" (English Translation: "its song matched its plumage"), she felt she might indeed claim to have produced a Phoenix.

The same night she dined with the Asquiths, taking the volume with her, where it was received with acclamation. She kept the book still, with all the signatures of those present written on the fly-leaf.

Among Jennie's most valued contributors was Lord Rosebery, who, on account of his great friendship with Randolph and out of kindness to her, wrote for the first number a short essay on Sir Robert Peel. Later, in one of the subsequent volumes, an article appeared which, to her regret, criticized his political opinions. She had gone to Scotland thinking the number was completed as she had seen it, but owing to the exigencies of time and space, the offending article had been substituted at the last moment. She was very much annoyed, but it could not be helped. Writing to Lord Rosebery, she told him how grieved she was that anything even approaching criticism of him should have appeared in her review.

Letter from Lord Rosebery - September 28, 1901, from Dalmeny House, Edinburgh: Lord Rosebery thanked Jennie for writing about the article but confessed he hadn't heard of it, having ceased to be a subscriber after a previous issue where he "perceived the cloven hoof of politics." He frankly stated he thought introducing politics into "The Anglo-Saxon" was a mistake but acknowledged she was a better judge. He added that he doubted he would ever see the article and was "quite sure that, if I do, it will not trouble me" while offering his "humble and hearty thanks to the Editress."

Looking back at the early period of the Review, Jennie often wondered how she should have succeeded without Pearl Craigie's intelligent help and advice. A woman of great sympathies, her unselfishness was realized by all who ever came in contact with her, and her valuable time was always at the disposal of anyone she could help. It was not for Jennie to dwell on her literary gifts, her works spoke for themselves. A brilliant and clever conversationalist, she could hold her own with all manner of men, and yet, in the more frivolous company which she often frequented and thoroughly enjoyed, she never talked over people's heads.

Jennie had many discussions with Mrs. Craigie about her plays. In reference to "A Repentance," which she asked Jennie to see and give her candid opinion upon, Mrs. Craigie wrote:

Letter from Mrs. Craigie - 1899, from 56 Lancaster Gate, W.: Mrs. Craigie welcomed Jennie's honest criticism, explaining the play was about Spanish Catholics and the character was meant to be a typical Carlist, not a hero. She noted her object was "not to display inhuman excellence, but a psychological diagram of the Carlist question!" She acknowledged this might be too experimental for the stage but felt it was worth trying. She mentioned that while some people loved the play, others didn't like it at all. She concluded with philosophical thoughts about the "squalid side of literary life," saying sometimes she longed "to retire to some lonely hilltop and meditate on the Four Last Things" but that "we cannot make terms with existence: we must cultivate our garden and a sense of humor."

Jennie thought the play most interesting, but too condensed. There was tragedy enough in the one act to make a substantial play of three. The critics were not overkind, and she wrote telling Mrs. Craigie that the general public were much better judges than the ordinary theater critic.

To her many gifts, Mrs. Craigie added that of being a very good musician and her nimble fingers could discourse very effectively. Jennie sometimes played together with her at concerts, and on one occasion, at the Queen's Hall, she and Mrs. Craigie and Mademoiselle Janotha played Bach's Concerto in D Minor for three pianos, with an orchestra from the Royal College of Music, which was conducted by Sir Walter Parratt. This was the only time Jennie could remember enjoying playing in public.

It was curious how sometimes "les beaux esprits se rencontrent" (English Translation: "great minds think alike"). Mrs. W. K. Clifford sent Jennie her play "The Likeness of the Night" for publication in "The Anglo-Saxon Review" before it was put on the stage. Shortly after the appearance of the number containing it, Mr. Sidney Grundy's play "A Debt of Honor" was given. There was no doubt a great similarity between the two, and this led to an animated correspondence in the press between Mrs. Clifford and Mr. Grundy.

The choice and study of the bindings afforded Jennie the greatest pleasure; there was nothing tentative about them. She knew they would be a success and please all bibliophiles, for most book-lovers are particular about the appearance of their books. She remembered once lending Pierre Loti's "Madame Chrysantheme" to Mr. John Morley (now Lord Morley of Blackburn). In one of his letters about it he alluded to people's fancies as to bindings.

Letter from J. Morley: Morley thanked Jennie for sending him the book, saying he would "take it in such doses as you prescribe, unless I find it too attractive to lay down."

The doses must have been microscopic, for he kept the book so long that she wrote to remind him that he still had it.

Letter from J. Morley - from 95 Elm Park Gardens, South Kensington: Morley expressed distress at being suspected of book-stealing, noting he had "suffered too much from that evil tribe." He explained he kept the book knowing she was away from home and apologized for its "dilapidated condition," suggesting he had considered having it bound but thought Jennie "might have fancies of your own about bindings, as I have." He thanked her for lending him the book, which had amused him greatly, and confessed that while devoted to French literature, he found "the modern French novel is rather too horrid for me, who was reared on George Sand."

In making up each quarterly volume of "The Anglo-Saxon Review," Jennie did not find the difficulty she had anticipated in procuring fitting contributors. The first number had established its reputation, and although critics were not wanting, it could rightly claim, on the whole, to be keeping up its standard of excellence. She aspired high; sometimes too high, as a letter from Lord Salisbury showed:

Letter from Lord Salisbury - July 2, 1899, from Walmer Castle: The Prime Minister expressed that while it would give him "great pleasure" to aid Jennie, he was "not capable of complying with your flattering invitation" as his "allowance of time and energy are only just enough to enable me to keep up with my necessary work." He added a note about Winston having made "a splendid fight" though "the Borough bears a bad name for fickleness."

Jennie was also disappointed at not getting an article from Mr. Cecil Rhodes, who, although not a literary man, could speak clearly and with great authority on his own particular subjects. She first met him in London in the early eighties. He was then a handsome young man, but with a delicate chest, and was just starting for South Africa, where he hoped the wonderful air would cure him. This it did, for although he died at a comparatively early age, it was not from consumption.

She remembered once having a most interesting conversation with him over his aims and ambitions. His whole soul was bound up in the future and progress of South Africa, and although he was not a self-seeker in any way, he was justly proud of having the immense province of Rhodesia named after him. In his heart of hearts he wanted his name to be handed down to posterity in this indelible manner, and he would have been bitterly disappointed had any other been chosen. When she questioned him as to this, he admitted it quite frankly. He was, she thought, a very happy man, for he never allowed small things to worry him, and his mind was not encumbered with the subtleties with which so many are hampered. A man of big ideas, he knew what he wanted, and made for the goal. He was singularly outspoken. On one occasion, discussing a sculptor, he said: "Why don't you let the fellow do you? You've got a good square face."

Letter from C. J. Rhodes - February 1899, from Vienna: Rhodes apologized for his delayed response, explaining her letter was misplaced among the hundred he received daily. He promised to visit Jennie upon his return in about three weeks. He mentioned they were "getting through to Egypt fairly well" though his companion Maguire was struggling with the servants. Rhodes added he was "learning the mysteries of bridge" and could see it was "an assured income to a thinking player," humorously noting the "annoyance, I would say amusement, is playing badly and seeing your partner's face."

Letter from C. J. Rhodes - from Burlington Hotel, W.: Rhodes said he would try to write something for Jennie's

Review on his ship voyage, adding "but do not announce it. I shall try to do something to help you and my cause, perhaps my cause first and you second, but I shall see you again." He encouraged her, noting she would "have lots of bother, some pleasure, and you will be doing something, which is best of all." He concluded by remarking that women "have great imagination and a much more delicate instinct than my sex, who are rough and brutal. I think you should have a fair chance."

Among many interesting contributions, it was with much satisfaction that Jennie received an article from Bernard Shaw, "A Word more about Verdi," which discussed Verdi's musical style and whether he was influenced by Wagner. Jennie ventured to disagree with Shaw's conclusion that Verdi was not influenced by Wagner, noting that in "Falstaff" she thought the orchestration was decidedly Wagnerian compared to Verdi's other operas.

It was with the greatest regret that Jennie ceased publishing "The Anglo-Saxon Review" in 1901, but circumstances over which she had no control obliged her to bring its career to an end. No one could be responsible for a publication of that kind without having many anxious and annoying moments, but she would always look back with pleasure and pride to that period, and to the ten volumes it produced. Her heart would never forget the gratitude she owed to those who worked so efficiently for her and with her.

Jennie Churchill in byzantine costume as the Empress Theodora

The South African War

Chartwell, 1964

The evening light was fading rapidly now, and Churchill's secretary had quietly lit several lamps around the studio. He sat heavily in his chair, but his voice gained strength as he continued. "The hospital ship Maine," he said, his eyes focusing on something beyond Sophia's shoulder. "When people ask about my mother's finest hour, they usually think of her social triumphs or political campaigns. But for me, it was watching her organize and lead a humanitarian mission during the Boer War."

"While you were captured by the Boers."

"Precisely. While I was sitting in a Pretoria prison, wondering if my career was over before it began, she was on the other side of the world, turning her social connections into life-saving medical care for wounded soldiers." Churchill's voice grew warm with memory. "She raised forty thousand pounds, fitted out a hospital ship, recruited American doctors and nurses, and sailed to South Africa herself to ensure the mission succeeded."

Sophia leaned forward. "That must have been extraordinary to witness."

"It taught me that true leadership isn't about position or title, it's about taking responsibility when others won't. Years later, when Britain stood alone against Hitler, I remembered her example. Sometimes one person's determination to act can inspire an entire nation to find courage it didn't know it possessed."

DEVONSHIRE, 1987

While beginning her work as a writer, Jennie was still part of London's social life. Rarely has the London social world been so stirred as by the fancy-dress ball given at Devonshire House, on the 2nd of July, 1897. For weeks, not to say months, beforehand, it seemed the principal topic of conversation. The absorbing question was what characters our friends and ourselves were going to represent. Great were the confabulations and mysteries. With bated breath and solemn mien a fair dame would whisper to some few dozen or more that she was going to represent the Queen of Cyprus or Aspasia, Fredegonde or Petrarch's Laura, but the secret must be kept. Historical books were ransacked for inspirations, old pictures and engravings were studied, and people became learned in respect to past celebrities of whom they had never before heard. The less well-known the characters, the more eagerly were they sought after. "Never heard of Simonetta? How curious? but surely you remember Botticelli's picture of her, one of the beauties of the Florentine court? No? How strange!"

"My dress is to be 'old Venetian' pink velvet, with gold embroideries , one of those medieval women. I can't remember her name; but that's of no consequence. Masses of jewelry, of course."

The men, oddly enough, were even more excited over their costumes than the women, and many paid extravagant sums for them. There is no doubt that when a man begins to think about his appearance, he competes with women to some purpose, money, time, and thought being of no account to him. On the night of the ball, the excitement rose to fever heat. Every coiffeur in London and Paris was requisitioned, and so busy were they that some of the poor victims actually had their locks tortured early in the morning, sitting all day in a rigid attitude, or, like Agag, "walking delicately."

Devonshire House, with its marble staircase and glorious pictures, was a fitting frame for the distinguished company which thronged its beautiful rooms. Every one of note and interest was there, representing the intellect, beauty, and fashion of the day, from the present King and Queen (then Prince and Princess of Wales) dressed respectively as the Grand Prior of the Order of St. John of Jerusalem and Marguerite de Valois, to the newest Radical member of Parliament, gorgeously attired as the Great Mogul. The Duchess of Devonshire, who looked exceedingly well as Zenobia Queen of Palmyra, and the Duke as the Emperor Charles V received on a raised dais at the end of the ball-room the endless procession who passed by, bowing, courtesying, or salaaming, according to the characters they represented.

Princess Pless, lovely as Cleopatra, was surrounded by a retinue in Oriental garb, some of whom so far sacrificed their appearance as to darken their faces. A number of the ladies were more becomingly than comfortably attired. A charming Hebe, with an enormous eagle poised on her shoulder and a gold cup in her hand, made a perfect picture, but, alas! in one attitude only, which she vainly tried to preserve throughout the evening, while the late hereditary Prince of Saxe-Coburg (Prince Alfred of Edinburgh), as the Duke of Normandy, a.d. 1060, in casque and chain armor, kept his vizor down until heat and hunger forced him to sacrifice his martial appearance. A beautiful and fascinating duchess, famous for her jewels, elected to appear as Charlotte Corday in cotton skirt and mob-cap, whereas Lady , , trembling on the verge of bankruptcy, was covered with gems of priceless value. The late Lady Tweedmouth was a striking figure as Queen Elizabeth, with eight gigantic guardsmen surrounding her, all dressed as yeoman of the guard. Many people copied the portraits of their ancestors, and Sir John Kaye, in chain mail, represented Sir Kaye of the "Morte d'Arthur." Many, too, were the heart-burnings over failures or doubles. In one case a well-known baronet had been perfecting himself for weeks in the role of Napoleon, his face and figure lending themselves to the impersonation. But what was his dismay at finding in the vestibule a second victor of Austerlitz even more lifelike and correct than himself. It was indeed a Waterloo for both of them.

Few danced, as in a raree-show of that kind people are too much occupied in gazing at one another or in struggling to play up to their assumed parts. Sometimes this was carried further than was intended. Toward the close of the ball, two young men disputed over a certain fair lady. Both losing their tempers, they decided to settle the matter in the garden, and pulling out their weapons, they began making passes. But the combatants were unequally armed, one being a crusader, with a double-handed sword, the other a Louis XV courtier, armed with his rapier only. He, as might be expected, got the worst of it, receiving a nasty cut on his pink silk stocking.

On the Saturday following this great entertainment Jennie went to Kimbolton to stay with the Duchess of Manchester, where most of the company were persuaded to don their fancy dress once more. Of course the ball was discussed ad nauseam. Many were the divergent opinions as to who looked the best, the majority giving the palm to Lady Westmoreland.

In the winter of 1898, persistent rumors of war with South Africa were prevalent, although few realized how soon England was to be plunged into its grim realities. At a shooting party at Chatsworth, Jennie remembered meeting Mr. Chamberlain, then Secretary of State for the Colonies. One night at dinner they discussed the situation, and he frankly told her he considered it inevitable. A few months later, hostilities were declared, and great was the excitement. But not even the most gloomy of pessimists could have foreseen or imagined the proportions the war was going to take, or the length of time it was to last. As is well known, it was very unpopular with many people, particularly with those who knew South Africa well and had lived there; but in the growing enthusiasm their voices were as of "one crying in the wilderness," and before long they were dubbed "Pro-Boers," or even traitors.

Mr. Selous, writing to Jennie on November 5, 1899, expressed his deep depression about the war, believing it to be unjust and impolitic. In his letter, he expressed concerns that the war could be fraught with grave danger to the British Empire. He noted that the Transvaal had been given every excuse to arm themselves after the Jameson raid, though Britain now accused them of planning to drive the British out of South Africa. Selous quoted Lord Randolph Churchill's earlier writings about how crushing the Boers in 1881 might have regained the Transvaal but lost Cape Colony due to Dutch sentiment. Though opposing the war, Selous hoped for a quick British victory, followed by good governance and a conciliatory attitude toward the Boers. He mentioned that his views had cost him many friendships, with people calling him a traitor.

A few days later, Selous wrote again stating that now that war had broken out, no Englishman could wish for anything but complete victory for British arms. He hoped Sir Redvers Buller would overcome all opposition quickly so the government could dictate peace terms. Selous mentioned that if these terms aligned with Lord Salisbury's statement that Britain sought neither gold-fields nor territory, he would support the government. Despite wishing to offer his services to Lord Methuen, Selous felt his views on the war's causes prevented him from taking up arms against people who had shown him nothing but kindness.

Jennie noted that Mr. Selous' pessimistic views regarding the Transvaal were not fulfilled, which must have been a great joy to him and to all those who had the welfare of South Africa at heart. The policy of good governance and a conciliatory attitude toward the conquered Boers, which he advocated, was followed by the Liberal Administration, bringing about a happy state of affairs. She sometimes wondered what would have been the condition of South Africa had the Conservative government remained in power and carried out their proposed measures.

In moments of great stress and struggle, inactivity becomes a positive pain. The people who were the most to be pitied during the war were those who had to remain at home. As a friend wrote to Jennie at the time, it was like being in a country house, seeing day after day other guests going out to hunt, while being compelled to remain indoors - nothing could be more depressing. People feeling this way soon started various movements to raise funds for alleviating the miseries of the sick and wounded. Everyone became interested and occupied in some scheme.

One day in October, Jennie received a visit from Mrs. Blow, an American lady who had lived for some time in Australia. Mrs. Blow suggested the idea of an American hospital-ship to be sent to South Africa. The project did not initially strike Jennie as practical, and for some days she gave it no thought. However, after meeting Sir William Garstin (of Egyptian fame) and discussing it with him, she was strongly advised to take it up. "Believe me," he said, "you will be making history apart from the excellence of the work." Then and there she made up her mind to do it.

On October 25, 1899, the first committee meeting was held at Jennie's house, with a number of her compatriots attending. Mrs. Blow was made honorary secretary, Mrs. Ronalds treasurer, and Jennie was elected chairman, with Mrs. Adair subsequently made vice-chairman. A large and influential general committee was formed. All worked with zeal and enthusiasm, and soon the whole enterprise was well underway. There was a general impression that the war would be short and sharp. Hospitals of all kinds were greatly needed, and they hurried with feverish activity.

Funds and a ship were their two great and immediate concerns. No stone was left unturned to procure money - much money, and it had to be all American money. The war was viewed with disfavor by Americans, who had a fellow-feeling for the Boers fighting for their independence. But the plea of humanity overran their political opinions, and once the fund started, money poured in. Concerts, matinees, and entertainments of all sorts and kinds were organized. Large firms of many nations contributed their specialties, until the amount of medical comforts became so great that they found some difficulty in storing them.

Checks and gifts from two shillings to £1000 were given by private persons, whose generosity seemed to know no bounds. On the other hand, they sometimes met with rebuffs, notably from an American multimillionaire who replied to Jennie's cable that he had "no knowledge of the scheme." Another wealthy individual, known for donating libraries, also refused, though his workmen subscribed £500. The committee had asked for £30,000 but eventually received £41,597, a noble sum to raise in two months, particularly under the circumstances.

Their research for a suitable vessel was not initially successful. They were particularly anxious to secure an American ship if possible and cabled to Mr. Roosevelt, then Governor of New York, but he couldn't help. Eventually, they received an offer through the chairman of the Atlantic Transport Company to lend them the Maine. This company had already offered the Maine to the English Government as a hospital ship, with captain and crew maintained at the company's expense. Though the Government had accepted, no steps had been taken to alter the cattle boat due to the great expense. Mr. Bernard Baker, President of the company, generously proposed to the Admiralty to hand over the Maine to the committee to fit out, and the Admiralty agreed.

The committee's chief difficulty was ignorance of the requirements for such a hospital. Compared with field hospitals, which had standardized requirements from the Army Medical Department, fitting out a hospital ship was far more complex. There was no precedent in England for a properly constituted floating hospital for war-times. Jennie haunted the precincts of the Army and Red Cross Medical departments, but they offered little help, being themselves stretched to the limit. However, they did supply men from the St. John Ambulance Brigade, whose training and military discipline proved invaluable aboard the ship.

The Atlantic Transport Company was more helpful, having equipped the Maine's twin ship, the Missouri, for the American Government during the Cuban war. The committee was determined that the staff of doctors and nurses should be American. Mrs. Whitelaw Reid in New York, with her knowledge of nursing and connection to the Mills School founded by her father, was able to send an efficient staff of doctors, nurses, and orderlies.

During October and November, the committee met almost daily. Jennie looked back on that time as perhaps the most absorbing of her life. The gloom and terrible depression which had settled on London at the unexpected reverses to the British arms did not affect them, and the daily accounts of horrors and suffering only doubled their activity. All their thoughts were centered on that small cattle boat which was to be converted into a haven of rest and comfort.

The Maine Committee worked with such will and fire that they carried all before them. The War Office and the Admiralty were badgered and heckled, but their cause was righteous, and they did not mind being importunate. Lord Lansdowne, the Minister of War, provided exceptional kindness and help, waiving aside red tape. It was largely owing to him and Lord Goschen, First Lord of the Admiralty, that their efforts were crowned with success.

On November 12th, they held their first general committee meeting. Jennie was able to proudly point out that although the scheme had been in existence only a little more than a fortnight, they already had a ship, a magnificent staff, hundreds of gifts, supporters worldwide, and £15,000. She suspected some present might have criticized the policy that necessitated sending soldiers to the front, but as her friend Mrs. Craigie (John Oliver Hobbes) had written, "The wounded are the wounded, irrespective of creed or nationality." Jennie quoted this effectively, adding that "deeds were better than words," and that the Maine would probably do more to cement friendship between England and America than any amount of flag-waving.

Though the Maine was an American hospital-ship, it was important to have it under British Government protection for the privileges this would bring. It was also necessary to be recognized as a military hospital-ship with an English principal medical officer of standing. This was initially met with discouragement from Lord Wolseley, the commander-in-chief, but he later changed his mind, expressing appreciation for the Americans' interest in British sick and wounded. Surgeon Lieutenant-Colonel Hensman was chosen, proving an excellent choice with his sense of duty and tactful manners.

The arrival of the American staff from New York created much excitement. They were offered reduced hotel rates and were lionized with luncheons, dinner parties, and entertainments, including one organized by London hospital matrons and nurses. They were invited to Windsor, where they were presented to Queen Victoria by Princess Christian. The Queen expressed her appreciation, saying, "I am very pleased to see you, and I want to say how much I appreciate your kindness in coming over to take care of my men."

Two days later, Jennie was invited to dine and sleep at Windsor, having an interesting conversation with the Queen about the war. The Queen asked many questions about the Maine and mentioned the visit of the surgeons and nurses, noting that the surgeons looked "very young." Jennie hoped this meant they would be "all the more energetic." The Queen also inquired about Jennie's sister-in-law, Lady Sarah Wilson, then reported to be a Boer prisoner, saying with a charming smile, "They will not hurt her."

The next day Mrs. Ronalds and Mrs. Blow came to the Castle to be personally thanked for their work. Jennie presented them to the Queen and felt proud of her handsome countrywomen as they came forward with self-possession and grace.

On November 17th, while visiting friends in the country, Jennie was awakened in the night by telegrams informing her that her son Winston Churchill had been captured by the Boers after an armored train in which he was traveling was trapped. The telegrams praised his gallantry in carrying wounded to safety and his coolness under fire. Jennie passed some terribly anxious moments, and were it not for the absorbing occupation of the Maine, she couldn't imagine how she would have endured that time of suspense. Among many telegrams, she received one from Empress Eugenie: "Prends bien part a vos inquietudes; espereaurezbientot nouvelle." [English Translation: I share deeply in your worries; hope you will have news soon.]

The committee wanted President McKinley to give them the American flag for their hospital ship. Jennie cabled him, adding that it would carry no political significance. After some delay, Secretary Hay replied that the President thought it unwise as his "motives might be misconstrued." Jennie tried again, suggesting a red cross on the flag, but the pro-Boer feeling in America was evidently too strong.

Meanwhile, Jennie had asked the Duke of Connaught to request a Union Jack from the Queen. A few days later, she received a letter from the Duke stating that the Queen had consented to present a Union Jack to the Maine as a mark of appreciation for the American ladies' generosity. The refusal from Washington placed Jennie in an awkward position, as the Queen believed the President was doing the same. Jennie decided the best policy was to preserve a judicious silence, and the American flag was not mentioned.

On the appointed day, the Queen's present of a huge Union Jack with a red cross on a white ground in the center was hoisted with great ceremony. The Duke and Duchess of Connaught, Princess Louise, and many distinguished people attended the luncheon and witnessed the presentation. The Duke made a felicitous speech, presenting the flag as a mark of the Queen's appreciation and noting that never before had a ship sailed under the combined flags of the Union Jack and the Stars and Stripes, hoping it marked an occasion of growing affection between the two countries.

On December 23rd, the Maine sailed for Cape Town. Jennie had decided to go with the ship, feeling the committee should be represented by a person of authority without a salary. Though the morning was dark and foggy, her heart was light because she had heard the day before that Winston, after escaping from Pretoria where he had been a prisoner, was safe at Lorenzo Marquez. The ship was in chaos, with decks covered in mud and workmen everywhere putting on final touches. With her friend Miss Eleanor Warrender, Jennie stood on deck as the vessel moved out of the docks. A momentary gleam of sun shone on them as those on shore burst into cheers, which were taken up by crews of nearby ships. "Mind you bring home Kruger, and we'll eat him," called some grimy colliers, but these cries were soon lost in the black fog which settled down upon them. Although they only reached the outer basin due to the fog, they felt they had started on their journey.

In January 1899, Jennie embarked on a journey to South Africa aboard the hospital ship Maine. She had anticipated some rough weather in the Bay of Biscay but was unprepared for the full gale that lasted six days, which authorities claimed was the worst experienced in many years. Encountering such severe weather in midwinter in a relatively small ship fitted as a hospital, with large hatchways and skylights and inadequate means of battening down, proved quite challenging.

For forty-eight hours, the ship lay to, adding to everyone's physical misery with the knowledge they were making no headway. Even experienced sailors found it trying to be buffeted from morning until night, with the impossibility of doing anything unless entrenched in a protective arrangement. Eating required extraordinary skill as no fiddles could prevent soup from being shot into one's lap or glass contents into one's face.

Jennie hadn't previously realized how one could suffer from color. The green of her attractive little cabin, which she had thought restful, became a source of acute suffering, forcing her to find a neutral-tinted cushion on which to rest her eyes. As she rolled in sleepless wretchedness, the sound of waves breaking on deck with the report of cannon balls reminded her of their mission, and she thought that if they went to the bottom, at least they would be counted as victims of the war.

Beyond the weather, the ship was in great confusion due to overcrowded holds and numerous items brought aboard at the last moment, creating serious obstacles to getting the vessel in order. Jennie did not dwell on the discomforts and hardships experienced by all.

On January 2, late in the evening, they anchored off Las Palmas, and with a sigh of relief, told each other the worst was over. In the morning, Mr. Swanston, the British Consul, and Captain

Wintz of H.M.S. Furious, who had been watching for them for days, came aboard bringing the latest news and fresh flowers. The news was scanty: General French had occupied Colesberg, and there had been a fresh attack on Mafeking. Otherwise, the situation remained unchanged.

They went ashore feeling giddy and battered, encountering the wrecked transport Denton Grange in the harbor, which had run ashore with three other vessels during the gale. Water was pouring through her hold, and all engines were hopelessly ruined. Jennie spoke with some of the dejected officers who were living on board.

Armed with cameras and long lists of purchases, they lunched at the Catalina Hotel, a pretty house with low verandas covered with bougainvilleas of different shades. The air was soft and balmy, and many English visitors were lounging about, looking peaceful and comfortable if slightly bored. Their friends provided them with a carriage and pair in which they crawled through the two feet of mud of the one long principal street of the town.

Las Palmas reminded Jennie of Monterey, California, there were the same square pink houses with green shutters and a center court or patio, tropical vegetation, and the sea at the door. But here the comparison ended, for Las Palmas was merely pretty, whereas Monterey with its seventeen-mile ocean drive, unparalleled gardens, and unique storm-swept cypress groves overlooking the ocean was perhaps one of the most beautiful spots in the world.

Excited and delighted with their day, they returned to the ship laden with spoils, birds, parrots, fruit, plants, coffee-pots, and much else. Jennie had an opportunity to judge the appearance of the Maine as they came alongside. Alas! The brilliant green stripe denoting their status as a military hospital-ship was a thing of shreds and patches, many of their stanchions were bent and twisted, and their would-be immaculate white paint was a foggy gray.

The seventeen days of their journey to Cape Town were busy ones. They were spared monotony by the work of getting the wards in order and rescuing hundreds of donations from the chaos of the hold. In the hurry of departure, many things had been forgotten, and many were put anywhere to be out of the way. They had very little time to appear shipshape before arriving.

After crossing the equator, evenings were spent star-gazing at the Southern Cross, though Jennie confessed she felt no keenness, having seen it often before and thinking its beauty a delusion. At first, they met no ships, and the absence of news was very trying. After a few days, however, they sighted a small steamer and instantly bore down on her, signaling for intelligence. What they got was: "Buller crossed Tugela. Ladysmith rumored relieved. Continued fighting", virtually no news, and they had to hold their souls in patience until arriving in Cape Town on January 23rd.

Cape Town, with its bay full of transports disembarking troops, the feverish activity of its docks, and streets crowded with khaki-clad soldiers, seemed indeed the real thing. Jennie's first impression of the bay at 6 a.m. with innumerable vessels and forests of masts, the clouds breaking on Table Mountain, and the rising sun turning all into a pink glory, would not soon fade from her memory. Though worn and tired, and realizing that their work was all before them, they rejoiced to be in measurable distance of it.

As they were rolling about outside the breakwater, through the kindness and exertions of Sir Edward Chichester who was in charge of the port, they were given a berth inside. As soon as possible, Jennie started off to see the Governor, Sir Alfred (now Lord) Milner, to get her letters and telegrams and gather what news she could. This was very meager. She later ascertained that Lord Kitchener's first order to all officers was to practice the utmost discretion, and any information about war news was strictly forbidden due to the mass of spies and disloyalty in Cape Town, with much valuable information being continually transmitted to the enemy.

The entire staff of the Maine were invited to a reception at the Mount Nelson Hotel, given in their honor by a committee of American ladies. It was pleasant to walk in the pretty garden, eating strawberries, and a marked contrast to the melancholy which prevailed at Government House, where Jennie dined that evening.

Upon arriving, the principal medical officer came on board and after visiting the ship, informed them that they were to be sent immediately to Durban to fill up with patients and return to England. Jennie remonstrated and explained the purpose and mission of the ship, pointing out that were it to be treated merely as a transport for convalescents, the international value of the gift would certainly suffer, and the large, expensive, and efficient medical staff on board would have nothing to do and would be greatly disappointed, as interesting serious cases were not likely to be sent to them. She pressed the point so much that at last he said the ship had better get orders from General Buller on arrival at Durban.

Upon arriving in Durban, the authorities came on board and told them they were to be filled with drafts from other hospital-ships and sent home at once. But with the help and influence of the Government of Natal, Sir Redvers Buller, and other influential friends, Jennie was able to successfully frustrate these attempts to send them back. The Maine not only remained in the harbor of Durban but had many interesting cot cases sent down. The absence of news was making everyone desperately anxious.

They had been asked by the Cape Town authorities to leave on the 25th for Durban. Although the notice was short, giving them only a couple of days after the long sea voyage of nearly a month, they were rather pleased to be able to say "Yes," and prove their readiness. A few hours after receiving their orders, however, Lord Roberts sent word that he wished to visit the ship the following day. Accordingly, he came and gave them a thorough inspection: wards, mess rooms, dispensary, operating room, everything was visited and much approved of. The only thing wanting to prove their efficiency was beds filled with the wounded.

Before starting, five civil surgeons and eight army reserve sisters were added to their number, the medical authorities having asked them to take them to Durban, their ultimate destination being Mooi River. They proved very troublesome on the journey, being indeed as exigeant as they appeared ignorant. One or two of the nurses actually brought maids to look after them! Jennie did not envy the hospitals which were to benefit by their services.

As they approached Durban, Jennie witnessed an astonishing storm which suddenly burst upon them. The electric barometer in her cabin dropped perpendicularly. Torrents of hailstones beat down on them as large as small plums, the wind increased to a hurricane, and was so violent that the ship stood still, although they had been going at ten knots. The awning aft was violently blown into the sea, carrying with it all its rafters and stanchions, smashing one of the big ventilators, and only just missing some of the sisters who were crouching on the deck.

The sea meanwhile presented a most curious appearance, being covered with millions of little jets about a foot high, due to the force with which the hailstones fell, and as they floated for a while, in a few minutes it was quite white. Inside Jennie's deck cabin, the din was terrific, the noise of the hailstones striking the skylight and windows with a sound like bullets. It was impossible to speak. One window was smashed, and the water and ice poured in everywhere. The hailstones had a pattern like agate.

The journey continued with many adventures, including Jennie's visit to Ladysmith after its relief and her successful efforts to prevent the Maine from being sent home prematurely. She received grateful letters from the officers who had been treated aboard the ship, and her work with the Maine proved to be one of the most thrilling experiences of her life, certainly the most important public work she had ever attempted.

Famous Letters Received

Chartwell, 1964

Churchill had grown visibly tired, but when Sophia began to pack her notebook, he raised a restraining hand. "One more thing, Miss Carter." He gestured toward an elegant writing desk in the corner of the studio. "My mother was perhaps the finest correspondent of her generation. Everyone wrote to her, statesmen, artists, royalty, ordinary people whose lives she had touched."

"She saved them all?"

"Not all, but many. They form a remarkable record of the age." Churchill's voice was barely above a whisper now. "But more than that, they reveal something essential about her character. She made people feel heard, understood, valued. Kings and commoners alike felt they could confide in her."

Sophia closed her notebook, sensing the interview was drawing to a natural close. "That's quite a gift."

"Indeed. And one that served me well throughout my own career. She taught me that politics, at its heart, is about human connection. Every great speech I ever gave, every successful negotiation I ever conducted, every moment of crisis I helped Britain navigate, all of it was built on her understanding that leadership begins with listening."

Churchill closed his eyes briefly, then opened them with effort. "She lived fully, Miss Carter. Never halfway, never cautiously. Perhaps that's the most important lesson of all."

LONDON, 1908

From reading her memoirs, letters were important to Jennie. In her memoirs, she's present letters in various languages - the complete letter - many in French. When people came back from trips, one of the first things they'd do would be to sit and read a large stack of letters. During this period, letter writing was an essential form of communication and played a crucial role in upper-class social life. In an era before telephones became widespread, letters served as the primary means of maintaining relationships, coordinating social engagements, and exchanging news across distances.

For society people specifically, letters were not merely practical communications but important cultural artifacts that reflected one's social standing. Proper letter writing was considered an art form and a social skill that demonstrated education, refinement, and good breeding. The quality of one's stationery, handwriting, and adherence to epistolary etiquette all signaled one's place in society.

Letter writing followed strict conventions, with different formats for different occasions. There were specific protocols for letters of introduction, invitations, congratulations, condolences, and thank-you notes. Society women often spent hours each day managing their correspondence, as it was crucial to maintaining their social networks and fulfilling social obligations.

The exchange of visiting cards and invitation letters formed the backbone of the social season in places like New York, London, and Paris. For those aspiring to climb the social ladder, mastering these written forms was essential to gaining acceptance in elite circles. Here is a sampling of some the letters included in Jennie's memoirs.

From General de Palikao to "My Dear Duke" (October 21, 1870) The General writes from Ostend, Belgium, where he had taken refuge after fleeing France on September 4 when threatened with arrest. He describes learning that his son was wounded at Sedan and taken prisoner. He expresses deep dismay about the capitulation at Sedan, writing "I had thought that it was easier to die than to suffer dishonor. The death of the Emperor at Sedan would have saved France, as well as his son; the capitulation has lost everything." He laments France's situation and mentions that he had offered his services to the government of National defense but withdrew this offer when Garibaldi was called to defend France, which he considered "an eternal shame."

From Napoleon III to Persigny (January 7, 1871) Writing from Wilhelmshohe, Napoleon responds curtly to Persigny, who had apparently been making efforts regarding the future of Napoleon's son without authorization. Napoleon writes: "I find it somewhat singular that anyone should busy himself with the future of my son, without taking account of my own intentions." He informs Persigny that Bismarck had contacted him about Persigny's communications, and Napoleon had told Bismarck "I have authorized nobody to busy himself with my interests, and those of my son, without first obtaining my consent."

From Isabelle, Comtesse de Paris (July 25, 1888) The Countess writes to thank Jennie for inspiring her to create a "Rose League" in France, modeled after the Primrose League. She sends circulars about this new organization and expresses hope that it will succeed "by following your example." She adds: "The Rose League will never be the equal of the Primrose League; but perhaps they may meet often in the future."

From Isabelle, Comtesse de Paris (October 7, 1888) The Countess thanks Jennie for sending a copy of the

"Primrose League Gazette" with "a very kind article on the Rose League." She writes: "The Primrose League is indeed kind to welcome so cordially its younger sister, the Rose League." She mentions sending a newspaper showing their new paper in its entirety and reports good news about the Rose League's progress, adding "it will be to you, above all, that we shall owe our success."

From Baron de Staal (October 31, 1902) A very brief note from the elderly Russian diplomat, writing: "Here is the very old face of a very old man who is half-dead but who likes you very much. Do not receive it too unkindly."

From King Milan of Serbia The exiled king writes of his personal troubles, particularly his son's marriage "to a perfectly impossible woman who is fourteen years older than himself,, to the great scandal of the country and the whole of Europe." He expresses his distress: "in my old age, and with my hair nearer white than gray, it is too hard. I have deserved better than this."

From an unnamed correspondent A brief note mentioning difficulty writing "A Tragic Idyll" and quoting Turgenev: "Life is a brutal affair."

Letter from soldiers aboard the Maine In April 1900, Jennie received a heartfelt letter of thanks from officers treated on the Maine, expressing "our sincere gratitude to the donors & committee of the American Hospital Ship Maine for their great generosity & kindness in sending the Maine to South Africa." They thanked her personally for "all the kind care and attention we have received."

Final Years

Chartwell, 1964

As Sophia gathered her things in the gathering dusk, Churchill remained seated, gazing out at his beloved gardens where the last light reflected off his carefully constructed lake. "She died too young, you know," he said quietly. "Sixty-seven. Just when she was beginning to see the fruition of everything she had worked for, my political rise, the vindication of her belief in Anglo-American cooperation."

"Do you think she knew? How significant her influence would be?"

Churchill considered this for a long moment. "I think she knew she was raising someone who would matter. Whether she imagined the scope of it..." He trailed off, then smiled slightly. "She once told my father's secretary that she wasn't returning his ceremonial robes because her son would wear them one day. So perhaps she did know."

Sophia paused at the studio door. "What would she think of it all? Of what you became?"

"I believe," Churchill said, his voice barely audible now, "she would say it was exactly what she expected. My mother never aimed low, Miss Carter. In anything." He closed his eyes. "The wind was in her veins, and she taught me to sail by it rather than against it."

As Sophia quietly let herself out, she could hear the old statesman murmuring to himself, words carried on the evening air: "Love conquered Hitler... Yes, I rather think it did."

LONDON, 1921

The girl who arrived at Cowes that summer day became a woman who helped reshape an empire. She proved that the power to change the world doesn't come from birth or tradition, but from courage, intelligence, and the willingness to break rules that need breaking. They still tell stories about Jennie Jerome - the American girl who became Lady Randolph Churchill. But the best story is the one she wrote herself, with every choice, every battle, every triumph and tragedy. Our book, was based on her memoirs.

Some called her a revolutionary. Others, a social climber. But history knows her as something rarer - a woman who refused to choose between love and power, and ended up changing both. By 1907, when Jennie began writing her memoirs, she had already lived several remarkable lives - as political wife, society hostess, and tireless advocate for her son Winston's burgeoning career. Now in her fifties and married to George Cornwallis-West, a man twenty years her junior, Jennie faced mounting financial pressures that sparked a new creative endeavor.

Jennie made new efforts to fund her life. She was a natural communicator and by 1907 was writing in earnest, being pressed by her publishers to deliver a memoir, a book if gossipy enough, that Edwardian society was drooling to read [3]. *The Reminiscences of Lady Randolph Churchill*, published in 1908 by Edward Arnold in England and Century in the US, was politely reviewed, considered a pleasant if somewhat superficial insight into society, and went through several editions [3].

The publication of her memoirs cemented Jennie's status as a woman of letters, not merely a society figure [7]. Though she avoided scandal and kept many of her most intimate experiences private, the book provided valuable glimpses into the upper echelons of British and American society during a transformative era. Her ability to navigate both worlds made her uniquely positioned as a chronicler of Anglo-American relations.

George Cornwallis-West, though handsome and charming, proved financially reckless. George, not without his own profligacies, wrote later that in money matters Jennie was without any sense of proportion. "The value of money meant nothing to her: what counted with her were the things she got for money, not the amount she had to pay for them" [3]. Despite their mutual extravagance, Jennie maintained her social position and continued her literary pursuits.

The marriage to George deteriorated gradually. Though they were happy for a time, arguments over money and his propensity for other women weakened the marriage [7]. After the failure of *The Anglo-Saxon Review*, Jennie tried her hand at writing plays. In 1909, her first play, *Borrowed Plumes*, which ran briefly at the Haymarket Theater, received poor reviews and lost money [7]. She also lost her husband to the play's leading actress, the legendary Mrs. Patrick Campbell. In July 1914, their divorce was finalized, and he married Campbell the following day [7]. Jennie chose to return to her more famous name, Lady Randolph Churchill [1].

The outbreak of World War I found Jennie, now sixty years old, at a personal crossroads. Yet characteristically, she threw herself into war work with the same energy that had defined her entire life. Jennie served as the chair of the hospital committee for the American Women's War Relief Fund starting in 1914 [1]. This organization helped fund and staff two hospitals during World War I.

During these crucial years, Jennie's relationship with her son Winston deepened as they faced the challenges of wartime Britain together [2]. Winston, who had been First Lord of the Admiralty, faced professional setbacks after the disastrous

Dardanelles campaign of 1915. When he resigned from the Admiralty and ultimately joined the army in France, his mother remained one of his staunchest supporters and confidantes [5].

Jennie wrote to Winston in February 1916: "I hear your speech was most successful & made a great impression... I do hope they may find the right post for you soon - I think you have been extraordinarily patient" [2]. Her unwavering belief in his abilities helped sustain Winston through this politically challenging period, demonstrating the evolution of their relationship since his childhood.

In the midst of war, Jennie found love again. On 1 June 1918 she was married for a third time, to Montagu Phippen Porch (1877–1964), a member of the British Civil Service in Nigeria, who was younger than her son Winston by three years [1]. Porch, a former member of the British Army, had served with the Colonial Service since 1906 [6]. Porch continued to serve in the British Army until the end of World War I, devoting his time to several successful ventures in Africa [6].

This final marriage brought Jennie a measure of stability and companionship in her later years, though Montagu's work would frequently take him to Africa for extended periods.

The post-war years found Jennie still active in society and supporting Winston's political career, which was once again on the rise as he served as Secretary of State for War and Air [5]. She maintained her reputation as a formidable hostess and continued to leverage her connections to benefit her son.

In February 1921, Jennie managed to sell for £35,000 a house she had bought in Berkeley Square: "a clear profit of £15,000," as Winston told Clemmie with undisguised relief. "She has already taken a little house in Charles Street. No need to go abroad. All is well. I am so glad" [3].

Her financial situation temporarily improved, Jennie embarked on what would be her final journey abroad. And so, in the spring of 1921, as Montagu returned to Nigeria to explore investment opportunities there, Jennie went off to spend the profit from the sale of the house, staying with her old friend Vittoria Colonna, Duchess of Sermoneta, in Rome [3]. The Palazzo Caetani, where Jennie had often stayed before the First World War, was being refurbished and Jennie was giving her friend advice on interior decoration. The two women enjoyed going to balls and shopping together: "We ransacked all the old curiosity shops and Jennie bought profusely; her zest in spending money was one of her charms" [3].

Among her purchases were elegant shoes that would tragically play a role in her untimely death. Jennie always prized her slim ankles and kept her skirts short enough to display them [3]. But wearing the new shoes (probably before her maid had scored the slippery soles) on a visit to her friend Lady Katharine Horner at Mells in Somerset, she fell down the staircase [3] and broke her ankle. Gangrene set in, and her left leg was amputated above the knee on 10 June [1].

Despite the amputation, complications arose. At age 67, she died at her home at 8 Westbourne Street in London on 29 June, following a hemorrhage of an artery in her thigh resulting from the amputation [1]. Like everything she did in her life, the leaving of it was highly charged and dramatic.

Jennie Jerome's influence on her son Winston Churchill was profound and multifaceted. What began as a distant maternal relationship in his childhood evolved into one of history's most consequential political partnerships. Winston himself wrote in his autobiography, *My Early Life*, that he loved his mother "dearly but at a distance" [2]. His verdict is too readily adopted by many Churchill historians. Closer reading of *My Early Life* reveals that the "distance" did not last beyond his father's death in January 1895.

Thereafter, Winston writes, Jennie became an "ardent ally, furthering my plans and guarding my interests with all her influence and boundless energy" [2]. Their relationship, he claims, was "more like brother and sister than mother and son. At least so it seemed to me" [2].

This transformation of their relationship proved pivotal to Winston's career. "She shone for me like the Evening Star," wrote Churchill in his autobiography. "I loved her dearly – but at a distance" [5]. Yet that distance closed considerably in his adulthood, as Jennie became his most trusted political advisor and champion [5].

Through Jennie, Winston gained invaluable connections to American society that would later prove crucial during both World Wars [8]. Her political ambitions are now centred on her son, Winston, and she uses her social influence, pulls strings with diplomats and generals and carefully helps his education introducing him to the right people and paving the way for his career by way of the Army, then journalism and ultimately, politics [8].

Jennie's American heritage gave Winston a unique perspective on international relations, particularly regarding the United States [4]. From his mother, Winston inherited not just her wit, energy, and determination, but also her understanding of the vital importance of the Anglo-American relationship. This understanding would prove pivotal during his leadership in World

War II, when cultivating American support became essential to Britain's survival.

Her confidence in Winston's destiny never wavered. A factoid is that when Randolph died Jennie did not return his ceremonial robes since, "my son would wear them one day" [9]. This unshakable belief in Winston's future greatness inspired him through numerous political setbacks, including the wilderness years of the 1930s when his warnings about Nazi Germany went largely unheeded.

Beyond political influence, Jennie instilled in Winston her love of writing [10]. His mastery of the English language, which would later earn him the Nobel Prize for Literature, owed much to his mother's own literary talents and encouragement. The volumes of correspondence between mother and son reveal a shared appreciation for powerful, precise language [10].

Lady Randolph Churchill was buried in the Churchill family plot at St Martin's Church, Bladon, Oxfordshire, next to her first husband [1]. Jennie Jerome, another of the Dollar Princesses, asked to be buried alongside her first husband, who brought her into the British aristocracy and elite society [4]. She is buried in Bladon, Oxfordshire, near her first English home of Blenheim [4].

Winston Churchill was devastated by his mother's sudden death, arriving at her bedside moments too late to say farewell [2]. As in the best of tragic operas, her son arrived at her bedside just too late to say goodbye to the woman he knew had done more than any other to shape his early life [2]. He wrote a friend: "I wish you could have seen her as she lay at rest, after all the sunshine and storm of life was over. Very beautiful and splendid she looked. Since the morning with its pangs, thirty years had fallen from her brow. She recalled to me the countenance I had admired as a child when she was in her heyday and the old brilliant world of the eighties and nineties seemed to come back" [2].

That quote from Winston about his mother after her death is particularly moving and provides a beautiful glimpse into their bond. It shows how, despite any distance in his childhood, he had developed a deep appreciation for his remarkable mother. Winston Churchill went on to become one of the most famous politicians in British history, leading the country through the Second World War, as his mother instilled a sense of importance and leadership [4]. The values Jennie imparted to Winston – courage, determination, and an unshakable belief in one's convictions – would guide him as he faced the darkest hours of World War II.

Perhaps the most fitting epitaph for this remarkable woman came from Winston himself. Winston, who had found a loving wife and no longer sought his mother's affection, wrote of her death: "I do not feel a sense of tragedy but only loss. Her life was a full one. The wind was in her veins" [4].

The girl from Brooklyn who captured the heart of an English lord left an indelible mark on history through her own achievements and through the son she raised to greatness [6]. Jennie Jerome Churchill's legacy lives on not just in the chronicles of high society or in the pages of her memoirs, but in the very character of the man who would one day save Western civilization. In Winston Churchill's courage, eloquence, and unwavering resolve, we see the enduring influence of the remarkable American woman who helped shape him [2, 5].

Churchill particularly valued how American entry into both World Wars came not from territorial ambition or traditional alliance systems, but from what he saw as a pure democratic idealism. This aligned with his own belief that the Anglo-American alliance represented not just a military partnership but a moral force for democracy and freedom. As he noted in his famous Iron Curtain speech, the English-speaking peoples had a special responsibility to defend these values.

The transformation of American society during World War II especially impressed Churchill. He watched as America, like Britain, underwent rapid socialization and mobilization of its industrial might for the war effort. This demonstrated to him that democracies, far from being weak and divided as the Axis powers believed, could unite with tremendous force when their fundamental values were threatened.

The legacy of Churchill's views on America can be seen in the enduring alliance between the two nations. Yes, love did conquer Hitler because Winston's vision of a partnership based on shared values, common language, and democratic principles were largely realized because an American Heiress, Jennie Jerome, married Lord Randolph Churchill. She wasn't an entitled young woman auctioned off to British royalty who spent her days planning balls and trips overseas away from her boring husband. Jennie Jerome dug in - and shaped both the lives of Randolph and Winston. Winston Churchill was American because of her. He often showed his understanding of both countries and cemented what many consider a "Special Relationship" that he continued to champion through the Cold War and into the modern era, remaining a cornerstone of international relations and democratic solidarity. Winston Churchill was an American. Jennie was his "Mum."

About Sophia

Our fictional Sophia Carter represents the pioneering female journalists who worked for major American magazines like Life and Look during the 1950s and 1960s. Women like Margaret Bourke-White, Life's first female photojournalist who covered

World War II and later documented Gandhi's final days, or Marguerite Higgins, who won a Pulitzer Prize for her Korean War correspondence. Dorothy Kilgallen of Look magazine made her mark covering high-profile trials and political stories, while Shana Alexander became Life's first female staff writer and columnist. These women broke barriers in a male-dominated field, securing interviews with world leaders and covering the most significant stories of their time. Like our fictional Sophia, they understood that the most revealing interviews often came not from asking about official policies, but about personal influences and private moments that shaped public figures.

Winston Churchill spent his final years at Chartwell, the Kent estate he had purchased in 1922 and lovingly transformed into his personal refuge. Following his stroke in 1953 and his retirement as Prime Minister in 1955, he increasingly retreated to this sanctuary where he painted, fed his golden orfe fish, and tended to his beloved black swans. He died at his London home on January 24, 1965, just months after our imagined conversation with Sophia would have taken place.

Today, Chartwell is preserved by the National Trust exactly as Churchill left it, his easel still positioned by the studio window, his maps and papers scattered across his desk. Visitors can walk through the rooms where he wrote his Nobel Prize-winning histories, stand in the garden where he built walls and dug lakes with his own hands, and understand how this quintessentially English estate became home to a man whose American mother had taught him that the whole world was his stage.

Comments and References

About fifty percent of the reference for this book came from the memoirs Jennie wrote "***The Reminiscences of Lady Randolph Churchill***" in 1907-1908, but edited third person to make it easier to read. We did not include citations from that book, but that source material ends with the chapter; "Famous Letters Received." These memoirs in raw form were difficult to read; one version on Amazon appears to be a photocopy of an edition the original printed book. The font is blurry and the writing style of the early 1900s is different than today. In her memoirs, Jennie rarely provides her thoughts, thus, our creative license. Most of our work was to rewrite, organize, and add conversations that might have happened, especially the chapter where Jennie meets Randolph. Both of the authors are also screenwriters and developing the TV series, so writing conversations is in our nature.

Jennie Jerome's memoirs ended in the early 1900's leaving out the final act of her life. But this was also the part of Winston's life when he wrote often about his mother and we didn't want to repeat in other excellent books about the two of them. In his autobiography "My Early Life" published in 1930, Churchill famously wrote that he loved his mother "dearly but at a distance." However, this oft-quoted line doesn't tell the whole story. Churchill scholars note that a closer reading of the autobiography reveals that this "distance" didn't last beyond his father's death in 1895, after which Jennie became what Winston described as an "ardent ally, furthering my plans and guarding my interests with all her influence and boundless energy." In the same autobiography, Churchill remembered his mother as "a fascinating but distant presence in his life as a boy." The book acknowledges that after his father's death, she helped advance his political career significantly.

In other writings, Winston described his mother more poetically, noting that she had "not blood but the wine of life coursing through her veins," highlighting her vibrant personality and passionate approach to life. One of his earliest known writings is actually a letter to his mother from May 1882, when he was just seven years old, describing his activities at Blenheim Palace, including riding a horse named "Rob Roy."

After Jennie's death in 1921, Winston wrote to a friend: "I wish you could have seen her as she lay at rest, after all the sunshine and storm of life was over. Very beautiful and splendid she looked. Since the morning with its pangs, thirty years had fallen from her brow. She recalled to me the countenance I had admired as a child when she was in her heyday." [2].

While these are the most notable written references, Churchill's correspondence throughout his life also contains numerous mentions of his mother. Their relationship evolved from the somewhat distant connection of his childhood to a close political partnership in his adult years, with Jennie playing a crucial role in launching and supporting his early political career.

The evolution of their relationship is particularly evident in their extensive correspondence, which has been compiled in books such as "My Darling Winston: The Letters of Winston Churchill and His Mother" (2018).

Credits and References

1. "Lady Randolph Churchill." Wikipedia, accessed April 2025.
2. "Great Contemporaries: Jennie, Lady Randolph Churchill." Hillsdale College, The Churchill Project, April 15, 2019.
3. Sebba, Anne. "Jennie Churchill and Her Attempts to Be an Independent Woman." International Churchill Society, Finest Hour 175, Winter 2017.
4. "The American heiresses who saved the British Aristocracy - Jennie Jerome, Lady Randolph Churchill." The Crown Chronicles, December 31, 2015.
5. "Churchill Archive Platform - Churchill and Women." Churchill Archives Centre, Cambridge University.
6. "Lady Randolph Churchill, Mistress of King Edward VII of the United Kingdom." Unofficial Royalty, June 28, 2024.
7. "Churchill, Jennie Jerome (1854–1921)." Encyclopedia.com.
8. "Jenny - Lady Randolph Churchill." Television Heaven.
9. Martin, Ralph G. "Jennie: The Life of Lady Randolph Churchill, Vol 1: The Romantic Years 1854-95." Goodreads.
10. "Churchill, Jennie Spencer (1854-1921, née Jerome, Lady Randolph Churchill)." ArchiveSearch, Cambridge University Libraries.

Photographs

Cover: Title: Winston Churchill Making "V" For Victory Sign., United Kingdom, License: All Media License, Issued by: Pond5 Inc.

Cover: Mrs. Randolph Churchill;Winston Churchill [Misc.], United Kingdom License: All Media License, Issued by: Pond5 Inc.

All other photos are in the public domain on WikiMedia.

About the Authors

Sandi Jerome is a screenwriter and author of fiction, non-fiction, and produced screenplays. She holds an advanced degree in screenwriting from UCLA and has written dozens of award-winning scripts, including one animated script produced by BlackOrb Studios. She did the book adaptations for ***HIJACKED***, a movie about the heroes of Flight 705 and ***JAKE AND CLARA*** a movie based on the book by David R. Stokes. She won a Native American in Media Alliance fellowship twice, and has been a finalist in the Nicholls Fellowship, Page International, Final Draft Big Break, and Austin Film Festival with five different scripts. She is the author of a YA fantasy series, ***KIRA AND HENRY***, a 2024 Kindle Book Review Semifinalist. After selling her technology company, she now writes full-time from her home in Florida where she developed the ***WILMA WALLABY - GIRL DETECTIVE*** series. She loves soccer and theme park food. Her husband, Keith Jerome, is Winston's fifth cousin, a few times removed. **Visit Sandi's website at SandraJerome.com.**

David R. Stokes is a Wall Street Journal bestselling author, ghostwriter, broadcaster, and retired pastor. His latest book, ***JFK'S GHOST***: Kennedy, Sorensen, and the Making of Profiles in Courage, was released by Lyons Press (Rowman & Littlefield) June 1, 2021. His earlier book, ***THE SHOOTING SALVATIONIST***, appeared twice on the Wall Street Journal Bestseller list in 2011. This story has been recently revised and republished with 30,000 words of new material. David has also written screenplays based on two of his novels, ***CAMELOT'S COUSIN*** and ***JAKE & CLARA***, and they are currently being represented for production in Hollywood. Retired FBI Agent and Bestselling author, Bob Hamer, says, "David Stokes combines his meticulous research with a writing style which makes you feel as though you are that fly-on-the-wall witnessing history as it unfolds."

David grew up in the Detroit, Michigan area and has been an ordained minister for more than 45 years. Now retired from pastoral ministry, he writes full-time. David has been married to his wife, Karen, since 1976, and they have been blessed with three daughters--all now grown and with wonderful children of their own. There are, in fact, seven grandchildren, a fact verified by hundreds--maybe thousands--of pictures, as well as an ever-growing collection of toys and gadgets joyously cluttering their home.His next book, THE HOPE NOT PLOT: A Novel of Churchill's Final Farewell will be published in fall, 2025. **Visit David's website: DavidRStokes.com.**

David at Blenheim

www.ingramcontent.com/pod-product-compliance
Lightning Source LLC
Chambersburg PA
CBHW071708120626
46550CB00001B/149

9781969767067